Contemporary Russia

Contemporary States and Societies

This series provides lively and accessible introductions to key countries and regions of the world, conceived and designed to meet the needs of today's students. The authors are all experts with specialist knowledge of the country or region concerned and have been chosen also for their ability to communicate clearly to a non-specialist readership. Each text has been specially commissioned for the series and is structured according to a common format.

Published

Contemporary India
Katharine Adeney and Andrew Wyatt

Contemporary Russia (3rd edition)
Edwin Bacon

Contemporary China
Kerry Brown

Contemporary South Africa (2nd edition)
Anthony Butler

Contemporary France
Helen Drake

Contemporary America (4th edition)
Russell Duncan and Joseph Goddard

Contemporary Japan (3rd edition)
Duncan McCargo

Contemporary Britain (3rd edition)
John McCormick

Contemporary Latin America (3rd edition)
Ronaldo Munck

Contemporary Ireland
Eoin O'Malley

Forthcoming

Contemporary Spain
Paul Kennedy

Contemporary Asia
John McKay

Also planned

Contemporary Africa
Contemporary Europe
Contemporary Germany

Contemporary States and Societies
Series Standing Order ISBN 978–0–333–75402–3 hardcover
Series Standing Order ISBN 978–0–333–80319–6 paperback
(*outside North America only*)

You can receive future titles in this series as they are published by placing a standing order. Please contact your bookseller or, in the case of difficulty, write to us at the address below with your name and address, the title of the series and one of the ISBNs quoted above.

Customer Services Department, Macmillan Distribution Ltd, Houndmills, Basingstoke, Hampshire, RG21 6XS, UK

Contemporary Russia

Third Edition

Edwin Bacon

First edition 2006
Second edition 2010
Third edition 2014

Published by
RED GLOBE PRESS

Red Globe Press in the UK is an imprint of Springer Nature Limited,
registered in England, company number 785998, of 4 Crinan Street,
London, N1 9XW.

Red Globe Press® is a registered trademark in the United States,
the United Kingdom, Europe and other countries.

ISBN 978–1–137–30739–2   ISBN 978–1–137–40827–3 (eBook)

A catalogue record for this book is available from the British Library.

A catalog record for this book is available from the Library of Congress.

Contents

List of Illustrative Material

Preface and Acknowledgements

The third edition of *Contemporary Russia* is substantially revised and updated. Updating self-evidently remains vital for any work with 'contemporary' in its title; events occur, key figures come and go, and the flow of new data never stops. Revision requires something more overarching than the mere addition of new information. Changing circumstances lead to changing interpretations. Occurrences such as the return to the Russian presidency of Vladimir Putin in 2012, the recent global financial crisis, and the slow down in Russia's demographic decline – all of these feed into new and revised interpretations of Russia today. Revision, in this case, has also involved changes in style and additions to areas of content. There is more coverage of cultural matters in the third edition than in the previous two, whilst it still maintains the same attention to socio-economic and political concerns.

As with earlier editions of *Contemporary Russia*, this third edition owes much to the insights of colleagues working in the range of specialist fields covered in its chapters. I am particularly grateful to John Berryman, Elena Chebankova, Richard Connelly and Mike Pushkin for their helpful comments on particular chapters. I am grateful too to the Department of Politics at Birkbeck, University of London, for providing research support for a trip to Russia in order to gather material. My father, Philip Bacon, likewise deserves acknowledgement for stepping in when the limits of research funding threatened to prevent the same.

Discussions with colleagues and friends too numerous to mention by name, from various areas of activity relating to Russia, have helped immensely as I have revised this book. If I mention fruitful conversations in Birmingham, Helsinki, London, Moscow, Rome and St Petersburg then I will not miss out too many interlocutors. They have my gratitude. As do the generations of students – at Birkbeck and at the University of Birmingham – who have annually reaffirmed my conviction that Russia's hold on the intellects and imaginations of those wanting to understand our world remains strong.

What has not changed between editions is the gratitude I owe to my family. Invaluable support and succour have come from my wife Deborah, and our daughters Eleanor, Charlotte, Emily and Joanna. They have my love and thanks as always.

EDWIN BACON

List of Abbreviations

AIDS	acquired immune deficiency syndrome
CEO	chief executive officer
CIS	Commonwealth of Independent States
CSTO	Collective Security Treaty Organization
EU	European Union
FIDE	World Chess Federation
FSB	Federal Security Service
G8	Group of Eight – a forum for eight nations in the northern hemisphere
GDP	gross domestic product
GUAM	semi-official grouping of states of Georgia, Ukraine, Azerbaijan and Moldova
HIV	human immunodeficiency virus
KGB	Committee for State Security – the national security agency of the USSR
LDPR	Liberal Democratic Party of Russia
MDR-TB	multi-drug-resistant tuberculosis
MFA	Ministry of Foreign Affairs (Russia)
NATO	North Atlantic Treaty Organization
NGO	non-governmental organization
OSCE	Organization for Security and Co-operation in Europe
RSFSR	Russian Soviet Federative Socialist Republic
SCO	Shanghai Co-operation Organization
UN	United Nations
UNICEF	United Nations Children's Fund (formerly United Nations International Children's Emergency Fund)
USSR	Union of Soviet Socialist Republics
WHO	World Health Organization
WTO	World Trade Organization

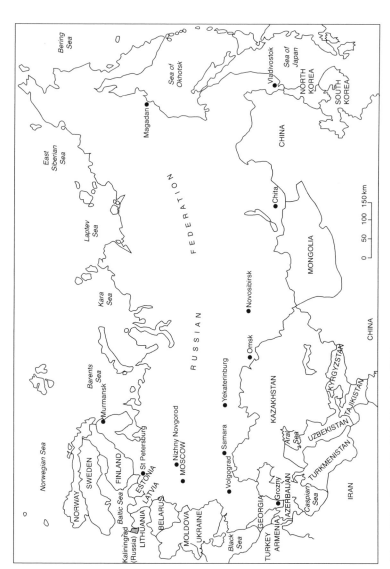

Map of Russia and its Neighbouring States

1

Introduction

Russia is one of the major powers in the world today. It is by some distance the world's largest country, played a pivotal role in world history in the twentieth century, and after undergoing the rare experience of state collapse in the 1990s is once again a key player at the high table of global affairs. It is also a country that seems to do its best to confound analysis and polarize opinion. Russia's history over the past century has seen the endurance of traumatic shocks beyond perhaps any other state in the world – staggering losses in two world wars, revolution, civil war, famine, rapid urbanization and industrialization, class war, political terror, the failure of a superpower state, regional conflict, domestic terrorism. At the same time, within such difficulties Russia has known great power and prestige, achievements of the human intellect and spirit, and a unifying sense of nationhood.

Contemporary Russia's woes thankfully do not reach the depths, nor yet do its achievements match the heights, of what has gone before. In many ways, both literal and figurative, Russia today represents a smaller incarnation of its former self. It covers less area than for many years. Its voice, though still important, carries less comparative weight internationally now that other global powers are rising. Critics cite examples of authoritarianism in Russia's governance, but, although such examples are evident, the Putin regime is neither willing nor able to emulate the totalitarian control of the Soviet years. For all that it remains a nuclear superpower and maintains a presence in space, Russia's global reach has diminished. None of this need represent a deeper diminution if what matters for a state is to seek its national interest – the interests of its people – peaceably within the community of nations. Such is at least the declared intention of Russia's rulers today, although a predilection for personally holding

1

tight to power and to a share of the nation's riches appears too as a distinguishing mark of Russia's current regime.

Distinction and particularity bring both burdens and privilege on a state. Russia's size, location and history dictate some unavoidable degree of exceptionality, and with good reason those who have written about Russia have long emphasized the same. Winston Churchill's description of Russia as a riddle wrapped in a mystery inside an enigma is now so much of a cliché that any Russia analyst who uses it might well be ashamed at their lack of originality. And yet, it is so overused because it has been so apposite. Russia appears to be a country riven with contradictions and paradoxes. At the same time, as if to reaffirm the inevitability of paradox, there are those who – like Russia's first post-Soviet foreign minister, Andrei Kozyrev – have sought only that Russia be a 'normal great power', rather than one encumbered with messianic mission or weighed down with doubts over its identity.

Let us begin our introduction to contemporary Russia by setting out some of its central ambiguities:

- Although two-thirds of it is in Asia, Russia is still the biggest country in Europe. The fact of its physical location translates readily into the question of where Russia sits historically, intellectually and culturally. This question has dominated much of Russia's development as a state over hundreds of years. Still today contemporary Russia is often defined – and often defines itself – in relation to the West. From the perspective of Western observers, it is enough like the West to be recognizably familiar, but sufficiently distinct to perplex with its difference.
- Russia's relationship with the West veers between the desire to join what President Vladimir Putin has called 'the mainstream of civilisation', and the view that Russian civilization is itself unique, superior, and represents an exemplar for others. The central intellectual debate in Russian history has been between the Westernizers and the Eurasianists. This debate retains force and relevance in the twenty-first century.
- Russia has a history going back several centuries as a major imperial power. During the twentieth century, as the overwhelmingly dominant nation within the Soviet Union, it became one of only two superpowers and dominated a large part of the world. Beyond its physical presence, the influence of its Communist ideology on twentieth-century global political affairs is difficult to exaggerate.

Nonetheless, contemporary Russia is in some ways a young state. In 1991 the authoritarian superpower which was the Soviet Union collapsed and a Russian state much reduced in power, strength and influence came into being.

- The Russia – or Russian Federation – which emerged as a newly independent country in 1991 set about establishing a framework for building a liberal democracy and a market economy. It organized free elections for president and parliament in a multi-party system, privatized its state-owned industries, and introduced a democratic constitution guaranteeing rights and freedoms according to international norms. A quarter of a century later Russia has still not experienced a democratic change of regime, its major companies are largely controlled by the state, and its record on rights and freedoms has been tarnished by a number of high-profile cases, including the trial of a dead man.

- Contemporary Russia remains much argued over by Western observers. Many adopt conceptualizations familiar from the Soviet era, when East and West represented civilizational alternatives locked in an elemental struggle for the future of the world. They emphasize the undemocratic nature of Russia, governed by a narrow and self-perpetuating elite, using the courts, the media and the security forces to keep its domestic opponents in check, and pursuing a foreign policy opposed to the interests of the West.

- Others argue that a quarter of a century after the Soviet Union collapsed, things have moved on. There is no longer any great ideologically-based systemic divide between Russia and the West. The media is largely free, and examples of misuse of the courts and the security services are rarely as clear-cut as opponents allege – and certainly nothing like that seen in the Soviet years. The notions of East and West are not so self-evident politically as they once were: the closed world of Soviet Russia has given way to a time where Russians, as so many other peoples, interact across the planet by means of technology and travel; Russian business interests are global in scope; Russia's international alignments shift according to events and interests, and are by no means fixed in an anti-Western stance.

- The tension between the formal and informal in Russian social and political life represents a notable conceptual barrier for many Western observers. The formal elements consist of the laws, regulations and procedures covering the conduct of politics, business, and many elements of everyday life. These matter and have genuine substance, but at the same time a good deal also gets done through relationships, favours, corruption, and the use of power in informal ways. Such informality operates at many levels of Russian life: from the traffic policeman soliciting a bribe, through the prosecution decision arrived at by consultation with the authorities rather than on the basis of evidence, to the cabals of political leaders at the highest level who have overlapping associates, business interests and career paths.

Many other examples of tensions and contradictions within Russia and its history could be put forward. However, the final tension to be considered here is that between those who buy into the idea of a uniquely mysterious and incomprehensible Russia, and those who reject that view as over-romanticization and see – or seek – a Russia that is simply, as the title of a 2003 paper by Andrei Shleifer and Daniel Treisman has it, a 'normal country'. Shleifer and Treisman argued that there exists a large gap between common perceptions of Russia and the plain facts. Their view was that Russia should be analysed straightforwardly as a typical middle-income capitalist country. All countries are, by definition, unique. All countries have their contradictions and historical paradoxes. To interpret Russia through a prism of preconceptions regarding its opacity and difference is – from this perspective – to set oneself on a path to *not* understanding Russia.

This book is written to increase the reader's understanding of contemporary Russia. To this end it consists of three essential elements:

- First, it takes on board the argument that the 'plain facts' about Russia need to be set out. Matters such as economic performance, demographic data, constitutional provisions, international agreements, even the rankings of the Olympics medals table – all of these and many more inform us about the state of Russia today and are reported here.
- Second, it asserts that conceptions and presumptions, myths and generalizations, impressions and orthodoxies, all have both analytical force and independent existence. Countries are neither understood nor treated on the basis of facts alone, but rather the accrual of knowledge on the basis of observed habits and traits leads to expectations patterned by history and culture. Furthermore, common assertions – like, for example, the view that Russia habit-

Moscow's most famous landmark, situated next to the Kremlin on Red Square. Its unique architecture is emblematic of Russia's distinctiveness.

Illustration 1.1   St Basil's Cathedral

ually reverts to authoritarianism – become independent variables in themselves. Whether right or wrong, they fill out the plain facts of political action and shape responses by political actors. Myths matter, although they might not match the facts. The more entrenched the myth, the greater the accumulation of plain facts needed to shift it. A good example of this came during Mikhail Gorbachev's rule in the Soviet Union (1985–91). Radical reformer though Gorbachev was, so ingrained were the inclinations of decades, that it took several years before these reforms could be widely accepted at home and abroad for what they were, rather than as some devious double game.

- Third, the analysis in this book seeks to present reasonably fairly the range of opinions which exist on so polarizing a subject as contemporary Russia. I do not measure out analytical content with any finely calibrated 'pro' and 'anti' gauge, seeking some impartial position in the dead centre. Such an approach would be tedious, difficult to maintain, and too generous to outlying views in particular cases. I do, however, endeavour to be clear about the differing perceptions of today's Russia that exist, both amongst Western observers, and within Russia itself.

The following chapters provide a detailed introduction to contemporary Russia, covering its history, society, politics, international relations, economy and culture.

Chapter 2 sets out a themed and chronological account of Russia's history, covering the origins of the state, the Mongol occupation, the early tsars, the Time of Troubles, the imperial era, the Communist years, the collapse of the Soviet Union, and the presidencies of Boris Yeltsin, Vladimir Putin (2000–8) and Dmitrii Medvedev. It ends with President Putin's return to power in 2012. Throughout the chapter key elements of Russia's history are drawn out, notably the role of the state, Russia's ambiguous relationship with the West, and the interaction of these issues with questions of modernization and national identity.

Chapter 3 introduces the Russian land and peoples. The first part deals with Russia's physical setting, environmental issues, borders, cities, the impact of Russia's geostrategic location on its development and history, and an outline of its demographic development and current demographic difficulties. The second part discusses the identity of the inhabitants of Russia, focusing particularly on the multi-ethnic and multi-confessional nature of the Russian Federation. It considers too the notion of national values. This chapter also focuses on Russia's regions, outlining the development of the federal structure of Russia in recent years, the centralizing policies of Putin and Medvedev, and war and terrorism in the North Caucasus.

Chapter 4 looks at Russian society today. In particular it covers four areas of great significance to the inhabitants of Russia; namely, living standards, demographic and health issues, education and judicial policy. The chapter gives key data about mortality and birth-rates, and sets out contemporary policy responses in health, housing, rural development and education. Discussion of the judiciary focuses on reforms and difficult cases. It also considers the gap between the rhetoric of the Putin regime about the rule of law, and the practice of state interference in the legal sphere.

Chapter 5 turns to the governance of Russia and considers questions around democracy, authoritarianism and regime change. Having

Table 1.1 Quick facts about Russia

Official name	Russia, or the Russian Federation
Capital	Moscow
Area	17,098,242 sq km (6,601,700 sq miles)
Population (2013 est.)	142.8 million
Population density (2013)	8.4 per sq km (21.6 per sq mile)
Population growth rate (2013 est.)	0.02%
Languages	Russian, and other minority ethnic languages
Religions	Predominantly Russian Orthodox, with a significant Muslim minority. Christianity, Islam, Buddhism and Judaism officially acknowledged as Russia's historical religions.
GDP (2012 est.)	$2.555 trillion
Per capita GDP (2012 est.)	$18 000
Distribution of GDP (2012)	60% services, 36% industry, 4% agriculture
Literacy	99%
Infant mortality (2013 est.)	7.2 per 1000 live births
Life expectancy (2013 (est.)	69.9 years
Government type	Federation with elected president and parliament
Administrative divisions	21 republics, 46 oblasts, 4 autonomous okrugs, 9 krais, 2 federal cities, 1 autonomous oblast
Executive	President, prime minister, and government
Legislature	Bicameral Federal Assembly; Federation Council, two members from each of the 83 regions, one representing the regional legislature, one representing the regional executive. State Duma, 450 members.
Party structure	Formally multi-party with United Russia dominating parliament (2011–16) and the other main parties being the Communists, the Liberal Democratic Party of Russia, and 'A Just Russia'.
Judiciary	Constitutional Court, Supreme Court and Higher Court of Arbitration – judges appointed by the Federation Council on the recommendation of the President.
Head of state	President Vladimir Putin (2000–8, 2012– term due to end in 2018)

outlined the development of Russia's political system, it establishes the main features of the Russian constitution and deals with the tensions inherent in Russia's decisions surrounding the form of democracy chosen in the early 1990s. Looming over political questions in contemporary Russia is the status of the Putin regime and of Putin himself, who moved back into the presidency from the prime ministership in 2012, after his protégé and placeman Dmitrii Medvedev had served as president for his four-year term – during which time he oversaw the extension of the presidential term to six years from 2012 onwards. This chapter sets out the formal powers of the executive, legislature and judiciary, and considers the regular changes made to the political process in recent years, such as the tightening then loosening of regulations on political parties, the abandonment then restoration of gubernatorial elections, and the shift from and then back to a mixed proportional and majoritarian system for parliamentary elections. Emphasis is also laid on the development of politics aside from the formal structures – the closing down of space for opposition, the importance of informal connections and power within the regime, and the options for those excluded from Russia's formal political process.

Chapter 6 focuses on economic transitions in Russia, from the centrally planned command economy of the Soviet era, through the economically catastrophic transition period of the 1990s to the relative prosperity of the early years of the twenty-first century, and on to Russia's attempt to deal with the effects of the global economic crisis of 2008 onwards and the plans for modernization of Russia's economy. The structure of Russia's GDP is set out, alongside discussion on the relative importance and performance of different sectors of the economy. The benefits of high energy prices will be put in the context of the potential dangers of over-reliance on income from gas and oil and of over-exposure to the European economies. The barriers to developing other sectors and investing to modernize the infrastructure and output portfolio are considered. Substantial attention is also paid to Russia's economic indicators and to developments in the agricultural sector.

Chapter 7 deals with the subjects of rights, freedoms and civil society. Having briefly noted the Soviet Union's poor record in this area, and the constitutional commitment of Russia to human rights and the existence of a healthy civil society, Chapter 7 sets out developments in these areas during the post-Soviet years, with a particular emphasis on the apparent worsening of the situation with regard to rights, freedoms and civil society during President Putin's third term (2012 onwards). An assessment of the formal legal situation, in terms of the Russian state's official and constitutional commitments to human rights, is compared to the experience of Russia's citizens today, and raises questions of the relationship between state and citizens regarding the right of people to collectively act independently of the state. Specific examples enable us to illustrate developments in contemporary Russia, and to consider too the counter-arguments made against critics of Russia's rights record. The chapter covers in some detail freedom of worship, the Chechen wars, rights in the military and in prisons, the securitization of areas of Russian life, the cases of Pussy Riot and Sergei Magnitsky, and the legislation of Putin's third term, including increased fines for unauthorized demonstrations and regulations requiring foreign-funded non-governmental organizations to register as 'foreign agents'.

Chapter 8 turns its attention to the more intangible aspects of Russian life – namely, ideas, culture and ideology. The 'Russian idea' is a distinctive, if partly mythical, aspect of national identity. This chapter draws out the provenance and central features of the Russian idea and explores the place of ideas and ideology in the national consciousness. It provides an account of official attempts to craft a national identity in recent years. The focus then turns to contemporary culture (both high and low), discussing the state of music, architecture, literature, drama, film and sport in today's Russia, and providing a brief overview of the new names, ideas and developments in these areas. The chapter concludes with an assessment of Russian media – focusing on the questions of ownership, independence and the state – and of the development of social media.

Chapter 9 turns its attention outwards, considering Russia's place in the world in the sphere of international relations. It traces the re-emergence of Russia as an independent sovereign great power in the twenty-first century, from the weakness of the 1990s, and investigates what lies behind Russia's current standing in the world through an overview of Russia's Foreign Policy Concept in its various iterations. The attempt to 're-set' relations between Russia and the US in the Medvedev–Obama years is set out, along with the subsequent difficulties experienced in the US–Russian relationship. Russia's avowedly pro-European stance is then analysed, since the relationship between Russia and the EU, as well as bilateral relations between Russia and European states, are of key significance. UK–Russian relations have been particularly problematic during the past decade, and the reasons for this are examined. The third major international relationship specifically focused on here is that between Russia and China, both considered as rising powers in recent years, and yet with markedly different trajectories and distinctly different roles with regard to one another. Significant attention is also paid to Russia's policy with regard to the former Soviet states in general, and to President Putin's ambitions to create a Eurasian Union including a number of these countries.

The final chapter of the book deals briefly with conceptualizations of contemporary Russia, drawing on the material in the preceding chapters. It considers different ways of reading Russia today, and sets out some potential paths along which Russia might develop.

2

The Historical Context

Contemporary Russia sits between East and West, between democracy and authoritarianism, between modernization and stagnation. In the last hundred years or so Russia has experienced upheavals on a scale beyond most other nations – revolutions, a staggering number of war deaths, dictatorships, empire building and collapse, superpower status, unprecedented decline and partial renewal. Its society has repeatedly experienced radical transformation. Its politics have been key to the way our contemporary world has developed. Today Russia stands as a prominent player in world affairs, one of the emergent nations, known as 'BRICS' (Brazil, Russia, India, China, South Africa), set to challenge US hegemony and Euro-centric conceptualizations.

It's a commonplace of course, but true nonetheless, that to understand a country requires an understanding of where it has come from. This book is about contemporary Russia, and so must start in earnest by understanding Russia's history. It is within the framework of this history that today's Russian leaders and people operate, whether that be economically, politically, culturally, socially or globally.

Russia is the world's biggest country, nearly twice the size of China and more than one and half times the size of the United States. And yet the area which it covers in the twenty-first century is smaller than at any time since the nineteenth century. At that time the Russian Empire was engaged in a process of expansion which had begun more than 300 years earlier, and was to continue until the invasion of Afghanistan by the Soviet army in 1979. Twelve years later, in 1991, the Soviet Union – one of two global superpowers and to many critics merely the Russian Empire by another name – ceased to exist. Each of its 15 constituent republics, including Russia itself, gained independence from the Soviet state. Expansion gave way to an immediate loss of lands which had been under Russian rule, be it the rule of a Russian Tsar or a Communist Party Secretary, for many years. When Russia emerged from out of the Soviet Union in 1991, the territory ruled from Moscow retreated by a third.

This geo-political introduction to contemporary Russia – or the Russian Federation, to use its other official name – serves to highlight a duality which is essential to our understanding of Russia today. There is a combination of decline and greatness which shapes much which goes on in the various areas of activity considered in this book.

For most of the 1990s and into the twenty-first century the socio-economic and political dividing lines in Russia ran through the question of how far this great nation should open itself up to the West in terms of economic policy, international allegiance, cultural identity, governance, and much more. The ancient question of whether Russia is a backward country trying to catch up with Europe, or a unique civilization carving out its own superior path through history still has a resonance in contemporary debate. During the Putin years (from 2000 onwards), the emphasis has shifted to a strong Russia confident in following its own lights into the future. Still though, the relationships between Russia and the West, between the past and the present, remain nuanced and prominent in official discourse and wider public debate. One thing is clear, with Russia perhaps more so than with most other countries, it is impossible to correctly read the contemporary scene without knowing what has gone before.

This chapter is about introducing the past to help us understand the present, and to that end the overview of Russia's history given here considers the development of ideas and moods in Russia's past within the framework of key events. We start our look at contemporary Russia with a *tour d'horizon* of its history over the past centuries, focusing on the tumultuous twentieth century and its aftermath. Box 2.1 provides a chronology of key events. This chapter then draws out the significant elements of Russian history in three phases: Russia before 1917, the Soviet period (1917–91), and the post-Soviet era.

Russia before 1917

The history of Russia is the history of a country whose geographical position, the biggest country in Europe but with two-thirds of its territory in Asia, stands at the heart of its identity. The ambiguous rela-

Box 2.1 Key events in Russian history

c. 882	Establishment of first Russian state with Kiev as its capital (Kievan Rus)
1237–1480	Mongol rule in Rus
1547	Ivan IV ('The Terrible') becomes first Tsar
1598–1613	'Time of Troubles' – civil war and foreign invasions, ends with founding of the Romanov dynasty
1682–1725	Reign of Peter the Great
1762–96	Reign of Catherine the Great
1812	Napoleon invades Russia and reaches Moscow before retreating
1861	Emancipation of the serfs, under the rule of reformist Tsar Alexander II
1905	'The 1905 revolution' – promise of limited parliamentary rights
March 1917	Tsar Nicholas II abdicates in the face of popular demonstrations and mutinies
October 1917	Russian Revolution; Communists seize power under Lenin's leadership
1922	Formal establishment of the Soviet Union
1924	Death of Lenin
1928–9	Stalin's power consolidated
1930s	Industrialization, collectivization of agriculture, and growth of labour camps
1937–8	The 'Great Terror' sees a wave of arrests and executions
1941	German invasion of Soviet Union
1941–5	Soviet Union fights on the allied side in Second World War
1945–8	Soviet Union consolidates control of Eastern Europe
1953	Death of Stalin; Khrushchev becomes leader of the Communist Party
1964	Khrushchev replaced by Brezhnev as Soviet leader
1982–5	Death of Brezhnev; successors Andropov and Chernenko each die in post
1985	Mikhail Gorbachev becomes Soviet leader
1989	Countries of Eastern Europe leave the Soviet bloc
1991	Boris Yeltsin elected President of Russia; collapse of Soviet Union
1993	Presidential–parliamentary conflict resolved in Yeltsin's favour by military means; new Russian Constitution adopted
1999	President Boris Yeltsin resigns on 31 December
2000	Vladimir Putin elected president
2004	Vladimir Putin re-elected president
2008	Dmitrii Medvedev elected president; Vladimir Putin becomes prime minister
2012	Vladimir Putin elected president; Dmitrii Medvedev becomes prime minister

tionship between Russia and the rest of Europe is apparent in a number of key historical moments. The first of these was the adoption of Eastern Orthodoxy as the religion of modern Russia's predecessor state, Kievan Rus, in the tenth century. Just like the countries of Europe, Russia has been predominantly a 'Christian nation' throughout most of its existence. Unlike most of Europe, however, the form of Christianity which Russia adopted was Eastern, not Roman. After Constantinople fell to the Turks in 1453 and hegemony in the Orthodox world shifted to Muscovy, the uniqueness of Russian civilization was emphasized still further, and Moscow became referred to as 'the third Rome'. According to this theory, ancient Rome fell because of heresy, and the 'Second Rome', Constantinople, was brought down by infidels. The 'Third Rome', Muscovy, would illuminate the world and never fall.

There is therefore an 'otherness' about Russia's cultural history, and this otherness was heightened by the fact that for most of the medieval era in Europe, from 1237 to 1480, the territories which make up contemporary Russia came under the control of the Asiatic Mongol Khanates, or 'hordes', of Ghengis Khan and his successors. So, as Europe moved into the Reformation and Renaissance of the sixteenth and seventeenth centuries, Russia, expanding from the principality of Muscovy, came on the European scene as a relative newcomer, undergoing the brutal and sadistic rule of Ivan the Terrible (1547–84) and the anarchic period of civil war and foreign invasion known as the 'Time of Troubles' (1598–1613).

The separation of Russia from the mainstream of European cultural developments and the imposition of Mongol forms of government have been seen by some historians as a key determinant of Russia's socio-political system subsequently. For those within and without Russia who emphasize the nation's Euro-Asiatic identity, distinct from but linked to the European lands to the west, these two and a half centuries of Mongol rule followed by brutal autocracy and chaotic internecine war serve as a formative feature of Russian identity. Only in 1613, with the establishment of the Romanov dynasty which was to last until the workers' revolution of 1917, did a degree of stability and 'normality' begin to appear. Nonetheless, the perceived separation of Russia from the European mainstream continued to play a key part in historical developments.

Peter the Great

Peter the Great (1682–1725) styled himself as Emperor of Russia, and it is from his reign onwards – until 1917 – that we talk about Imperial Russia. Peter oversaw a period in which the Russian state was modernized and increased its power through a mixture of discipline and administrative reform. This combination of approaches appears as a motif throughout Russian history to the present day. For Peter the Great the humiliating defeat of Russian forces by the Swedes at Narva in 1700 can be seen as the trigger for fundamental reforms which began by introducing foreign expertise and technology into the armed forces. Driven on by military priorities, he sought rapid reform in many areas – notably tax rises and a social reorganization which affected both peasantry and nobility, with lifetime conscription into the army for one peasant from every twenty households and a strict 'table of ranks' for the nobility.

Nothing symbolized reform more in Peter's reign than the construction of a new capital city, St Petersburg, as a 'window on the West' (see Chapter 3, Box 3.3); nothing except perhaps his infamous tax on beards, whereby men who continued with the 'Slavic look', rather than adopting the clean-shaven Western fashion, would be singled out for the regime's fiscal disapproval. Alongside these symbolic representations of Peter's Westernizing intent, came the introduction to the Russian court and nobility of Enlightenment philosophies which were flourishing in Europe. West European craftsmen were also brought to Russia, to pass on their expertise, and Russian nobles and students were sent abroad to likewise steep themselves in the latest ideas and approaches.

The scale and speed of reform in Russia under Peter the Great was almost revolutionary. Nonetheless, as many leaders of Russia have discovered, reforming and re-shaping this vast Euro-Asiatic country from above represents no easy task. Peter's authoritarian approach to making Russia more European caused resentment amongst some of the elite, which in turn encouraged a response in the form of the growth of police surveillance. The number of trials for treason increased, and often relied on torture and denunciation for evidence. The Orthodox Church, a naturally traditionalist – and indeed bearded – institution, was made into a department of state. Without drawing too close a parallel, presentiments of the Stalin years can be discerned in all of these responses, as in the attempt at forced and fast modernization from above, by a ruler who saw himself as dragging Russia forward into a future both desirable and – from the military-security perspective – necessary.

Catherine the Great

The influx of Western political thought continued throughout the eighteenth century and flourished particularly during the reign of German-born Catherine the Great (1762–96). Intellectual life in Russia was transformed as knowledge of European languages grew and indicators such as the number of books published and the number of students studying in universities showed a dramatic increase. However, there was a duality present in the attitude of the regime to the influence of Enlightenment thought. The desire to embrace the new ideas of European thinkers, and to benefit from a closer relationship with Europe, had to be kept in increasingly uncomfortable tension with the autocratic nature of the Russian state itself.

Catherine's enthusiasm for Enlightenment philosophy waned after its contribution to the French revolution and the subsequent anti-royalist terror in France. Having encouraged a relatively free press and the growth of intellectual activity, she turned against – and indeed jailed – writers such as Nikolai Novikov and Aleksandr Radishchev, whose writings applied radical European ideas to the situation in Russia.

Russia's history over the first half of the nineteenth century was dominated by military and diplomatic, as well as intellectual, engagement with Europe. Under Catherine the Great Russia's territory had been increased, by military action, in the south and west. In the latter case, and not for the last time, much of what had previously been Poland was absorbed into the Russian Empire. After Catherine's reign, as the French Empire spread across the continent under the leadership of Napoleon Bonaparte, Russia – led by Alexander I – at first reached an accommodation with the French which bought time. In 1812, however, Napoleon attempted the invasion of Russia. Napoleon's efforts famously resulted in his army reaching Moscow, which had been set on fire by the retreating Russians, before succumbing to the ferocity of the Russian winter. In the retreat from Moscow in 1812, Napoleon's renowned *grande armée* was destroyed, and by 1814 Russian troops following in their wake had entered Paris.

For years the Russian nobility had imported Western European ideas and customs into Russia without a great deal of experience of Western Europe itself. For many of those Russian officers who entered Paris in 1814, the firsthand experience was formative, and played a role in the debates which were to dominate Russia over the next several decades. These debates consisted of two elements in particular:

- Demands for the Tsar to cede some of his autocratic powers to representative bodies began to be put forward amongst the more liberal members of society's upper stratum. Most notably, the Decembrist Revolt of 1825 entailed a group of military officers putting together a low-level, poorly organized revolt in support of a demand for some representation. Although the actions of the Decembrists in themselves posed little danger to the Tsar's powers, their symbolic significance as the first liberal challenge to autocracy was seminal.
- The intellectual debate between the Slavophiles and the Westernizers flourished in the years after the Decembrist revolt. The Slavophiles saw in Russia a unique and superior civilization, and idealized the era before Peter the Great's Westernizing revolution. The Westernizers preferred to pursue Western intellectual ideals, not to copy what existed in the West but to engage with the ideas of Western thinkers in their search for a new way to order society.

Alexander II

The debates and ideas of the post-Decembrist years in Russia met with little encouragement from the Tsar, Nicholas I (1825–55). Suspicious of the nobility and determined that Russia should not succumb to the revolutionary fervour sweeping Europe in 1848, Nicholas proved a reactionary monarch, clamping down on dissent and standing by his slogan of 'Orthodoxy, Autocracy, and Nationality'. Not until the reign of his son, Alexander II (1855–81), were further far-reaching reforms introduced in Russia. Alexander's natural reformist tendencies were given more urgency by the defeat of Russian forces in the Crimean War, coinciding with his accession to the throne in 1855. Military defeat highlighted the need for Russia to catch up with the West economically, technologically and socially. In simple terms, war was a huge burden to an already heavily indebted state, and the technological advances of a rapidly industrializing Europe were absent from a Russia whose social structure was still founded on serfdom.

Alexander II gradually but radically reformed his realm, most notably overseeing the abolition of serfdom in 1861 (four years before the abolition of slavery in the United States). Some 50 million serfs and state peasants, approximately 80 per cent of Russia's population, were granted personal freedom. At the same time, rural and urban local councils (the *zemstva* and *duma* respectively) were established in many regions of Russia, to which poorer members of society could be elected, albeit that the indirect election system favoured the nobility and property-owning classes. Alongside these major reforms, during Alexander II's reign, censorship declined, universities encouraged more egalitarian access, and an independent judiciary was established.

Liberal though Alexander's reforms were, their consequences were not all as beneficial as intended. Emancipation of the majority of the population brought hardships, as established rural structures were overturned, the land-owning nobles struggled to continue agricultural production, and the peasantry had to bear higher taxes under the system developed to compensate the nobility. In the second half of the nineteenth century, Russia also experienced rapid population growth. These factors combined to create social upheaval, as a population more transient than ever sought seasonal work in the growing urban settlements. Meanwhile, reforms in local government and in education encouraged the growth of more radical hopes and expectations, amongst those who wanted not reform but revolution. The Tsar, like Soviet leader Mikhail Gorbachev over a hundred years later, faced the difficulty of conducting fundamental changes without bringing down the regime. He succeeded in the short term, in that the Tsarist regime remained in place into the twentieth century. However, Alexander II himself was assassinated by revolutionary terrorists in 1881.

The causes of revolution

Each of the reform periods noted above was accompanied by a discourse of reform which implicitly, and sometimes explicitly, sought to import values from the West. The development of political thought, with its roots in Europe, can be seen throughout the nineteenth century in Russia. After victory against the French armies of Napoleon, Russian troops, many members of the educated nobility amongst them, saw and experienced Western Europe, occupying Paris in 1814. By 1825 the Decembrist uprising sought the beginnings of constitutional reform and representation in Russia, only to be met by the determined autocracy of Tsar Nicholas I (1825–55). During the reign of Alexander II (1855–81) the liberal movement, with its basis in Enlightenment thought, saw a little progress with the creation of local representative bodies, as the Tsar facilitated a widening of debate on policy, although he was not willing to concede actual decision-making powers.

The European Enlightenment did not, however, only give birth to a weak Russian liberalism, but also to a more robust and radical strain, the revolutionary socialist movements. In Russia there existed both a Marxist revolutionary movement with its roots in European political thought, out of which the Communists emerged to rule Russia for most of the twentieth century, and also a revolutionary socialist movement, the Populists, which looked to Russian traditions as opposed to Western European thought as a model for the future. The Populists saw the organization of the traditional Russian peasant *mir* (village) as a model for a democratic future, and the more radical Populists, from whose ranks came the terrorists who assassinated Alexander in 1881, explicitly counted amongst their heroes the leaders of past peasant revolts, such as Pugachev and Razin.

To rather crudely summarize, as Alexander II carried out his programme of reforms he was opposed by conservative members of the nobility and the land-owning class, who objected to the loss of their serfs as well as more subtly to the sense, so brilliantly portrayed in Chekhov's play *The Cherry Orchard* (1904), that the relatively privileged world which they knew was being irreparably changed. He was also opposed by the radical revolutionaries, who did not want to see reform of the system, but rather an entirely new system, in which there would be no role for the tsar and the nobility. In between sat the liberals, whose aim was evolutionary reform of the system in a more democratic, more representative direction.

By the end of the nineteenth century Russian society had grown in number and complexity. The forces for reform were legion but scarcely univocal, as the demands of intellectuals, newly emancipated peasants, diminished nobility, nascent entrepreneurs and industrialists, and many other forces moved together and apart. The successors of Alexander II – Alexander III (1881–94) and Nicholas II (1894–1917) – appeared to have learnt from his assassination the danger of reform. They returned to the notion of 'Orthodoxy, Autocracy, and Nationality', and allowed only cautious reform, aimed primarily at economic growth, under figures such as Sergei Witte (Finance Minister, 1892–1903) and Petr Stolypin (Prime Minister, 1906–11). Whilst such incremental change occurred, the contradictory demands and discontents of many simmered. Military defeat in the Russo-Japanese conflict of 1904–5 acted as a signal for widespread discontent, with violence spreading in urban and rural areas. In January 1905, in St Petersburg, troops fired on peaceful demonstrators, sparking further unrest. By October 1905 Tsar Nicholas signed a manifesto promising an elected parliament, and the unrest of the '1905 revolution' subsided.

The Soviet period, 1917–91

Russian history is for the most part dominated by a strong 'garrison' state. However, partly as a factor of the size of Russia, partly stemming from the nebulous concept of an authoritarian political culture, the Russian state has repeatedly seemed profoundly insecure about itself and so constantly sought to expand its control over society. This insecurity is not ill-founded though, as there are regular episodes in Russian history where the authority and power of the state collapses and 'society' rises up. Such a perspective offers one approach to the advent of rule by revolutionaries in Russia in 1917.

The Bolshevik Party – later to become the Communist Party of the Soviet Union – came to power in October 1917. As noted above, there had been a 'revolution' in Russia twelve years earlier in 1905, when largely uncoordinated unrest across the Russian Empire resulted in Nicholas II agreeing to the creation of a parliament, or Duma, whose actual influence on policy was minimal to begin with and faded thereafter. However, the hardships and social upheaval of the First World War, in which as many as two million Russians died, created fertile soil for revolutionary and reformist movements to flourish, and protest became increasingly frequent.

In February 1917 unrest in Petrograd – as the Tsarist capital St Petersburg was then known – developed into a revolution which forced the abdication of Tsar Nicholas on 2 March and the creation of a Provisional Government, based on the largely liberal Duma. At the same time the revolutionary movements recreated the Petrograd Workers' Council – or 'Soviet' – which had first existed in 1905, and similar Soviets came into being in other cities. A situation of 'dual power' existed, with the Provisional Government and the Soviets both claiming legitimacy. It is only a slight oversimplification to say that the elite and the masses stood at loggerheads.

In October 1917, the Bolshevik Party staged a seizure of power in the name of the Soviets. In its implementation if not its effect, this event was more akin to a coup than a revolution. And in the immediate situation of Petrograd in 1917 it represented simply another twist in a year of violence and upheaval which had seen a workers' uprising, the abdication of the Tsar, the creation of a Provisional Government, a failed attempt by the revolutionaries to seize power in the 'July Days', a failed counter-revolutionary reaction led by former Tsarist General Kornilov in September, and now a seizure of power by the Bolsheviks, the most radical of a number of socialist parties, in October.

Earlier in 1917 Lenin had said that he did not expect to see a revolution in his lifetime. The idea that a Bolshevik uprising in October might leave them in power for most of the century would have been greeted by many observers at the time as tenuous to say the least. However, that is what happened. The Communists' first few years in power were – like the 'Time of Troubles' over three centuries earlier – years of civil war, foreign intervention, and economic uncertainty. Russian novelist Boris Pilnyak captured this chaos, and what he saw as the essence of Russia's elemental spirit, in his work *The Naked Year*. He portrayed the worst year of the civil war, 1919, as a time when the civilized Western clothes of Russia were stripped away to reveal beneath them the true Asiatic nature of the Russian masses. Such a force was more ready to be harnessed by the radical revolutionaries, be they urban Bolsheviks or rural Socialist Revolutionaries, than by the weak and sparse liberal elite. The tradition of peasant revolt against landowners was replayed again under the initially supportive gaze of Lenin and his government. By a combination of propaganda, populist measures, ruthlessness, military skill, and a strong minority of popular support, the Bolshevik regime survived and prospered.

By the late 1920s, with the rise to power of Josef Stalin, the state was ready once again to fully reassert control. Forced collectivization of agriculture, state-planned industrialization, centralization, state-induced famine, a vast labour camp network and political terror all combined in the 1930s to rebuild a state which was now not merely authoritarian, but totalitarian, seeking to dominate every aspect of its citizens' lives. During the Stalin years, millions of victims were incarcerated in the labour camps of the Gulag or were executed during the

'Great Terror', and all aspects of public life came under the dictatorial control of the regime.

Playing catch-up?

As we have noted above, a clear pattern supports the discourse of a perennial need for Russia to emulate Europe, and 'the West' in general. From this point of view the motivation for reform and accompanying upheaval in Russia has regularly been realistic self-interest, driven by a combination of economic decline and related security threats. Be it the perceived need to build a modern navy under Peter the Great, a modern army under Alexander II, or a more high-tech military industrial complex under Mikhail Gorbachev in the 1980s, a realist motive lay behind these times of upheaval. The dictum that 'war is the locomotive of history' applies to Russia perhaps more than to anywhere.

We can add to these examples the defeat of Russia in war with Japan, which precipitated the revolution and constitutional reform of 1905, and the defeat of the Russian forces on the eastern front during the First World War, which served as a catalyst for the collapse of the Tsarist regime and the rise of the Communists in 1917. We can add too the industrialization of the 1930s under Josef Stalin, who explicitly stated in 1931 that Russia had to catch up or be crushed, as war was coming within the next decade (the Stalin years will be considered in more detail below).

None the less, if we are adopting the catch-up approach to understanding the major features of Russian history – and this is certainly not the only approach possible as we shall see later – then a more idealist, as opposed to realist, explanation for these periods of reformism can also be offered.

There are two main difficulties with the catch-up approach outlined above, and an awareness of these related problems is extremely helpful for our understanding of contemporary Russia:

● First, Russia has not spent its entire history in unsuccessful pursuit of a superior European ideal. Although the periods discussed above provide examples of such a pursuit, the whole picture – both of Russia itself and even of those particular periods – is more complex. In particular, there was not always a coincidence of modernization and Westernization in Russian history. Although Peter the Great, Alexander II and others all used selective borrow-

Illustration 2.1 Contrasting historical influences on contemporary Russia, Red Square, Moscow, May 2008

A Russian Orthodox icon of Christ peeps out from behind a temporary standard erected to commemorate 'Victory Day', marking the end of the Second World War. Note that this standard includes the cyrillic letters, 'CCCP', meaning USSR.

ing from and imitation of the West, they were also evidently constrained by the Russian context within which they ruled. There were other periods too, such as the reigns of Alexander III (1881–94) and Nicholas II (1894–1917), and perhaps – though this is less clear cut, given Marxism's European origins – the Stalin years, when overcoming backwardness was attempted within more traditional approaches, such as autarky and repression. In other words, there were strategies which sought to synthesize modernization and Russian-ness.

- The second difficulty with the catch-up approach is that the idea of a backward Russia is, understandably, not one which is held dear by most Russians. This has a resonance in Russia today, in the policies of the ruling regime and the opinions of the people. A sense of injured national pride, and of being patronized by the West in the post-Communist era, has without doubt helped to shape the political discourse of contemporary Russia.

Jumping ahead of our chronology momentarily, it is worth noting that Vladimir Putin brought the duality of Russia's history into focus when he came to power, initially as acting president, on 31 December 1999. Russia's second post-Soviet leader succeeded President Yeltsin with – as he himself put it – the task of combining the universal principles of democracy and a free market, with Russian reality. Putin called Communism 'a blind alley, far away from civilisation'. However, he was not about to junk the entire Communist experience. Putin made clear early in his presidency, in an address to the Presidium of the State Council, that there was much to be proud of in Russia's past, and that the wholesale rejection of what had gone before was untenable:

> Where shall we then put the achievements of Russian culture? Where shall we put Pushkin, Dostoyevsky, Tolstoy and Tchaikovsky? Where shall we put the achievements of Russian science – Mendeleyev, Lobachevsky and many, many others? Much of what all of us take pride in – what shall we do with all this? ... And do we really have nothing, except the Stalin camps and repressions, to recall for the whole Soviet period of our country's existence? Where shall we then put Dunayevsky, Sholokhov, Shostakovich and Korolev and the achievements in outer space? What shall we do with Yurii Gagarin's flight, as well as the brilliant victories of Russian arms – from the times of Rumyantsev, Suvorov and Kutuzov? And the victory in the spring of 1945?

(For details of Putin's Russian heroes see Box 2.2.)

Putin's argument provides a particularly pertinent context to understanding contemporary Russia. During his years as Russia's leader, he has sought to recreate a sense of national pride and identity of Russia as a 'great power'. The most tricky element in this narrative of renewal was the question of what to do with Communism itself, an ideology rejected by Presidents Yeltsin, Putin and Medvedev. For most of the twentieth century the Soviet regime represented itself as at the leading edge of global historical development. One does not have to be an apologist for the Communist system to note that this case was not a wholly ridiculous one. There was a logic to it, a mix

Box 2.2   Putin's Russian heroes

In a speech to the Russian State Council, President Putin singled out the following fourteen men as indicative of the great achievers in Russian history.

Aleksandr Pushkin, 1799–1837. Known as the founder of Russian literature, and Russia's greatest ever poet.

Fyodor Dostoevsky, 1821–81, was one of the great novelists of the nineteenth century. His best known works are *Crime and Punishment* (1866) and *The Brothers Karamazov* (1879).

Isaak Dunayevsky, 1900–55. Composer, particularly popular during the Stalin years and best known for his film music which fostered an upbeat view of Stalin's Soviet Union.

Yurii Gagarin, 1934–68. In 1961 he became the first person to travel into space.

Sergei Korolev, 1907–66. Instrumental in the development of the intercontinental ballistic missiles which undergirded the Soviet Union's status as a nuclear superpower.

Prince Mikhail Kutuzov, 1745–1813. Commander of the Russian forces which repelled Napoleon's invasion of Russia in 1812.

Nikolai Lobachevsky, 1792–1856. Mathematician and founder of non-Euclidean geometry.

Dmitrii Mendeleyev, 1834–1907. Developed the periodic table of chemical elements.

Marshal Pyotr Rumantsev, 1725–96. Hero of the Seven Years' War with Prussia in the mid-eighteenth century, and of later wars in Europe. Governor-General of Ukraine from 1764.

Mikhail Sholokhov, 1905–84. The only non-dissident Soviet writer to win the Nobel Prize for Literature (1965). His best known work is *Quiet Flows the Don*.

Dmitrii Shostakovich, 1906–75. One of the twentieth century's finest composers, and arguably its greatest symphonist.

General Aleksandr Suvorov, 1729–1800. Famed military commander of the latter half of the eighteenth century, Suvorov was known for his development of 'military science'.

Pyotr Tchaikovsky, 1840–93. Composer; his best known works are the *1812 Overture*, the opera *Yevgenii Onegin*, and the ballet *Swan Lake*.

Lev Tolstoy, 1828–1910. One of the great novelists of the nineteenth century. Tolstoy wrote *War and Peace* (1865–9) and *Anna Karenina* (1873–7).

of interpretation and fact which together created a powerful discourse and a powerful state.

Putin's selection is a conservative group, in the sense that all of these would have been acknowledged in the Soviet era as great men of Russian history. However, Putin has also paid tribute in official speeches to a number of fiercely anti-Soviet figures – notably Nobel Prize winning author Aleksandr Solzhenitsyn (1918–2008), civil war General Anton Denikin (1872–1947) and philosopher Ivan Il'in (1883–1954).

To make the case for Russia leading the world in the twentieth century let us go back to our discussion of political thought, and the influence of European thought in particular. A distinction should be drawn between liberal thought and revolutionary thought. It is the latter which transformed twentieth-century Russia. Revolutionary thought had both European and Russian strands. The Populists in the nineteenth and early twentieth centuries saw the uniqueness of Russian civilization, with its overwhelming peasant majority and particular forms of local governance, as the basis for a future socialist society.

Those Russian socialists who took their lead from the writings of European counterparts had a more global perspective. Men such as the founder of the Soviet state, Vladimir Lenin, drew on Western European political thought as developed by Karl Marx and Friedrich Engels. Marxism concentrated not on the peasantry, but on the industrial working class – the proletariat – and a rejection of capitalism. Revolution would come from the proletariat, revolution would eventually be global, and the final stage of history would be communism – an end to exploitation and oppression, the emancipation of mankind and the fulfilment of humanity's potential in a technologically advanced, rationally managed society. Russian and Soviet communism, as it developed in the twentieth century, placed itself unequivocally at the head of the Marxist camp, and the Populists were soon repressed following the Bolshevik revolution of October 1917.

Soviet Marxism placed an emphasis on being at the cutting-edge of a developing global movement. Marxism provided a world view within whose framework every aspect of life could be placed. Its adherents claimed it to be scientific and rational, with the implication that it was therefore infallible. And the Marxist view was that global workers' revolution was inevitable. This emphasis on scientific rationalism and the ongoing development of history to its end-point, communism, carried with it a contemporary edge in most areas of life. Communism was a creed for the newly emergent industrial working class, predominantly the younger generation:

- it embraced modern technology;
- it rejected superstition and religion in favour of mankind's ability to construct a better world itself;
- it sought common ownership of goods and planned production to meet the needs of the people, as opposed to the vagaries of the market; and
- it was a teleological ('goal-oriented') ideology, with a momentum and a purpose.

That a successful workers' revolution leading to a socialist regime occurred first in Russia, rather than in the more industrialized states of Western Europe, took a little explaining in terms of the expectations of Marx. Lenin's explanation was that the chain of capitalism broke at its weakest link – Russia – and that global revolution would follow. Global revolution did not follow, at least not in terms of the European powers becoming Communist. However, much of the former Russian Empire became united under Communist rule as the Soviet Union by the early 1920s, and thereafter – particularly in the Cold War era after the Second World War – numerous countries around the world became part of the Communist bloc. The Soviet Union established itself as the leader of this growing Communist camp, which stood in opposition to the US-led capitalist bloc. In its own terms, the Soviet Union was on the cutting-edge of history's inevitable progress to communism. In some sense the Russian nationalist concept of Moscow as 'the Third Rome', which would illuminate the world and never fall, can be said to have been taken up by the Communists.

In reality, the Soviet experiment soon soured. Whatever one's politics, for most people there can be little argument that the Stalin regime, which imprisoned in labour camps or executed around 20 million of its own citizens between 1929 and 1953, scarcely represented the fulfilment of Marxism's emancipatory mission. Historians and politicians have disputed whether the authoritarianism, repression and dictatorship of the Stalin years in particular represent a failure of Marxism or of its Soviet implementation. Some have sought the roots of Soviet totalitarianism in the political culture of Russia. Stalin implicitly encouraged parallels between himself, Ivan the Terrible and Peter the Great, and the suggestion that Russians are somehow predisposed to rule by a 'strong hand' is fairly often cited in the literature.

Although the Stalin years represent the epitome of totalitarian dictatorship, from Lenin through to the late 1980s the Soviet Union was marked by:

- repression of opponents;
- the existence of a single party with no participation in politics by any other means;
- strict state censorship and ownership of all media;
- a preference for the rights of the state over the individual;
- a judicial system accustomed to political judgements; and
- the socialization of all citizens into the Soviet ideal.

Lenin ordered the arrest and execution of ideological opponents. Khrushchev's reformist reputation stems largely from his closure of many labour camps and his condemnation of Stalin in the Secret Speech of 1956, but none the less he himself instigated a brutal anti-religious campaign. In the Brezhnev years (1964–82) dissidents were subjected to compulsory psychiatric treatment, after all, the argument went, if they oppose the Soviet regime, they must be mad.

Can we then still speak of the Soviet Union in any sense as leading the world? In short, yes, if only because of its development into one of two global superpowers by the middle of the century, and its consolidation of this position for over three decades. Even in the 1930s, as the Stalinist repressions swung into action and millions died in labour camps or state-induced famine, there was support for the Soviet regime on the European left. Stalin's repressions were largely hidden from the world. Only in 1956 did Khrushchev begin to acknowledge them. Only after the Soviet archives opened in the late 1980s and early 1990s was their extent fully revealed.

To many observers at the time, the Soviet Union seemed to be demonstrating the superiority of the planned economy in comparison with the market. While the Great Depression devastated the economies of the United States and much of the capitalist world in the 1930s, the Soviet Union enjoyed rapid economic growth as it industrialized with unprecedented speed. As the Marxists had stated, capitalism appeared to be collapsing under the weight of its inherent contradictions, whilst the new scientific rationalism of the Communist regime apparently flourished. During the Second World War, the contribution of the newly industrialized Soviet Union to the defeat of Nazi Germany can scarcely be over-exaggerated (see Chapter 8).

From this perspective it is easier to gain that sense of unstoppable momentum which is central to understanding communism's place in the world in the middle decades of the twentieth century. Similarly, an elaboration of the extent and speed of the global political map's reddening in the immediate post-war decades, provides us with an insight into the influence of Soviet Communism. By merely counting the number of states which became Communist between 1945 and 1975 – albeit that many were coerced into the Communist camp – one might have concluded that Marx's prediction of world revolution was not completely far-fetched. With the benefit of hindsight and the knowledge of Soviet Communism's eventual failure, it is too easy to forget the enthusiasm and commitment of those in the Soviet Union and elsewhere who genuinely believed that they were pushing forward in history's vanguard.

We began this section by noting two problems with the catch-up approach to Russian history. The Soviet experience is by and large a demonstration of the first problem; namely, the fact that Russia has not spent its entire history in unsuccessful pursuit of a superior European ideal. For much of this period the Soviet Union travelled a path not taken by the Western nations – albeit that the provenance of Marxism was European, even if the 'actually existing socialism' of the Communist world had Russian snow on its boots.

The second problem is that the idea of a backward Russia is not one which is held dear by most Russians. When considering the Soviet era, many Russians hold a broadly positive view, particularly of the post-Stalin years. In opinion polls in the post-Soviet decades, when Russian citizens are asked to name the best Russian leader of the twentieth century, Leonid Brezhnev repeatedly tops the list, with his time in office being voted the best period to live in (Bacon and Sandle, 2002: 4–5). Again, this perception cannot be dismissed as fanciful. Many Russians of that generation look back on those years as a time when living standards steadily increased, full employment and job security were the order of the day, inflation was virtually non-existent, crime levels were low, and national pride was high.

From communism to contemporary Russia

Using different but complementary approaches to Russian history, we have illuminated much of the context helpful to our understanding of contemporary Russia. It is worth emphasizing again – as will become apparent later – the resonance of history in contemporary Russian political debate. Politicians and population alike in Russia today are well-versed in their past, and given the nature of Russia's recent history it is perhaps not surprising that it plays a significant role in shaping the contemporary agenda. In the final section of this chapter we will consider the transition from communism to the present day. Much of what is covered here will be revisited in later chapters; again our emphasis is on providing the context for studying contemporary Russia.

As noted above, the Brezhnev years (1964–82) regularly come out on top in opinion polls of the best era in which to live from the last hundred years of Russian history. As well as the everyday factors – and somewhat romanticized nostalgia – which influence people's opinion of these years, the Brezhnev era was a time when the Soviet Union competed as an equal with the United States in the space race and the arms race; a time when Soviet musicians, dancers and composers were renowned the world over; and a time when Soviet sportsmen and women regularly competed with and beat the world's best. In 1980 the Olympic Games were held in Moscow, in what was the first – and until Beijing 2008, the only – Olympics held in a Communist state. The event was intended to crown the achievements of a great superpower, and was seen in the Soviet Union as an unqualified success despite a boycott by many Western countries. Had it been suggested that within little more than a decade the Soviet Union would have weakened to the point of collapse, few would have believed it. And yet, underneath the surface, there was much wrong with the Soviet regime by the 1980s.

Mikhail Gorbachev

Mikhail Gorbachev, when he came to power in 1985, began to refer to the Brezhnev years as an 'era of stagnation'. He characterized it as a time when an ageing leadership clung to power and gave little thought to the future development of the country. After Brezhnev died in 1982 his two successors, first Yurii Andropov and then Konstantin Chernenko, both took power as sick men and died after very little time in office. The economy stopped growing, and Gorbachev inherited what he called 'a pre-crisis situation'. The later joke was that in 1985 the Soviet Union stood on the edge of the abyss, and under Mikhail Gorbachev it took a great step forward.

Gorbachev's characterization of the Brezhnev years provided the context in which he began his reform programme. It could also be argued that the military weakness of the Soviet superpower was exemplified by the inability of Soviet forces to secure victory in the Afghan War (1979–88). For a state which owed its superpower status almost entirely to its military strength, this failure in a low-tech conventional war was compounded by the Soviet Union's inability to compete with the United States in the high-tech stakes. As the arms race between the superpowers moved increasingly towards the development of smart conventional weaponry and missile defence shields (the so-called 'star wars' programme announced by US President Reagan in the early 1980s), Gorbachev, along with many of the generals and most of the party leadership, saw that reform was needed in order to catch up with the West.

The Soviet economy was shrinking, and Gorbachev's solution was to radically reform socio-political relations, gradually reducing the reach of the authoritarian state and giving the people a genuine democratic vote for many key positions – though never for his own. Unfortunately for Gorbachev, a simultaneous reduction in authoritarian control and an invitation to elect political leaders led many in the national republics which made up the Soviet Union to vote for leaders who sought independence from the Soviet state. The biggest of these national republics was Russia itself, and once Russia, under its newly elected president, Boris Yeltsin, declared independence from the Soviet Union in 1991, no Soviet state remained. If Gorbachev inherited a pre-crisis situation, then by the end of his period in office it had turned into a terminal crisis for the Soviet Union.

In December 1991 the leaders of Russia, Ukraine and Belarus met and declared that their republics were forming a Commonwealth of Independent States. By the end of the month the majority of Soviet republics had signed up for this Commonwealth, and those that had not signed up insisted resolutely on complete independence. The Soviet Union no longer existed.

Boris Yeltsin

When Boris Yeltsin rose to power in Russia in the late 1980s and early 1990s he did it with the support of the emergent broad democratic movement, Democratic Russia. Yeltsin, like many post-Soviet politicians, had been a member of the Communist Party of the Soviet Union for much of his adult life, and was brought into the Party's highest body – the Politburo – by Mikhail Gorbachev in 1986, having been put in charge of the Party in Moscow in December 1985. Yeltsin soon came to national and international attention as something of a maverick with a populist touch. He advocated faster and more far-reaching reform than that proposed by Gorbachev, and in 1987

Yeltsin resigned from the Politburo. Gorbachev removed him from his senior position as head of the Moscow Communist Party, but, to the surprise of many, then gave him a ministerial post in the Soviet government. In the past, this might have been the end of Yeltsin's influence, but, as Gorbachev's reforms opened up the Soviet electoral system, Yeltsin was able to gain election first to the new Soviet parliament – the Congress of People's Deputies – in 1989, and then, in 1990, to the parliament of the Russian republic.

In the Russian parliament, Yeltsin, with the support of the reformist deputies, was elected Speaker – at that time the highest position in the Russian, as opposed to the Soviet, political hierarchy. In March 1991, Gorbachev organized a referendum across the Soviet Union on the preservation of the Soviet state. Yeltsin again saw his opportunity and, with the support of the Russian parliament, placed a second question on the referendum ballot, asking the people of the Russian republic to support the creation of a Russian presidency. Approval was duly gained, and in June 1991 Boris Yeltsin became the first ever directly elected leader of Russia, albeit that he remained constitutionally – if not democratically – in an inferior position to Soviet President Gorbachev. It was from this position of strength that President Yeltsin moved to take Russia out of the Soviet Union.

In August 1991, Gorbachev's conservative opponents in the higher echelons of the Soviet government and party structures staged a coup attempt. Gorbachev himself was put under house arrest, a state of emergency was declared by the coup plotters, and troops were brought in to take control of Moscow. The Russian parliament and president became the focus of opposition to this coup. Thousands of supporters gathered there to hear Yeltsin – having climbed up on one of the tanks sent to enforce the coup – declare the state of emergency illegal and call for the immediate return of Gorbachev to Moscow and to his position as head of the Soviet Union. Although there was the real danger of an assault on Yeltsin and his parliament by special forces under the command of the coup plotters – and indeed three civilians were killed in skirmishes outside the parliament building – within a couple of days the coup had collapsed and Gorbachev came back to Moscow. However, he returned to a very different political landscape. Yeltsin's moral authority and popularity had been boosted by his opposition to the coup. Furthermore, he could point to the fact that he had been elected to his position by the Russian people, whereas Gorbachev, in contrast, had never stood in a democratic election. It was from this strengthened position that Yeltsin moved rapidly through the Soviet endgame, and to the creation of the Commonwealth of Independent States noted above.

After communism – from Yeltsin to Putin

The collapse of the Soviet Union at the end of 1991 marked the culmination of an astonishingly short period during which the Soviet bloc, which had shaped world affairs since the end of the Second World War, disappeared. In 1989 the Soviet 'satellite states' of central and eastern Europe embarked on a democratizing path, establishing constitutions, political institutions, independent judiciaries and multi-party systems. In the economic sphere, they moved away from state planning and towards a market. When an independent Russia emerged out of the failed Soviet Union in 1991, it likewise intended to take this path.

It is a commonplace of political life that to be in opposition is easier than to govern. In the last years of the Soviet Union many disparate forces had been able to unite together around a common cause, that of democratic opposition to the Communist regime. Once the common goal had been achieved, these disparate forces began to fracture around the question of 'What next?' In broad terms, the democratic opposition, Yeltsin included, wanted to establish democracy and a market economy. When it came to the specific implementation of policy, however, many differences and questions emerged:

- What about the sequencing and pace of reform? Should economic reform precede political, or vice versa? Should everything be done at once, taking the 'shock therapy' route, or would a more gradualist approach be beneficial?
- What about relations with the other former Soviet republics? A good number of those in the broad Yeltsin camp had fought for a democratic Soviet Union, but had not envisaged its total disappearance.
- And when it came to democratic transition, what form of democracy should be adopted? Parliamentary or presidential? An electoral system based on proportional representation or a majoritarian system? A single chamber or a bicameral parliament?
- And what about relations between Russia's regions and the centre? How should powers be divided between the centre and the regions across Russia's vast territory?

There was clearly much to decide. Unfortunately the decision-making process was not clear. Yeltsin had risen to power in Russia with the support of the parliament, or Supreme Soviet, which, thanks to Gorbachev's democratizing moves, had at last been able to lay hold of the authority to which it had been nominally entitled throughout the Soviet period. Once elected president, though, Boris Yeltsin had a mandate direct from the people, rather than having to rely on the maintenance of a parliamentary majority. However, many of his powers as president were granted to him by the parliament, under the terms of the much amended Russian Constitution. This Constitution had been in force since 1978; it was a Soviet Constitution in desperate need of replacing. Yeltsin wanted to replace it with a constitution setting out a presidential democracy; the parliament wanted to change it for a constitution establishing a parliamentary democracy.

There was deadlock, and for the best part of two years (1992–3), when the newly independent Russian state was in desperate need of fresh legislation and clear governance, President Yeltsin and his parliament were at an impasse. One solution would have been the holding of simultaneous presidential and parliamentary elections; Yeltsin was confident of re-election, many parliamentary deputies less so, and so the parliament rejected this option. Yeltsin was unable to dissolve parliament himself, as this lay outside the bounds of his constitutional powers.

Finally, after move and countermove, and an inconclusive national referendum, President Yeltsin unilaterally – and in constitutional terms, illegally – dissolved the parliament in late September 1993 and announced new elections for the following December. Parliament refused to accept its dissolution, and, with the Constitutional Court ruling in its favour, it remained in session. After a stand-off of several days, fighting broke out in Moscow, as troops loyal to the parliament attacked the building of a national television station. Yeltsin responded by ordering a full-scale assault on the parliamentary building, where only two years before he had led the parliament in its opposition to the Soviet coup plotters. The parliament building was shelled, over a hundred of its defenders were killed, and Yeltsin stood as the undisputed ruler of Russia. On 12 December a national referendum passed a new and heavily presidential Constitution on the same day as the people voted for the new parliament that this Constitution created.

It is this Constitution of 1993 that remains in force in Russia today. Its provisions include the right of the President to issue decrees with the force of law, and the clear separation of the executive (presidency and government) and legislature (parliament). No member of parliament may serve in the government at the same time as being a parliamentary deputy, and the only oversight which parliament has over the government is the ratification of the president's choice of prime minister. Should parliament reject the president's nominee, then the president can dissolve parliament. These provisions are discussed in more detail in Chapter 5.

Yeltsin stood again for the presidency in June 1996 and was re-elected in a second-round run-off against his Communist opponent, Gennadii Zyuganov. This victory owed much to the support of a coterie of rich businessmen and media owners, who collectively became known as the oligarchs, because of their subsequent influence on the president. For much of his second term in office, Yeltsin was in visible decline both physically and mentally. He underwent a major heart operation after his re-election in 1996, and throughout his period in office was prone to bouts of heavy drinking.

Ironically, having sent troops against his parliament in his pursuit of a heavily presidential constitution, Yeltsin increasingly seemed unable to govern Russia as the twentieth century came to an end. A presidential constitution demands a strong president – Boris Yeltsin was physically weak, owed a political debt to the increasingly powerful oligarchs, relied heavily on a small group of advisers known as 'the family', and had to make a series of bilateral agreements with regional leaders in which he negotiated the division of power between the centre and the components of the Russian Federation.

It became ever more apparent that the Russian state was weak, and this impression was emphasized by the fact that between 1998 and 2000 Russia had five prime ministers. Boris Yeltsin was casting around for a successor, and the fact that three out of the four prime ministerial appointments which he made in this period were of men with security service backgrounds indicates the sort of figure for which he was searching. Yeltsin wanted a technocrat rather than a politician to succeed him, someone able to strengthen the state, and someone who would both protect his legacy and guarantee him a safe and comfortable retirement. By the end of 1999 Yeltsin believed he had found that man. Vladimir Putin had risen from relative obscurity to the post of prime minister in August of that year, and on 31 December Yeltsin resigned the presidency and – in accordance with the Constitution – appointed Putin acting president pending an election in March 2000. Putin duly won this election. Boris Yeltsin enjoyed a quiet and comfortable retirement until his death at the age of 76 in April 2007.

From Putin to Medvedev and back to Putin

Vladimir Putin became President of Russia in May 2000, at the age of 47, and remained in that position until May 2008, having served the constitutional limit of two *successive* four-year terms. On leaving the post of president, he was immediately appointed prime minister by his successor as president, Dmitrii Medvedev. In 2012, at the end of his term as president, Medvedev stood aside so that Putin could stand again, successfully, for the presidency, the term of which had by then been extended by constitutional amendment to six years.

The Putin years can be said to stretch from 2000 onwards until whenever he finally leaves the political scene in Russia. Although Putin did not, for constitutional reasons, serve as president between 2008–12, to most observers he remained the most powerful figure in Russia, the 'national leader', even whilst his loyal protégé Medvedev enjoyed the formally superior position of president. Much of what has happened in Russia under Vladimir Putin forms the basis of the subsequent chapters in this book. None the less, it is worth presenting here a brief overview of his years in power, particularly in relation to the frameworks of Russia's history established in this chapter.

Vladimir Putin has devoted considerable effort to placing twenty-first-century Russia within a historical narrative, drawing on precedents from the nation's past and engaging in the debate on Russia's relationship with the West. As noted earlier (see Box 2.2), Putin attempted at an early stage to create a sense of Russian continuity within, and to some extent despite, the Soviet era. He consistently sought to downplay communism *per se* whilst at the same time holding on to the notion of Russia as a great nation. A good example of this approach can be seen in his move, within months of becoming president, to replace the Russian national anthem of the 1990s with an anthem made up of new words to the music of the old Soviet era national anthem. Putin sought to build bridges with émigré communities descended from those forced out of Russia by the Bolsheviks. He also abolished 7 November, formerly Revolution Day, as a national holiday.

These symbolic moves are just that – symbols. None the less, a good deal of effort was put into the creation of a narrative which emphasized pride in Russia and in great Russians, even from the

Soviet years, whilst remaining critical of communism and its leaders (this narrative is explored in some detail in Chapter 8). Such a balancing act could not always be carried off successfully, particularly in relation to the seminal event of the twentieth century – the Second World War. To laud the achievement and sacrifice of the Russian people without appearing to celebrate the leader of the state in that period, Josef Stalin, has proved difficult.

The importance to Putin of creating an appropriate national narrative was apparent too in the way in which the Yeltsin years were presented. Increasingly during his period as president, Putin and his team talked of the 1990s as a period of chaos and weakness, comparable to the 'Time of Troubles' at the turn of the seventeenth century. This fitted well with the idea that a strong 'tsar' and a strong state were required after Yeltsin.

The process of strengthening the power of the Russian state became a key feature of Putin's presidency, particularly in the first term. The oligarchs, who had exercised significant political influence under Yeltsin, were reined in by Putin. The message was clear – they should stay out of politics and stay loyal. Some of the most prominent oligarchs refused to do so and went into exile – for example, Boris Berezovsky and Vladimir Gusinsky – or ended up in prison, as is the case with Mikhail Khodorkovsky. Similarly, Russia's regions were brought more firmly under the control of the federal authorities.

The process of 'strengthening the state' was tackled by a variety of means, including greater state oversight of political parties, an end to elections for regional leaders, political interference in the judicial process, and increased state control over the media – partly via companies in which the state owns a majority share. At the end of the 1990s almost all commentators agreed that the Russian state needed strengthening. More than a decade on, the consensus is that democracy and pluralism have declined in Russia during the Putin years. Within this consensus, however, there is room for analysis and debate. Throughout the rest of this book, questions over the legitimacy, wisdom and outcome of Putin's methods and goals are considered.

Political developments in Russia during Putin's first two terms as president (2000–8) took place in a climate of rapid economic growth. Increasing standards of living, accompanied by the state's ability to pay off debts and spend more on public goods, came on the back of high energy prices providing a boost to the largest sectors of the Russian economy, the oil and gas industries. Economic success is one of the reasons why Putin's popularity remained remarkably high throughout this period. The global economic downturn of 2008 onwards affected Russia badly, particularly in its early stages, and has brought a harsher reality to bear. Putin's popularity in the early years of his third term (2012–18) has not quite matched what went before, although it still remains comparatively high. Mass demonstrations in Moscow in 2011–12, around the election period which saw Putin return to office, called for a fairer and more open political system, and were met with the prosecution and imprisonment of a number of demonstrators and prominent oppositionists. Although most Russians were not ready to take to the streets, opinion polls in 2012–13 did point to an increased sense of fatigue with the Putin regime. The policy emphasis in Russia is once again – as this chapter demonstrates it so often has been – on the need for modernization.

3

Land and People

Russia covers roughly 17 million square kilometres, significantly larger than its nearest rivals in terms of being the world's largest country – namely Canada, the United States and China – each of which covers between 9 and 10 million square kilometres. Before it collapsed in 1991, the Soviet Union was a third bigger again. Yet Russia easily retains its lead position, even with the post-Soviet loss of the vast territories of Central Asia (Kazakhstan, Kyrgyzstan, Tajikistan, Turkmenistan and Uzbekistan), the Transcaucasian countries (Armenia, Georgia, Azerbaijan), the Eastern European lands (Belarus, Moldova, Ukraine), and the Baltic States (Estonia, Latvia and Lithuania).

In terms of population, Russia ranks ninth in the world with a population in 2013 of 142.8 million. The Soviet Union before its collapse had ranked third in terms of global population, and at the beginning of the twenty-first century, Russia ranked seventh. Russia's population has declined markedly in the post-Soviet era, decreasing by an average of 390,000 per annum between 1993 and 2009, even allowing for immigration of around 5 million over the same period. As Chapter 4 details, Russians suffered from a high death rate, particularly amongst men, and a low birth rate. Russia's population began to grow again in 2010, but there is no guarantee that this represents a longer-term trend. Most demographic predictions for the coming decades set out a number of scenarios, of varying degrees of negativity. Russia's official demographic predictions remain relatively optimistic, with the Russian statistical agency's medium prediction being for a population of 139 million in 2030. The United Nations' medium prediction, on the other hand, estimates that Russia's population will have fallen to 136 million by then.

Russia's capital city, Moscow, ranks sixth in terms of the world's most populous cities, keeping to a strict definition of city boundaries. If estimates are made for urban areas, Moscow slips to nineteenth in the global rankings. Moscow and St Petersburg are the two cities in Russia which have the status of federal regions. Moscow is Europe's biggest city, with a population of 11.5 million in 2010, though if the Moscow urban area is included that figure rises to 15.8 million. St Petersburg is Europe's third biggest city, with a population of 5.0 million. London comes in second, between these two Russian giants, with over 8 million.

Moscow is a European city and the centre of the country's political, economic and cultural life. It is too easy to forget the vast Asiatic expanse of Russia when so much in terms of contact with the West is mediated through crowded, commercial, cosmopolitan Moscow. Almost a fifth of Russia's population live in the *millioniki* – those cities which proudly boast a population of more than a million (see Box 3.1) – and 60 per cent of the population live in the Central, Volga and Southern federal districts of Russia. Or, to put it the other way round, those areas officially classified as 'the North' (the Far East, Siberia and northern European Russia) make up 70 per cent of the territory of the Russian Federation, but contain only 8 per cent of the population. According to the 2002 census, over a quarter of Russia's population can still be classified as rural dwellers.

The final point to make by way of creating a true picture of Russia which moves beyond the Moscow-centric European perception is that it is a multi-ethnic federation. Over 190 different national groups were identified in Russia by the 2010 census. Although over 80 per cent of the population are ethnically Russian, the diversity of the country is represented in its federal structure, in its religious make-up (with around 10 per cent of the population being Muslims), and – most acutely – in ongoing conflict between the state and ethno-religious rebels in the North Caucasus, particularly during the Chechen wars. All of these issues are dealt with in this chapter, which outlines the physical, demographic and social bases of the Russian state.

The physical setting

Covering as it does a seventh of the earth's land surface, Russia stretches more than 10,000 kilometres across Europe and Asia, from the port of Kaliningrad on the Baltic Sea (an enclave cut off from the

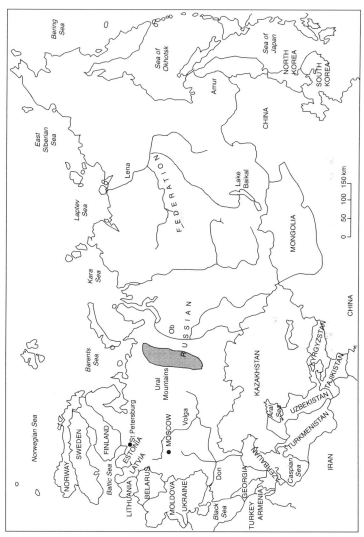

Map 3.1 Russia: main physical features

Box 3.1   The '*millioniki*' – Russian cities with over a million inhabitants (largest to smallest)

Moscow, population 11.5 million (see Box 3.2).

St Petersburg, population 5.0 million (see Box 3.3).

Novosibirsk, population 1.5 million. Russia's third largest city, the largest in Siberia, and the furthest million-plus city from Moscow.

Yekaterinburg, population 1.4 million, a key gateway for the Urals region, and the third largest city economy in Russia.

Nizhnyi Novgorod, population 1.3 million, the nearest million-plus city to Moscow.

Samara, population 1.2 million, an administrative and industrial centre on the Volga river in southern European Russia.

Omsk, population 1.2 million, on the main route between Yekaterinburg and Novosibirsk.

Kazan, population 1.1 million, capital of the majority non-Russian region of Tatarstan.

Chelyabinsk, population 1.1 million, situated in the southern Urals region.

Rostov-on-Don, population 1.1 million, centre of the Southern Federal District.

Ufa, population 1.1 million, capital of Bashkortostan.

Volgograd, population 1.0 million, formerly Stalingrad, situated on the Volga at its nearest point to the Don.

Perm, population 1.0 million, in the Urals region, known as Europe's most easterly city.

Krasnoyarsk, population 1.0 million, Siberia's third largest city, an aluminium producer located on the Trans-Siberian railway.

rest of Russia) to Cape Dezhneva in the far north-east (the easternmost point in the Eurasian land mass, named after the Cossack explorer who was the first European to sail round it). Russia extends over eleven time zones, and journeying overland on the Trans-Siberian railway from one end of the country to the other will take the traveller over a week. The distances involved have been a problem for successive governments seeking to make their mark across such a vast land area.

There are a number of other points about geographic conditions in Russia which help us to understand its development and present situation. First, most of Russia is of course located very far north. Half of its land mass is above the latitude of 60° north – that is, north of a line running through Oslo, the Shetland Islands, the southernmost tip of Greenland, the middle of Canada, and southern Alaska. Sub-Arctic conditions prevail along its north coast, and through all of Siberia apart from the far south-east, since the high mountain ranges on Russia's southern and eastern borders exclude warm tropical air masses from further south in Asia. Average winter temperatures, a mild –1° in the south-west, fall as low as –45° in the diamond-mining centre of Yakutsk, where temperatures only rise above freezing point for four or five months a year.

Second, Russia has relatively low levels of rainfall. It is a long way from the Atlantic Ocean and protected by mountains from the Pacific. The Arctic Ocean is too cold, and the Black and Caspian Seas too small to provide much water vapour. Peak rainfall in the better agricultural areas occurs in late summer and autumn, rather than earlier in the growing season. This growing season, particularly in the more northerly parts, lasts for a relatively short period, when intensive efforts have to be made. Just 13 per cent of the land area, virtually all located south of a line from St Petersburg in the west to Novokuznetsk in south-western Siberia, is used for agricultural purposes. Of the rest, 45 per cent is forested, and the remainder largely tundra, mountain and swamp which are too cold for cultivation. Even the most fertile areas in the so-called black earth (*chernozemnyi*) region along Russia's border with Ukraine often suffer from the lack of rainfall.

Russia is not then well placed for productive agriculture. It is, however, blessed with an abundance of natural resources, with substantial coal, oil, natural gas and iron ore reserves as well as non-ferrous metals, gold and diamonds. There are very few naturally occurring minerals in which Russia is not self-sufficient. Indeed, so much of its territory is undeveloped that there may well be many resource deposits yet to be discovered. Many of the easily accessible resources in European Russia and the Urals regions are being depleted, however, and most of the important deposits are now found in more remote and inhospitable parts of the country.

Attempts to exploit these more inaccessible resources were heightened during the industrialization drive under Stalin from the 1930s onwards, largely on the back of forced labourers who had no choice about where they worked. Consequently, millions of people lived, and died, in remote regions where they might never have settled

Box 3.2   Moscow

Moscow was founded in 1147 by Prince Yurii Dolgoruky. With Constantinople falling to the Turks in 1453, Moscow came to be seen by the Russian Orthodox as the home of true Christianity – the 'Third Rome'. From Muscovy, Ivan the Great (1462–1505) united the Russian principalities.

In the sixteenth century, Moscow grew to become one of Europe's largest cities, and by that time the Kremlin, Red Square and St Basil's Cathedral were all established. Moscow remained the seat of Russian power until Peter the Great moved the court to St Petersburg in 1713. Moscow was re-established as the capital in 1924. May Day parades of troops, tanks and missiles on Red Square – watched by a line of Communist leaders from the mausoleum containing the preserved body of their predecessor Lenin – symbolized for many the power of the Soviet state. In 2008, this military element was restored to an annual Red Square parade, but this time for Victory Day on 9 May, commemorating the end of the Second World War, rather than for May Day. Despite the Putin regime's rejection of communism, the embalmed body of Lenin still lies in his mausoleum on Red Square.

A visitor to Moscow in the mid-1980s would have found a sterile city compared with the one seen today. Communist Party slogans stood in place of advertising, there were relatively few cars, shops were dull and poorly stocked, and conformity and cleanliness were abiding features. By the mid-1990s all this had changed, as Moscow became a vibrant city, full of traffic, advertising, shopping malls, restaurants, political demonstrations, noise, crime, beggars and a chaotically hedonistic nightlife. From 1998 onwards, Moscow also became the scene of terrorist acts such as the blowing up of random apartment blocks in 1999, and suicide bombs on the metro system in 2004 and 2010, and at Domodedevo airport in 2011.

In recent years Moscow has seen vast capital projects, such as the rebuilding of the Cathedral of Christ the Saviour, the construction of the Manezh shopping centre next to Red Square, and the ongoing development of the Moscow International Business Centre – complete with contemporary skyscrapers including Europe's two largest towers, the Federation Tower at 506 metres, and the Russia Tower at 612 metres (see Illustration 6.1). The flipside of these vast construction projects is the destruction of many Moscow buildings, including the Soviet-era hotels Moskva, Rossiya and Intourist. Heritage campaigners have fought, largely in vain, for the preservation of landmark buildings across the city in recent years.

Contemporary Moscow is also marked by the curse of many of the world's major cities – traffic congestion. Growing prosperity has brought ever greater numbers of cars onto the streets, despite the fact that Moscow's efficient metro train system carries a staggering 9.5 million passengers a day, more than the underground systems in London and New York combined. Official figures state that in 2013 two and a half million people a day came into Moscow from the surrounding regions, including 1.3 million travelling in by car.

Box 3.3   St Petersburg

St Petersburg was founded in 1703 as Russia's 'Window on the West', built on the orders of Peter the Great, the westernizing Tsar who saw Russia's future firmly in Europe. The city became his capital, and remained the capital of Russia until the Soviet era.

In 1914, with the outbreak of the First World War, St Petersburg changed its name to Petrograd, which sounded less Germanic. Petrograd was the scene of the Russian revolution in 1917, and in 1924 was renamed again: Leningrad, after the revolutionary leader and founder of the Soviet Union, Vladimir Ilyich Lenin.

For around 900 days during the Second World War, from September 1941 until January 1944, Leningrad remained under siege by the German armed forces. Over half a million inhabitants died during this period. In 1991, with the Soviet Union on the brink of collapse, a city-wide referendum restored the name of St Petersburg.

Still spoken of as one of Russia's two capitals, St Petersburg enjoys a rivalry with Moscow, sharpened by the fact that Russia's current and previous presidents (Vladimir Putin and Dmitrii Medvedev) come from there, as do many of their senior colleagues.

under a market economy. As the Gulag system of forced labour camps declined from the mid-1950s onwards, compulsion largely gave way to material incentives and continued ideological exhortation as a means of attracting workers to the industrial cities of Siberia and the far north, such as Norilsk. None the less, it was the economic system of central planning and subsidy which sustained many of them. Since the collapse of the Soviet Union and the introduction of a market-based economic system, the plight of these remote settlements and their inhabitants has worsened as many are simply unable to survive economically. Russia's economic life, as exemplified by its major transport routes, is overwhelmingly centred on European Russia and on the east–west route of the Trans-Siberian railway, which runs across the south of the Federation.

The environment

The particular difficulties of Russia's physical setting outlined above have in many cases been exacerbated by problems of pollution and environmental degradation. Although the process of industrialization produces environmental difficulties the world over, a number of factors exist which mean that contemporary Russia still carries an especially negative environmental legacy from the Soviet era. In addition to this, the process of global climate change presents Russia with an uncertain path ahead. The locations of Russia's major cities, transport infrastructure and economic resources all stem to a large extent from climatic factors. Furthermore, Russia's size means that the impact of changes in the climate will differ across the country.

In 2013, Russia's Environment Minister announced the allocation of $3.3 billion specifically for the cleaning up of pollution remaining from Soviet-era industry. More than two decades after the collapse of the Soviet Union, Russia's government had carried out an inventory which identified ten priority projects, and no fewer than 77 sites of environmental pollution for which no owner could be found. The relative lateness of the Soviet Union's industrialization – in comparison to the rest of Europe – coupled with the desire to catch up rapidly (as noted in Chapter 2) and to prove the superiority of the Communist system, meant that the middle decades of the twentieth century saw rapid and large-scale industrialization. This prioritization of rapid industrialization left little room for serious consideration of environmental effects, and many of the environmental problems being faced in contemporary Russia stem from decisions made in the Soviet years.

The Communists' ideological stance with regard to the relationship between mankind and nature seriously exacerbated the environmental problems that generally accompany industrialization. The Communist view was constructivist, believing that enlightened human beings could build, on the basis of ever-increasing knowledge, a better world. Although this approach is most often thought of in terms of its application to building a new society and economy, it applied also to the natural world. Natural resources existed for people to use, exploit, and improve with little attention paid to the potential consequences. So, for example, the 'virgin lands scheme' initiated by Nikita Khrushchev (Soviet leader 1953–64) saw 30 million hectares of previously uncultivated land in Kazakhstan and southern Russia put to the plough, sowed with grain, and doused with chemical fertilizers and pesticides, in a grand scheme to increase grain supplies massively. Ecological issues were scarcely considered and, after the scheme's initial success, soil erosion and environmental degradation set in.

There are numerous other examples of the environmental devastation wreaked during the Soviet era, most notably the Chernobyl nuclear power station disaster of 1986. Details of one other case in

Box 3.4 Closed cities

It is estimated that 1.3 million Russians live today in 'closed cities', towns with restricted access under the purview of security-related state bodies such as the State Corporation for Atomic Energy (Rosatom), the Ministry of Defence and the Russian Space Corporation. There are at least 40 such closed cities in contemporary Russia.

Closed cities were set up in the Soviet era as urban centres closed off from the world around them. Not only were foreign visitors barred from them, but so too were citizens of the Soviet Union, unless they had the correct documentation. These cities were declared 'off bounds' for security reasons, as they contained key military facilities or were centres for research into defence technology, usually nuclear.

When the Soviet Union collapsed many of the larger closed areas (such as Chita, Kaliningrad, Vladivostok, Nizhny Novgorod and Murmansk) were opened. None the less, a number of smaller closed cities remain. Ten cities are closed under the instructions of the State Corporation for Atomic Energy, and a further unknown number cordoned off by the Defence Ministry.

The world of the closed city is fascinating. In the Soviet years, isolation was compensated for by prestige and privilege – the inhabitants were engaged in work which would see the Soviet superpower lead the world in military power and as a reward they lived well in comparison with workers elsewhere. In the 1990s, subsidies to these cities were hit by the economic downturn. None the less, the cities remain, and offer a tantalizing research subject from the sociological point of view.

Generations of families have lived their lives in relative isolation, and have married and brought up children within the community. Human rights activists are concerned that the laws on closed cities allow restrictions on basic rights, such as freedom of information and freedom of movement. Levels of security vary between the cities, but in most of them employees with access to restricted information cannot travel abroad, beyond a limited number of former Soviet countries. Residents, regardless of their access to restricted information, can only invite close family members to visit them.

particular illustrate the sorts of ecological problems caused. Although the Aral Sea is no longer, since the collapse of the Soviet Union, ruled from Moscow (it straddles the border between Uzbekistan and Kazakhstan), the fate of this particular body of water is illustrative of the lack of environmental concern displayed by the Soviet authorities. The relative shortage of water in the Soviet Union led to numerous schemes being touted for the diversion of rivers. Happily many of these got no further than the planning stage. However, the irrigation of cotton and rice fields by the diversion of water from rivers feeding into the Aral Sea in Central Asia from the 1960s onwards resulted in what was the world's fourth-largest inland sea shrinking in size by three-quarters. Former fishing ports now find themselves some distance from the shoreline, increasing levels of salinity have killed virtually all of the fish and many crops, and salinity of the air, accompanied by contaminated dust from the dried-out seabed, has increased rates of cancer, respiratory diseases and miscarriages. Life expectancy in communities close to the Aral Sea had fallen from 64 years in the late 1980s to 51 years by 2005 as the drying up of the sea produced toxic salt which is responsible for health problems and the poisoning of arable land in regions around what is left of the sea.

As if all this were not enough, from the 1930s to the 1990s the Soviet armed forces used Vozrozhdeniye Island in the Aral Sea to test biological weapons, including anthrax and strains of diseases made resistant to antibiotics. With the shrinking of the sea, Vozrozhdeniye is less and less the isolated testing ground it once was. The shore is now only six miles away. The island's name means, with a sad irony, 'Regeneration' – although what is left on it is the most likely cause of the sudden deaths, in separate incidents, of a large shoal of fish in the Aral Sea in 1976, and thousands of antelopes on the nearby steppe in 1988.

In the 1990s, the authorities in Kazakhstan, where the 'small', or northern, Aral Sea is situated, began to investigate ways of reversing the environmental catastrophe which was occurring. In 2005, a dam was completed which doubled the water flow from the Syr Darya river into the North Aral Sea, and sea levels have risen rapidly since. It's a different story in the southern Aral Sea, the two sections of which are reduced to highly salty water replete with bacteria.

The Aral Sea is not in Russia, but serves as a clear example of the lack of environmental concern which is the Soviet Union's legacy to all of its successor states. There is a story that when the heavily polluting Baikalsk paper and pulp mill was built in the 1960s, a Soviet minister, challenged about a development which would see toxic waste pumped into the world's largest freshwater lake, declared that 'even Lake Baikal must work for the advancement of the Soviet regime'. It was only in November 2008 that the Baikalsk mill, now controlled by billionaire Oleg Deripaska, was closed down.

Perhaps the worst ongoing environmental disaster on Russian territory is in Norilsk, a city in remote northern Siberia which regained its closed status in 2001. Norilsk has been named, in a study by the US-based Blacksmith Institute in 2007, as one of two Russian cities in the top ten most polluted sites in the world. The other Russian city named in this report is Dzerzhinsk, a chemical industry city 250 miles east of Moscow. The 'white sea' in Dzerzhinsk is the nickname given to a lake of chemical waste, the clean-up of which is one of the priority projects identified in 2013 as part of the Kremlin's designated 'year of environmental protection'.

The Norilsk region contains over a third of the world's nickel reserves and two-fifths of its platinum-group metals, as well as important cobalt and copper resources. Norilsk was first seriously developed by forced labour in the 1930s. By the early years of this century it was claimed that the Norilsk Mining Company produced a seventh of all industrial pollution in Russia, and the maximum allowable concentration of toxic air pollution was exceeded most days of the year (*Guardian* 2008). Given such conditions, it is scarcely surprising that average life expectancy for factory workers in Norilsk is notably below the national average. That national average in 2013 was 64 years for men.

Norilsk and Dzerzhinsk are at the extreme end of environmental problems in today's Russia. None the less, the legacy of the Soviet era continues to be felt more widely. Russia has just under a quarter of the world's supply of fresh water, but the ecosystems of 200 of its rivers are being undermined by the effects of the dams built as part of the hydroelectric programme of the 1960s and 1970s. In the late 1980s and into the 1990s, when increased political freedom meant that environmental concerns became more openly expressed, such concerns were of low political priority when set against a growing economic crisis. A lack of public investment over recent decades has resulted in a situation today where, according to official statements, around two-thirds of Russia's public water supply is not fit to drink. Only recently have Russia's politicians begun to give serious thought to the passing of clearer environmental laws. President Medvedev (2008–12) talked of enshrining high environmental standards in new laws and introducing sanctions for polluting businesses.

Medvedev's stated environmental aims dealt not only with long-standing issues of pollution, but also with wider environmental issues around the question of climate change. He spoke with regret about how far Russia is behind in the development of renewable energy technology, and in waste disposal and recycling. Environmental issues came to a head in Russia in 2010, when a summer heatwave, with temperatures reaching 40°C, caused vast forest and peat fires and smothered Moscow in smoke. Pollution levels were five times their usual level and death rates increased threefold. Predictions of climate change suggest that by 2030 there could be an average

Box 3.5   The rise and fall of the Russian Empire

9th century	First Slavic settlements, in present-day Ukraine and Western Russia. Known as Kievan Rus period
1237–40	Mongol (Tatar) Invasion, led by Ghengis Khan's grandson, Batu Khan. Russia under Tatar control
1480	End of Tatar rule in Rus
1552	Battle of Kazan signals beginning of empire building
16th–17th centuries	Expansion through Siberia to Pacific coast
18th century	Conquers present-day Western Ukraine, Belarus, Lithuania, Latvia and Estonia; Russians settle Alaska and parts of Northern California
1809	Finland acquired from Sweden
19th century	Conquers Central Asia, the Trans-Caucasus and Bessarabia
1867	Sells Alaska to the United States for $7,200,000 (or 2¢ an acre)
1875	Exchanges Kurile Islands with Japan for possession of whole of Sakhalin
1917–23	Constituent parts of Empire reconquered by Bolsheviks; Finland, Baltic states, Poland, Western Ukraine and Bessarabia lost
1922	Country renamed Union of Soviet Socialist Republics
1941–5	Stalin reincorporates into the Soviet Union parts of the Russian Empire lost after 1917; Yalta Conference (1945) gives USSR control over most of Eastern Europe
1989	Collapse of Communist rule throughout Eastern Europe
1991	Belovezha Agreement between leaders of Russia, Ukraine and Belarus dissolves the Soviet Union into 15 independent states

Further reading: Hosking (1997)

temperature increase across Russia of 1.5°C, though this would vary between regions. In addition, rainfall levels and occurrences of extreme weather, particularly flooding, may increase.

Russia ratified the Kyoto protocol on climate change, which could not come into force without such ratification, in 2004. It remains, however, the third biggest producer of CO_2 in the world, after China and the US. Russia stayed within its relatively modest target for emissions, and under President Medvedev (2008–12) appeared to place increasing emphasis on the need for a clear climate policy as part of his push for modernization and energy efficiency. President Putin, returning to office in 2012, has placed less emphasis on the issue. In December 2012, Russia, along with Canada, India, Japan and the United States, opted against taking on further commitments under Kyoto 2.

Russia's development over the centuries has been shaped by the fact that much of its vast area is not easily habitable, and certainly not amenable to farming. Global warming might therefore bring some benefits, in particular by decreasing the area covered by permafrost and increasing both arable land and the growing season. Any such impacts from climate change are not, however, adapted to easily – farming habits and expectations need to be adjusted, land cultivated for the first time, and infrastructure built. At the same time, the changes brought about by warming will have negative effects in terms of shortening the lifespan of buildings, increasing the area of marshland, and, in Russia's south, creating more droughts and water shortages.

Geostrategic location

Russia has long been a player in the international affairs of a number of regions, straddling as it does two continents and having land borders with no fewer than fourteen sovereign states. In security terms this geostrategic position has often translated into wide-ranging threat assessments and the fear of encirclement by hostile powers. An important point to appreciate is that, situated on the Great Eurasian plain, Russia has few natural borders such as mountain ranges or oceans. Russia's international borders have shifted over time; indeed, a clear answer to the question 'Where is Russia?' remains elusive.

Russia, including the Russian enclave of Kaliningrad, has land borders with:

- Azerbaijan
- Belarus
- China
- Estonia
- Finland
- Georgia

- Kazakhstan
- The Korean People's Democratic Republic
- Latvia
- Lithuania
- Mongolia
- Norway
- Poland
- Ukraine

Since the military conflict with Georgia in August 2008, Russia has also recognized Abkhazia and South Ossetia – with which it also shares land borders – as independent states. However, neither Abkhazia or South Ossetia are recognized internationally as anything other than Georgian territory.

In addition, Russia has sea borders with Japan and with the United States. The state of Alaska, which was sold by Russia to the United States for $7.2 million in 1867, lies just 56 miles across the Bering Strait.

In the aftermath of the collapse of the Soviet Union at the end of 1991, many Russians felt that parts of several former Soviet republics – in particular, Northern Kazakhstan, Eastern Ukraine, Belarus, the Narva region of Estonia, and Abkhazia and South Ossetia in Georgia – should be incorporated in the new Russian state. Border disputes have complicated bilateral relations with a number of Russia's neighbours, such as the continuing controversy with Japan over ownership of the Kurile Islands, seized by Russia at the end of the Second World War. The popular post-Soviet mood was reflected in the speeches of more nationalistic politicians, with, for example, the former mayor of Moscow, Yurii Luzhkov, calling on a number of occasions for the transfer of the port of Sevastopol, in Ukraine, to Russia. The Communist Party of the Russian Federation did not recognize the collapse of the Soviet Union, and the head of the Liberal Democratic Party of Russia (LDPR), extreme nationalist Vladimir Zhirinovsky, even called for the re-establishment of Russia within her 1860 borders, including Finland, Poland and Alaska. Such a call might have been treated with wry amusement by observers, had the LDPR not garnered almost a quarter of the votes in the 1993 general election and scarcely less than 10 per cent of the national vote in the following five Duma elections up to 2011.

Russian politicians of all political hues continue to distinguish between the 'near abroad' of former Soviet republics, and the rest of

Table 3.1   Russian public opinion on the collapse of the Soviet Union, 2000–12 (percentage of respondents, omitting 'don't knows')

Do you now regret the collapse of the Soviet Union in 1991?

	2000	*2005*	*2010*	*2012*
Yes	75	65	55	49
No	19	25	30	36

Source: Levada Centre (2012).

the international community, though this tendency decreases as time passes. A similar phenomenon is evident amongst the Russian public at large. Three-quarters of Russians voted for the preservation of the USSR in the referendum held by Mikhail Gorbachev in 1991. Since then, far more Russians have continued to regret the collapse of the Soviet Union than have celebrated it, though again, this tendency is diminishing with time (Table 3.1).

The Yeltsin, Putin or Medvedev administrations have not sought to change the borders of Russia as constituted at the collapse of the Soviet Union in 1991, although some would claim that military conflict with Georgia in August 2008, and the subsequent recognition of Abkhazian and South Ossetian independence, comes perilously close to a *de facto* border change. The nearest that the restoration of any union between the former Soviet states has come on any formal level is in the shaky relationship between Russia and Belarus. These two states signed the Treaty on the Formation of a Union State in December 1999. This was more a statement of intent than substance, however: Russia would prefer Belarus to become a component of the Russian Federation; Belarus wants a more equal relationship. Relations between the two countries have subsequently fluctuated, but a formal mutual commitment remains. Beyond that, as Chapter 9 sets out, the Putin administration seeks to create a Eurasian Union, akin to the European Union. Such a union is being developed, but with the involvement of only a few states (Belarus, Kazakhstan, Kyrgyzstan, Tajikistan).

The peoples of Russia

Russia has always been a multi-ethnic country. The first Russian state, Kievan Rus, from its foundations around the ninth century, consisted of Slavs, Varangians (Vikings) and Finnic peoples. As Russian colonists moved southwards and eastwards across the Eurasian continent over the centuries, they found themselves coexisting with a wide variety of ethnic groups, including Caucasian, Finno-Ugric, Hunnic, Turkic and Mongol peoples, as well as a wide variety of indigenous inhabitants across the expanses of Siberia.

Russia today remains a multi-national country. Results of the most recent census, carried out in 2010, counted over 190 separate ethnic groups. Of the total population of 143 million, 80 per cent are Russian. According to the 2010 census, six other ethnic groups had populations of more than 1 million: Tatars number over 5 million, whilst the proportion of Ukrainians has dropped from over 2 per cent in the 2002 census to 1.4 per cent in 2010. Bashkirs, Chuvash and Chechens number around 1.5 million each, and the Armenians just over the million mark. A further eleven ethnic groups number more than 500,000 each.

When the Soviet Union ceased to exist at the end of 1991, more than 25 million ethnic Russians suddenly found themselves living abroad, in one of the fourteen non-Russian Soviet republics. The reality of this situation took some time to sink in, for people and politicians alike. Many of the newly independent states had not only been part of the Soviet Union for decades, but had been part of the Russian Empire before that. One of the great projects of the Communist state had been the creation of the 'new Soviet man' (or woman), to whom nationality would be far less important than solidarity with workers across the globe. On a less ideological level, there was substantial geographical mobility within the Soviet Union; young people went to universities or served in the armed forces far away from their homes, skilled workers moved to different parts of the country as the planning system established certain industries in particular areas. Naturally, there was a significant amount of 'intermarriage', though it was not often thought of in those terms, particularly amongst related ethnic groups. The cities in particular reflected such mobility. Across the non-Russian republics of the Soviet Union, Russians made up 16 per cent of the population as a whole, 24 per cent of the urban population, and 30 per cent of the population in capital cities.

Put yourself in the shoes of a Russian from Moscow who, say in the late 1970s, married a Ukrainian from Kiev and then lived, with their children, in Minsk (the capital of the then Soviet Republic of Belorussia). Such a family may have had little perception of themselves as anything other than a normal Soviet family unit settled in an area of their country, in a city not too far removed either geographically or culturally from their own home cities. Suddenly, as 1991 turned to 1992, they woke up one morning to find themselves living in a new country – Belarus, separate from both Russia and Ukraine. Should they stay there, in a relatively small country with an uncertain future? After all, their children were presumably Belarusians. Or should they return to their home country? And, if so, to which country, since Ukraine and Russia were now two separate states?

With 25 million ethnic Russians suddenly finding themselves living abroad in the early 1990s, similar dilemmas were widespread, and the solutions settled upon were as varied as the number of complex combinations of circumstances. Many Russians returned to Russia in the 1990s, in a reversal of the trend of 500 years of expansion outwards from the Russian heartland. Between 1989 – the date of the last Soviet census – and 2001, there was a total immigration to Russia from the other former Soviet republics of more than 5.5 million people, and a net immigration of just under 4 million. This flow rose to a peak in 1994 and seemed, by the beginning of the twenty-first century, to have more or less come to its natural end so far as Russians returning to Russia is concerned.

As in many other countries, the immigration issue in Russia is controversial politically. The Russian situation is particularly complex since the distinction between immigrant and returnee has not always been clear. In some ways there were good reasons for allowing the relatively lax immigration policies of the 1990s. First, for ethnic Russians entering Russia there were few difficulties with cultural and linguistic assimilation – though economic integration was not so straightforward given the state of the Russian economy in the 1990s. Of course, it must be remembered that those returning to Russia were in many ways coming back to a different country from the one they left – to Russia, not the Soviet Union. Second, net immigration of 4 million went some way towards off-setting the decline in population caused by emigration, low birth rates and high death rates.

Despite these factors which would seem to undermine the arguments of the anti-immigration lobby, from the end of the 1990s onwards the Russian authorities began to tighten up the rules on immigration, bringing them more into line with those in most European states. Responsibility for overseeing migration issues was transferred in 2002 to the Ministry of the Interior, which oversees the Russian police force. This move was accompanied by much discussion amongst politicians, including government spokesmen, of the alleged higher propensity of immigrants for criminal activity. By the early years of the twenty-first century, the immigration of those ethnic Russians who suddenly found themselves living abroad at the Soviet collapse had all but run itself out. Immigration debates took on more of a racial character, as the majority of immigrants were from Central Asian states and of Central Asian ethnicities, coming to Russia to find work. In 2010, the Federal Migration Service estimated that there were around 7 million foreign workers in Russia, 4 million of whom were there illegally. By 2012 the World Bank's estimate was that 12.5 million migrants came to Russia to work each year, again with over half doing so illegally.

Labour migration, particularly of unskilled workers from the former Soviet republics in Central Asia, continues to be a source of both valuable labour and xenophobic tension in Russia today. A report by the International Fund for Agricultural Development said that the economies of two Central Asian states in particular, Tajikistan and Kyrgyzstan, were dependent on remittances sent back from labour emigrants working abroad, and that figures for Uzbekistan were also high (IFAD 2007). Lawyers working on behalf of migrant workers in Russia report thousands of complaints each year about poor labour conditions, low wages and xenophobic mistreatment. Official rhetoric and action in recent years can also be characterized as a crackdown on illegal immigration, with the current Russian administration increasing the penalties for entering the country illegally, introducing more stringent registration regulations, and placing more responsibility on employers to ensure that their workers are in the country legally.

War and terrorism in the North Caucasus

During the first two decades and more of the post-Soviet era, the unity and peacefulness of the Russian Federation has been most threatened in the North Caucasus region. The North Caucasus area in Russia is divided into the republics of Adygea, Chechnya, Dagestan, Ingushetia, Kabardino-Balkaria, Karachaevo-Cherkessia, North Ossetia and the regions of Krasnodar, Rostov and Stavropol. Over 80 per cent of the region's population are Sunni Muslims. The Chechen wars (1994–6, 1999–2000) became known for the brutality of the conflict and its accompanying terrorist atrocities. Since the Chechen conflict formally ended, and a settlement reached which involves the Russian government turning a blind eye to the nature of the regime overseen by Chechen president, Ramzan Kadyrov, in return for loyalty to the Kremlin, the impression could be gained from Western media that peace has returned to the North Caucasus. It has not. As opposed to the first, the second Chechen war saw the involvement of Islamist jihadists who saw the conflict as part of their wider, global struggle. In recent years, jihadist violence in the region has widened beyond Chechnya into neighbouring republics, and jihadists from the region have gone to fight for their cause in conflicts around the world.

Chechnya is a republic within the Russian Federation, on its southern border with Georgia. The age-old desire for independence was at the root of the Chechen conflict when it flared up in the immediate post-Soviet years. Chechnya's geographical position made it a far more likely candidate for secession than another occasionally independence-minded republic, Tatarstan. The latter is firmly within Russian territory and surrounded by other regions of Russia. Chechnya, on the other hand, is on the periphery of Russia. The history of the Chechen people is one of repeated conflict with Russian invaders. Even when firmly part of the Soviet Union, Stalin felt that the Chechens were not to be trusted at the end of the Second World War, and so organized the brutal forced re-settlement of the entire Chechen people to Central Asia. It was not until the 1950s that the Chechens returned to their homeland.

In November 1991, as one by one the Union Republics of the Soviet Union declared their independence, the Chechen leadership – under former Soviet air force general Dzokhar Dudaev – declared their republic independent. The difficulty was, however, that Chechnya was not one of the 15 Union Republics, but was a republic within the Russian Soviet Federative Socialist Republic (RSFSR), as Russia was officially known in the Soviet era. The newly elected Russian president, Boris Yeltsin, whilst actively encouraging the Union Republics – including his own – to secede from the Soviet Union, was determined that Russia itself would not break up. He declared a state of emergency in Chechnya and insisted that it remain within Russia.

An uneasy stand-off between Chechnya and Moscow held until December 1994, when Yeltsin sent troops into Chechnya to try and subdue the rebel republic. The Russian army was used as a blunt instrument, engaging in indiscriminate bombing and shelling of the capital, Grozny, where many of the remaining inhabitants were ethnic

Russians unable to flee to family in the Chechen mountains. The Chechen rebels, on the other hand, were skilled at guerrilla and terrorist tactics. By the summer of 1996 the stalemate was broken by a deal which gave some autonomy to the Chechens, but no real hope of independence.

In late summer 1999 Chechen rebels encroached into the neighbouring Russian republic of Dagestan. This was followed in September of that year by a series of devastating bomb attacks on apartment blocks in Moscow and elsewhere, which were blamed on the Chechens. Yeltsin, backed by his new prime minister, Vladimir Putin, sent troops into Chechnya again. The result was similar to that of the first Chechen War, with the exception that reported brutality on both sides was if anything fiercer. Putin, soon after becoming president in 2000, talked in terms of the Russian troops in Chechnya being the first line of defence for Europe against militant Islam. After the terrorist attacks on New York and Washington of 11 September 2001, he repeatedly placed the Chechen conflict within the framework of the global war on terrorism.

At the same time, the Chechen rebels increasingly adopted the symbols of radical Islam and tactics of Islamist terrorists, as well as developing links with other Islamist terror networks. They took terrorism to the heart of Moscow on several occasions, using suicide bombers on the Moscow metro, outside a city-centre hotel, and at a summer rock festival. In October 2002, a group of Chechens took several hundred people in a theatre audience hostage. The siege was ended by Russian special troops, who stormed the building, killing all the terrorists. Tragically, over a hundred of the hostages were also killed, not by terrorists but by the gas that the Russian troops pumped into the theatre to debilitate those inside. Within a week in August and September 2004 Chechen terrorists planted bombs which destroyed two separate passenger airliners, detonated a device outside a metro station in Moscow, and – in horrific scenes which captured global attention – killed hundreds of school children after taking them hostage in Beslan, southern Russia.

The horror of the Beslan school siege turned out to be the culmination of this period of terrorist attacks. President Putin's policy for dealing with terrorism in the North Caucasus was to cede regional power to local leaders, on condition that they remained loyal to the Kremlin and kept order within their own republics. To the extent that Russia is no longer engaged in a quasi state-to-state conflict with Chechnya, this policy has been a success, and Moscow announced a formal end to the anti-terrorist operations in the republic in March 2009. The price paid for this has been supporting, both politically and economically, the undemocratic regime of Chechen President Ramzan Kadyrov in power. Whilst to a great extent, Chechnya has been pacified, as noted above, violence has spread into the wider North Caucasus, and this violence has clear internationalist, jihadist roots.

Ongoing violence in the North Caucasus causes hundreds of deaths a year in contemporary Russia. According to the figures provided by the Caucasus Emirate (the jihadist organization fighting against the Russian state), in 2012 there were 568 separate attacks in the region, the majority in Dagestan, resulting in 652 deaths. Nor is it only the North Caucasus itself that is afflicted with such violence, as terrorist attacks further afield spring from the same source, including the March 2010 double suicide bombing in the Moscow metro system, which resulted in around 40 deaths and wounded many more.

Religion in Russia

As well as being multi-ethnic, Russia today is also religiously diverse. Religious activity has increased since the collapse of communism. Survey evidence from 2012 reports that almost 80 per cent of the adult population describe themselves as Russian Orthodox believers, with a further 8 per cent adhering to another faith and only 5 per cent willing to declare themselves definitively atheist. Half of all Russians claim to attend religious services at least once a year, although only 5 per cent claim to attend weekly – although these figures probably exaggerate religious attendance as survey responses are known to report higher levels of religiosity than is found from counting the numbers attending.

The dominant religion in the country is Russian Orthodoxy. There are also many other Christian confessions, a substantial Islamic minority, and established but small Jewish and Buddhist communities, as well as a few adherents of pre-Christian pagan religions. Of Russia's 83 regions, 5 are Islamic republics and 1, Kalmykia, is a Buddhist republic. Table 3.2 provides data on the number of registered religious communities at the beginning of 2006.

Table 3.2 does not provide a complete picture because a number of religious groups either do not wish to, are unable, or cannot afford to register. Estimates from religious groups themselves suggest that up

Table 3.2   Registered religious organizations in Russia, January 2006

Russian Orthodox Church		12,350
of which, Moscow Patriarchy	12,214	
Muslim		3,668
Pentecostal		1,486
Baptists		965
Evangelical Christian		812
Jehovah's Witnesses		408
Lutheran		288
Old Believers		285
Jewish		284
Roman Catholic		251
Buddhist		197
Presbyterian		187
Methodist		115
Other		1,217
Total		22,513

to 9,000 Muslim groups and over 1,000 Christian groups remain unregistered.

The religious revival in Russia dates from 1988, the millennium of the conversion of Russia to Christianity, which, thanks to official support from previously anti-religious Soviet authorities, became a nationwide celebration. It has a number of elements. The Orthodox Church has been resurrected as a national symbol, as indeed it was before the 1917 revolution, although it now maintains its independence from the state. The Orthodox Patriarch – up until his death in December 2008, Aleksii II, and since February 2009, Kirill I – blesses the president on his inauguration, and in times of political crisis has played a mediating role. Other politicians from across the political spectrum have been keen to associate themselves with Orthodoxy. The post-Communist period has seen the building or restoration of many churches, cathedrals, monasteries, seminaries and theological academies. Charitable and educational work by churches has become increasingly common after decades of complete prohibition, and the option to study the foundations of the Orthodox faith, as well as a number of other traditional faiths, has been put on the school curriculum. The Orthodox authorities continue to argue for the restitution of land and property lost in the Soviet period. While the current (1993) Russian Constitution and the 1997 Law on Freedom of Conscience and Religious Associations guarantee religious freedom, there have

Founded in 1524, its buildings mostly date back to the seventeenth century. The Soviet government closed the convent and turned the cathedral into a museum. The convent re-opened as such in 1994.

Illustration 3.1   Smolensky Cathedral, in the grounds of Moscow's Novodevichy Convent

been concerns about an overly close relationship between the Orthodox Church and the Russian state, and about harassment of some religious minorities, a topic examined in detail in Chapter 7.

Islam is the second largest religion in Russia, and – along with Christianity, Judaism and Buddhism – is recognized in the preamble to the 1997 Law on Freedom of Conscience and Religious Associations as one of Russia's traditional religions. As a proportion of the population of the Soviet Union, Muslims made up a greater percentage than is now the case in Russia, since the break-up of the USSR brought independence to Kazakhstan, Uzbekistan, Kyrgyzstan, Tajikistan, Turkmenistan and Azerbaijan. None the less, there are more than 14 million Muslims in the Russian Federation, around 10 per cent of the population. Virtually all of Russia's Muslims are Sunni Muslims, though in a few areas – significantly

---

Box 3.6   What is Russian Orthodoxy?

Contemporary Orthodoxy, like all religions, encompasses many different elements and interpretations. While we can hardly do justice to the
richness of the tradition, the following distinctive features are noteworthy:

- *The role of tradition:* the split with Catholicism in 1054 was a rejection of changes that the Western Church wished to introduce. Since
  then, Orthodoxy has seen itself as being the closest of all the
  branches of Christianity to the traditions of the early Church.
  Doctrinally and in practice there have been few changes since the
  eighth century. Participation in an Orthodox service indeed involves
  an experience of changelessness and timelessness. Doctrine does not
  change, because faith is seen as a matter of practice, not doctrine, an
  attitude that often causes confusion among foreign observers.
- *Greater emphasis on mysticism and spirituality:* Western religion,
  like Western thought, has since the Enlightenment been dominated by
  a tradition of rationalism; that is, the belief that the human mind is
  capable of explaining everything, eventually. This attitude applies to
  theology as much as to philosophy: theological statements must be
  susceptible to proof and human reason. Orthodoxy does not reject
  truths that arise out of reason, but takes much more seriously extra-
  rational sources of truth: the symbolic, inspiration and spiritual tran-
  scendence. The religious icon, the form of the service, Russian
  religious music, the emphasis on artistic aspects of worship all arise
  out of an emphasis on experience and adoration rather than analysis.
- *Less hierarchical:* at least in the experience of worship. There are,
  for example, no pews in a Russian Orthodox church, and the congre-
  gation is able to come and go as it pleases, giving rise to a much
  more flexible and informal atmosphere than is familiar in many
  Western denominations. There is no equivalent in Orthodoxy of the
  Pope, no individual with universal jurisdiction. What holds the
  Church together is that its members understand it as a communion of
  the faithful.

Chechnya and Dagestan – there is a tradition of Sufism. In the current
demographic downturn afflicting Russia, the Islamic population is
notable for its growth rate compared with the rest of the population.

The size of the Jewish community is far smaller, with the 2010
census reporting that only around 160,000 Jews remained in Russia,
down from over half a million in 1989, and 230,000 in 2002. The
emigration of Jews from Russia, mainly to Israel, has been particularly marked since the end of the 1980s, when restrictions were eased.
From a peak of over 180,000 émigrés in 1990 the figure fell to an

average of around 60,000 in the first half of the 1990s and it has fallen still further since. Around 1.1 million Russian-speaking Jewish émigrés now live in Israel. Reasons behind this emigration are varied, and there is no doubt that economic factors played a major role, as they did with emigrants of all faiths or none from Russia in the immediate post-Soviet years. To some extent, though, Russia's tradition of anti-semitism was also a factor, particularly with the rise of fascist and far right movements during the 1990s and beyond (see Chapter 5).

The place of Buddhism as a legally acknowledged traditional religion in Russia owes more to its longevity and its identity with specific groups of people than to any large Buddhist community. Estimates of the number of Buddhists in Russia are not easy to come by, but the country's only Buddhist republic, Kalmykia, has around 150,000 Kalmyks, and a figure of about twice that for the number of Buddhists in Russia would not be far wide of the mark.

Who are the Russians? Culture and traditions

The culture of a group is not a fixed or given set of attitudes and ways of behaving. However, members of a society do tend to share beliefs about themselves as a collective, and about right ways of acting, and these beliefs have an important impact. They are embodied not just in social discourse, but in religious practices, art and literature, folk traditions, notions of social justice, and national symbols. Generalizing about these matters is a risky business: values are not shared by everyone, and social beliefs and practices change over time. However, at the risk of stereotyping, there are cultural beliefs which, while not necessarily shared by all sections of society, are none the less central to understanding contemporary Russia.

The importance of the 'Russian Idea'

The term 'Russian Idea' indicates a set of interpretations, by Russian thinkers of various political and philosophical persuasions, of what is distinctive about Russia. These formulations are not identical, but they do tend to share common features. The most important of these is that Russia is different from the West. Western societies are often lumped together and stereotyped as being overly individualistic, excessively materialistic, immoral, and generally unpleasant places to live in. Russia is defined, crudely, as not the West. Russians allegedly share a uniquely spiritual, communal existence, a life which concentrates not on the squalid pursuit of individual material goals, but on what is most important in existence. Values such as spirituality and communality are, of course, not easy to measure. However, figures for attendance at religious services or membership of those organizations which make up civil society are far lower in Russia than in the United States – casting great doubt on claims that Russians are somehow more spiritual and communal than Americans. None the less, even if hard statistics do not back up the common perception, the widespread existence of that perception has influence in itself. It contributes to the construction of a national identity, and from there into the formulation of voting preferences and policies. (For more details on civil society, see Chapter 7).

Proponents of the Russian Idea, the 'Slavophiles' of the nineteenth century and their modern-day successors, idealize the role of the Orthodox Church in 'Holy Russia', the co-operative values of the peasant commune and, often, the desirability of political autocracy. The way in which these are conceived is, it scarcely needs to be said, an idealized version of reality. There is no point in history where Russians did live in this way. Furthermore, basing a system of thought on how different the society is from Western societies is not a feature unique to Russian culture. Thinkers in many other countries – for example, in the Islamic world or East Asia – like to argue that their societies are less materialistic, or more co-operative, though the precise emphasis obviously varies from culture to culture, and it must be said that the level of egalitarianism found in many versions of the Russian Idea is high by comparison with most other parts of the world.

The 'Russian Idea' tends to have a distinctive view of the role of the state and the nature of political leadership. One way to understand this is to compare Russian political ideas to those of the founding fathers of the American Constitution. In 1788 James Madison, in *Federalist No. 51*, wrote that the political arrangements proposed were necessary because this was a government of human beings:

> If men were angels, no government would be necessary. If angels were to govern men, neither external nor internal controls over government would be necessary. In framing a government which is to be administered by men over men, the great difficulty lies in this: you must first enable the government to control the governed; and in the next place oblige it to control itself. (Hamilton 2008)

The American political system is therefore one that manifests a suspicion of power. There has been a tendency in Russia, on the other hand, to invest new governments with inflated expectations, as if they were indeed governments of angels not of men. Governments of this kind do not need to be politically restrained, hence the lack of countervailing political institutions compared to some other parts of the world. Governments of truth also like to believe that they have unique access to the way in which the country should develop, which is a feature of administrations from Peter the Great through Stalin to Putin. If you know the answer, you are building the New Jerusalem, so political opposition serves little purpose, and hence the concept and the practice remain underdeveloped in Russia.

This concept of the place of the state and its powers has become increasingly evident during the Putin and Medvedev presidencies (from 2000 onwards). Although formally holding to democratic procedures, the notion that there should be opposition forces offering genuinely alternative views has had little purchase with the Putin regime. The space in which opposition forces might operate has been squeezed by bureaucratic control over party formation, state oversight of the media, and the occasional use of the legal system to disrupt opposition organization or key oppositionist figures. In terms of the Russian Idea, the Putin administration put a good deal of effort into creating a national narrative which was in line with Russian traditions. A new public holiday, National Unity Day, symbolized this well in its fusion of Orthodoxy, a distinct – that is, non-Western – national identity, and the need for unity amongst the diverse groups that make up Russia.

One important consequence of this conception of politics is that it tends ultimately to undermine government when rulers turn out after all not to be perfect. When their actions begin, as is inevitable, to favour some groups over others, and fail to realize their utopian promises, disillusionment sets in. This disillusionment has periodically in Russian history – including the end of the periods of rule of Mikhail Gorbachev and, to a lesser extent, his successor Boris Yeltsin – led to legitimacy crises and a real breakdown of state power. Predicting the decline of the ruling regime in Russia has ever been fraught with difficulties. None the less, it has been noticeable that since Vladimir Putin's return to the presidency in 2012, his ratings have fallen a little. It is perhaps inevitable that, in this age where information and opinion can be freely shared over the internet, the longer someone is in power, the less they are able to avoid an increasing attitude of cynicism towards them and the notion that their time has past. Whether this is enough to terminally undermine his political position, however, is a more difficult call to make in a country where the Putin regime has sewn up most of the levers of power.

Russia's first three post-Soviet presidents, Yeltsin, Putin and Medvedev, as well as the last Soviet leader, Gorbachev, have all proclaimed their belief in the rule of abstract law. None the less, Russia remains a country where connections, influence and political expedience regularly appear to undermine the equitable application of the law. Not for nothing was the team around Boris Yeltsin at the end of the 1990s known as 'the Family'. In anointing Putin his successor, Yeltsin made sure that the first act of the new president would be to grant him immunity from prosecution.

The Slavophiles versus Westernizers controversy

One consequence of the controversy surrounding the Russian Idea has been that intellectual life in Russia, both throughout the nineteenth century and again in the present day, has seen a marked tension between those who want a society and political system unique to Russia, and those who are less convinced about Russian 'specialness' and want to adapt practices used elsewhere to Russian circumstances. The tensions between these two positions have been an important driving force in Russian politics. In opinion polls clear majorities regularly state a preference for a uniquely Russian path of development, rather than a Western one.

Social mood

The national mood in Russia has changed with some volatility over recent decades. In the 1950s and 1960s there was, amongst the elite at least, and probably more widely in Soviet society, a sense of national pride and optimism. Soviet successes in the space race saw the launch of the first artificial satellite (Sputnik) in 1957, and then four years later Yurii Gagarin became the first man in space. The sense that the Soviet Union was at last beginning to fulfil its promises was memorably captured in the boast contained in the 1961 Programme of the Communist Party that the country would catch up with and overtake the United States in economic terms by 1970, and that by 1980 Soviet citizens would be living under true communism.

Of course, by the end of the 1980s the Soviet Union was on its last legs, and it finally collapsed in 1991. In the rest of the 1990s, against a background of economic decline, mass poverty, lawlessness and environmental devastation, such promises, and the optimistic era from which they came, became a distant memory. Commentators who are more critical of the Communist experience stress the negative influences on morality of the 'double life' Russian citizens were compelled to lead under Soviet rule, paying lip service to an ideology of public service and striving to build a Communist utopia, while in practice not being able to discuss social problems which everyone knew to exist and being party to a culture of irresponsibility both at work and in public life. Those who dislike the economic policies of the post-Soviet years stress how these have directly led to a rise in undesirable behaviour such as greed, nepotism, corruption and organized crime. Whatever the case, the first post-Soviet decade created a mood in Russian society of deep pessimism, powerlessness and hopelessness about future possibilities, moral decay, cynicism and general despair.

Under Putin's leadership the national mood undoubtedly changed. Putin himself retained exceptionally high levels of personal popularity throughout his first two terms in the presidency, scarcely falling below 70 per cent approval ratings in the opinion polls. Such figures were retained throughout 2008 as he became prime minister, and his successor as president, Dmitrii Medvedev, enjoyed only slightly lower levels of popular support in the same period. On his return to the presidency in 2012, Putin enjoyed an initial jump in popularity, but approval levels through 2013 settled around the 50 per cent mark – acceptable for a third-term president, but not reaching the popularity levels that he previously enjoyed.

4

Social Structure and Social Policy

So much that is written about contemporary Russia majors on how different it is from something called 'the West'. In contrast, it is entirely possible to look at many aspects of Russian society today and emphasize how much more like 'the West' they have become in the twenty-first century. In terms of social structure and social policy, this case is relatively straightforward to argue. In the past decade or so, Russians as a whole have enjoyed a rising standard of living, with wages increasing threefold since the turn of the century. For many better-off Russians, lifestyles have become increasingly akin to those enjoyed by the more well-off across the developed world. Nearly a quarter of Russians were born after the collapse of the Soviet Union, and even the oldest of these only experienced the socio-economic collapse of the 1990s as young children and have come of age in a Russia where living standards have increased year on year.

Similarly, albeit from the very low base of the 1990s, those staples of social policy – education and healthcare – have seen increased official attention and investment in recent years. Even where some key socio-economic indicators are negative in international comparison, the notion that this represents some East–West divide does not invariably stand up to scrutiny. For example, it is certainly the case that Russia is marked by an unusually large gap between the richest and the poorest in society, but the accepted measure of such a gap (the Gini coefficient) shows that it is greater in the United States and in China than in Russia.

None of this is to say that Russia's social structure and social policy is just like that in 'the West'. The point rather is that understanding the complexities of social issues in a country as large and diverse as Russia is not best served by oversimplification. Much in the area of social policy has improved in Russia, largely on the back of the economic growth which began in the late 1990s, but there still exist major problems – for example, regional discrepancies, the treatment of particular diseases, and the potential for a significant demographic crisis looming. This chapter brings together the key threads in terms of contemporary Russia's social structure and social policy. Both the Soviet period and the difficulties of the 1990s provide essential background for identifying the baseline experiences and expectations of Russians in regard to social policy, and explaining the developments which have led to today's social structure. After summarizing this historical background, we move on to considering living standards, demography, health policy and education policy. The chapter concludes by setting out the notable developments in judicial policy accomplished largely during the presidency of Dmitrii Medvedev (2008–12).

Social policy before and after the Soviet collapse

The Soviet Union was known for its 'cradle to grave' model of free social welfare provision. While the reality of this provision was often wholly inadequate for people's needs, the immediate post-Soviet period saw a deterioration in many respects. The disruption of even this basic level of provision caused severe difficulties for the population as a whole. During the Soviet era, Russia went from being a rural country to being predominantly urban, both in terms of its demographic structure and its political priorities. The population became much more highly educated, and the number employed in administrative and professional capacities grew substantially. None the less, Soviet social structure took a different shape from that found in industrial democracies. The basis of social divisions was access to administrative power, rather than wealth. In terms of monetary income differentials, the Soviet Union was notably egalitarian. However, the Party-state elite exerted monopolistic and unaccountable control over resources and people. Unsurprisingly, this led to the development of an elaborate system of special privileges. Officials had access to goods that were unavailable to the wider population – networks of special schools for their children, closed hospitals with superior facilities, luxurious dachas (country retreats), and their own holiday resorts. Such privileged access was, partly by its nature and partly by deliberate policy, concealed from the view of most citizens. This apparently egalitarian state of affairs suited Soviet propaganda well, especially when contrasted with income differentials in the capitalist countries. However, the actual impact of monetary income on the life of a Soviet citizen was relatively minimal, with the problem being access to goods, rather than the ability to pay for them.

In many former Communist countries, the period of transition from communism to whatever followed it – democracy in some cases, · authoritarianism in others, and various points in between for the rest – proved to be a time of great social and demographic upheaval. According to estimates put forward by UNICEF, the post-Communist transition process was responsible for over 3 million early deaths. The UN Development Programme posits a population deficit of over 10 million 'missing men'; that is, premature deaths plus the number otherwise expected to be born, as a consequence of the transition process.

Russia after the collapse of communism was faced immediately with social and demographic problems on a huge scale. A report published in the UK's leading medical journal in 2009 showed that, of the countries which emerged out of the Soviet collapse, Russia was an extreme case in terms of demographic impact (Stuckler *et al.* 2009). Life expectancy declined by almost five years between 1991 and 1994. As noted in Chapter 2, such large-scale human hardship has been far from uncommon in Russia's twentieth-century history. The historian Christopher Read has even written of 1990s Russia having witnessed 'economic mass murder' with excess deaths comparable to Stalin's purges (Read 2001:230). In fact, best estimates suggest that excess pre-war deaths in Stalin's Russia were over 10 million, while the highest serious estimate for the Yeltsin years is 3.5 million. There is, too, a clear difference in intent between the famine, forced labour and executions of the Stalin years, and the severe economic hardship of the 1990s. Although to some extent economic transformation lay at the root of policies in both eras, direct causes of early death are less easy to establish in the Russia of the 1990s than in the Soviet Union of the 1930s. Such factors as poverty, increasing income-differentials, declining standards of medical care, and psycho-social stress are all cited as causes of excess deaths during the post-Soviet transition in Russia, alongside more immediate causes such as drinking, smoking and accidents. *The Lancet*'s research showed that the chief explanations as to why Russia fared even worse than other post-Communist countries in this respect were the rate of privatization and the lack of engagement with social organizations on the part of the Russian population.

Suddenly, in the 1990s, money became, as across most of the world, the key factor in obtaining goods and services. What is more, while the Soviet Union had been a shortage economy with next to no access to Western consumer goods, post-Soviet Russia witnessed an influx of Western shops, brands and technology. In the Yeltsin years (1991–9), while most Russians were suffering materially and physically from the transition process, a few were getting very rich, and their lifestyle was visible to all. Following on from an era when goods were few, privileges relatively hidden, and egalitarianism the state creed, the in-your-face wealth of these few super-rich 'new Russians' was particularly galling for the majority who appeared to have lost out. The notion that wealth would 'trickle down' and spread through the economy seemed to be an empty excuse for most of the 1990s, and it was only really in the boom years of high oil prices when wealth did indeed begin to spread more widely. Even then, though, at the end of Putin's second term in 2008, around half of all Russians were still seeing their wages rise more slowly than prices.

Standards of living

The immediate post-Soviet period saw a sharp decline in overall living standards in Russia. This was then followed by a gradual improvement from around the turn of the millennium. The United Nations Human Development Programme estimated that, in purchasing power parity terms (that is, adjusting national incomes for relative prices), as of the year 2000, Russia's per capita gross national income was US$8,395. This was just a fifth of the US$40,230 figure in the United States, 28 per cent of the US$29,001 in the United Kingdom, and put Russia, according to these data, on a par with countries such as Lebanon and Brazil. By 2012, Russia's per capita gross national income was US$14,461, a third of the figure for the United States and nearly half that for the United Kingdom. In 2012, the CIA's estimate of Russia's gross domestic product at purchasing parity power per capita was US$17,700. According to these data, Russia ranks 76 of the 229 countries in the world, and is on a par with countries such as Malaysia and Latvia.

The decline in living standards in the first decade after the Soviet collapse had a number of identifiable causes:

- the dramatic reduction in state subsidies for basic services such as rents, public transport and energy;
- the hyperinflation of 1992 which led to rises of some 2,500 per cent in price levels and the wiping out of personal savings;
- the economic slump and rise in unemployment;
- the non-payment of wages and an inadequate welfare system; and
- the collapse of the rouble in 1998, which again wiped out the savings of many Russians.

As noted above, income inequality also sharply increased after the collapse of the Soviet Union. Using the Gini coefficient (a standard measure of income inequality in which the higher the figure, the greater the inequality), the late Soviet figure of 26 had risen to 40 in 2000 and then 42 in 2007, where it remained in 2013 . In terms of international comparison this places Russia, according to the CIA, 84th out of 136 countries for income equality, with the United States being less equal at 94th, and the United Kingdom more equal at 76th. These figures are a useful corrective to aggregate data showing economic growth or gross income per capita. Similarly, regional variations facilitate a more nuanced perspective on the living standards of Russians. That Moscow is not Russia is a helpful maxim to bear in mind if one wants to understand fully contemporary Russia. According to the United Nations, in 2009 Russia's GDP per capita – adjusted for purchasing power parity – was US$18,869. In Moscow it was US$40,805. Only two other Russian regions – sparsely populated and oil- and gas-rich Tyumen and Sakhalin – have higher GDP per capita. However, Moscow also has a vast gap between its richest and poorest inhabitants.

Just as Russian politics polarized in the early 1990s, with the concept of the 'middle ground' giving way to an almost elemental struggle between reform and reaction, so standards of living moved in opposing directions. The 'new poor' and the 'new rich' appeared. Among the 'new poor' were many professional people – teachers, academics, scientists – whose wages scarcely pretended to keep up with the rising costs of everyday life, even when they were being paid, which often they were not. A common sight in the centre of Moscow in 1992 and 1993 were groups of people, from all walks of life, standing outside metro stations selling their possessions in order to buy the necessities of survival. The practice ended on this large scale in the mid-1990s not because the problem went away, but because the city authorities put a stop to it. Popular resentment of the 'new rich', more commonly known as the 'new Russians' – that is, the section of the population that prospered materially in the post-Communist period – was fuelled by conspicuous consumption. Their expensive foreign cars, lavish lifestyles and luxurious new dachas were evident to all. For some of the 'new Russians', the word 'rich' seems inadequate. A very small, but highly visible, proportion of the population made serious money in the privatizations of the mid-1990s, when vast state-owned resources were sold at prices which turned out to be gross underestimates of their true market value.

For the men in control of these resources, foreign cars and lavish lifestyles were only the beginning. In 2003, one such businessman, 36-year-old Roman Abramovich, bought one of London's top football clubs, Chelsea, and proceeded to astonish the world of European football by using his wealth to pay huge transfer fees and wages for almost any player the club desired. With an estimated personal fortune of around US$7 billion, made chiefly in the oil industry, he could afford to transform the landscape in the home of the world's most popular sport.

Abramovich remained close to Putin. A number of other high profile 'oligarchs', however, fell into disfavour with the Russian government. Men such as Vladimir Gusinsky and Boris Berezovsky both left Russia for 'voluntary' exile in western Europe during Putin's first term in office (2000–4), under threat of prosecution should they ever return to Russia. Berezovsky died in England in 2013, shortly after failing to win a London High Court case against Abramovich surrounding the ownership of an oil company. Press reports claimed that in the weeks before his death, he had petitioned President Putin to be allowed to return safely to Russia.

The most well-known case of a Russian oligarch falling out of favour in Putin's Russia is that of Mikhail Khodorkovsky. In the summer of 2003, Khodorkovsky was imprisoned in Russia and charged with financial irregularities (Box 4.1). Putin's stated desire, in a deliberate echo of a Stalinist phrase used to describe the 1930s campaign against the Soviet Union's 'rich peasants' (kulaks), was to 'destroy the oligarchs as a class'. Many observers have noted, however, that only those oligarchs who display politically opposition-ist tendencies seem to attract the negative attentions of the Russian state. The major energy companies previously controlled by these oligarchs (for example, Khodorkovsky's Yukos, Abramovich's Sibneft) have now – after auctions, mergers and renamings – come under state control within the structures of such companies as gas giant Gazprom and oil giant Rosneft. Key figures on the boards of these companies are central players in the Putin regime:

- Igor Sechin, chairman of the management board of Rosneft, was Russia's deputy prime minister between 2008 and 2012;
- Viktor Zubkov, chairman of the board of Gazprom, was Russia's prime minister between 2007 and 2008; and
- Zubkov's predecessor as chairman of Gazprom's board was Dmitrii Medvedev, who became president of Russia in 2008 and served as prime minister from 2012 onwards.

Critics of the oligarchs under President Yeltsin – and there were many – accused them of taking advantage of the Soviet collapse to gain control of lucrative and strategic industries, in order to enrich themselves and exert undue influence over the governance of the country. Under the Putin regime the state has regained control of these industries, but critics would still assert that such control manifests itself in enrichment and accumulation of power.

Berezovsky, Gusinsky, Abramovich and Khodorkovsky belonged to the super rich of the new Russians. By 2013, there were an estimated 110 dollar billionaires in Russia, third in the world behind China's 122 and the United States' 442. Below these billionaires, many others made a great deal of money in the chaotic marketization of the post-Soviet period. It is folly to use generalizations in judging any particular individual; none the less, there are features of the 'new Russians' as a whole which apply sufficiently well to be worth identifying:

- There was an element of elite continuity from the post-Soviet era, as those who had access to, or *de facto* control of, resources – such as factories or local networks of influence – were in a favourable position when it came to gaining ownership on privatization. Research by David Lane and Cameron Ross (1999) showed elite continuity in the older areas of economic activity, but less continuity in new areas such as retail and commerce.
- There is some truth in the assertion that no one who made money in Russia following the collapse of the Soviet Union did so without paying bribes, protection money, back-handers and so on. The

common view, in Russia as much as outside, is that corruption has been so rife that material success is itself a sufficient indicator of guilt. Some mitigation might be offered on two grounds. First, a market economy needs to be regulated by a complex framework of laws, none of which existed under the Soviet command system. Factors such as political upheaval and lack of expertise meant that the development of a privatized, proto-market environment outpaced the construction of a renewed legal framework. Inevitably, old and inadequate laws were broken. Second, there were those who saw the arrival of an 'incipient acquisition class' as a necessary precursor to the creation of a regulated market economy. Once wealth had been acquired, so the argument went, then it would be in the interests of those who held it to support a protective legal framework. Two decades later, there are cautious signs that a legal environment of this nature is emerging, though these are vitiated by an apparent willingness on the part of the judiciary to take the side of the state when required. (For discussion of legal affairs, see later in this chapter.)

- There was a shadowy crossover between corruption and organized crime in Russia. Turf wars between groups seeking control of profitable areas of activity – for example, banking or trade – resulted in hundreds of contract killings of business people.
- Success in the marketizing economy often came more easily to the younger generation, who did not need to adjust from the old way of doing things and were far more likely to have gained business expertise abroad or with Western companies. Of course, by no means all Russian companies in the first decade of the twenty-first century are tainted by corruption and links with organized crime. As the market economy has become established, so have respectable companies – for example, in manufacturing and the service industries – with high quality products, staff, and standards of customer service.

Below the level of the seriously rich, Russia has a growing middle class emerging out of Moscow, St Petersburg and other urban centres. According to data used by the United Nations, the percentage of the Russian population which could be reliably termed middle class, on the basis of income and professional status, was around 20 per cent by the end of the first decade of the century. In terms of Russia's future with regard to modernization of the economy and regime stability, the middle class has the potential to be a key player, despite its relatively small size. It is disproportionately made up of younger, better educated people who would not easily tolerate a decline in living standards and are committed to the modernization of the country. These are the people with increasing amounts of disposable income who are behind the retail booms – and related real estate developments – in major cities. They travel abroad regularly, buy consumer goods, and contribute taxes to the state. The emergence of a middle class has been seen by theorists of democratic transition as a key driver in establishing a liberal democratic system in Russia. However, although an identifiable middle class is apparent, there is still some way to go before it becomes the bedrock of support for deeper democracy. Members of the middle class do not yet represent the 'average citizen' in Russia in the same way as they are often deemed to do by politicians in most Western countries. There is a disparity between statistical indicators of the middle class based on income, and what might be deemed middle-class attitudes. The assumption that middle class equals liberal is not yet one that can be readily made in Russia.

The proportion of the population living in poverty in Russia, according to official estimates, was around 1 in 5 of the population in 1994. By the turn of the century around 1 in 3 had incomes below the official subsistence minimum. Official figures released at the beginning of 2004 showed that during President Putin's first term in office, the proportion of people living below the poverty line of US$70 per month had fallen from 1 in 3 to 1in 5. By 2012, official data placed 13 per cent of all Russians below the official poverty line. However, there are three caveats that might undermine an otherwise impressive reduction in poverty:

- Independent experts assert that official figures do not give a true picture. In particular, the subsistence minimum is set lower in relation to the cost of living than would be the case in many European countries, and so a smaller proportion of people live below it.
- The reduction in poverty has happened largely during a period of economic growth, with a key factor behind it being the increase in state expenditure on pensions and wages. It is less clear that root causes of poverty have been addressed.
- Having around 18 million people living below even the official poverty line remains a major problem for Russia to tackle.

When Russians are asked what the most worrying problems facing Russian society are, the top three factors cited are to do with poverty

Illustration 4.1 Afimall City, Moscow

One of many new shopping malls opened in Russia's major cities in recent years to cater for the growing urban middle class.

– unemployment, inflation, and a generalized fear of the impoverishment of the population (see Figure 4.1). The situation has improved since the 1990s, and has changed in terms of who are the most affected. In the 1990s in particular, state employees and pensioners took the brunt of the economic collapse. While we are a long way from saying that pensioners no longer suffer from poverty, it is certainly the case that pensions have increased in recent years, with the average reaching around US$300 a month in 2013. For those in work, average real wages have risen more than threefold since 2000. Since his return to presidential office in 2012 in particular, Putin has appeared keen to increase wages in the state sector, with average wages of teachers and doctors increasing 20 and 18 per cent respectively in 2012–13. None the less the picture presented for the poorest remains a bleak one and some sections of the population are in particular need. These groups include one-parent families (increasingly common given rising divorce rates, rising numbers of extra-marital births, and the high mortality rates among middle-aged men), the unemployed and migrants.

Figure 4.1   Top three problems facing Russian society, 2009–2012

What problems facing our society alarm you most? (Top three from list of
18 options covering politics, economic, social problems and ecological
issues. Percentage of respondents choosing the option.)

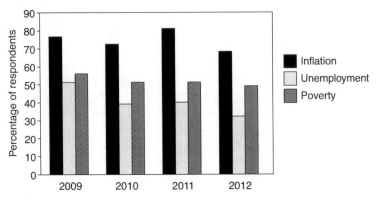

Source: Levada Centre (2012).

Despite increases in pensions and wages, many Russian people
worry about increasing prices (see Figure 4.1). The cost of housing in
Russia means that only a quarter of Russians can afford to buy their
own accommodation. In a campaign article ahead of his election to
the presidency in 2012, Putin pledged to dramatically increase this
figure to 60 per cent by 2020, partly by the expansion of a programme
to subsidize mortgages for young families and state employees. It is
not just the cost of housing that causes concern, however. Running a
household is made more difficult by substantial increases in the cost
of utilities, with both electricity and gas prices experiencing a 15 per
cent rise in 2013.

Demography

Questions of demography have loomed over Russia more than is the
case with most countries in recent decades. As we have noted elsewhere (Chapter 2), excess deaths in the Stalin years amounted to tens
of millions from famine, forced labour, displacement and war.
Demographic issues played some part in the collapse of the Soviet
Union, with an increasing awareness that Islamic Soviet republics

had a faster growing population than did Russia itself, leading to misgivings about the future ethnic mix of the USSR amongst its predominantly Russian political and military leaders.

In the 1990s, the impact of economic hardship and the dismantling of the centralized economy and welfare system was, as noted earlier, associated with perhaps several million excess deaths and a dramatic decline in the birth rate. By the turn of the century, demographic forecasts in relation to Russia began to take on an almost apocalyptic tone, amid talk of dramatic population decline and associated notions of the Russian nation and state gradually dying away. Such talk did not simply stem from alarmists and political opponents. In 2001, a United Nations report forecast that – assuming constant fertility rates – by 2050 the population of Yemen (then just approaching 20 million) would exceed the population of Russia (then over 145 million), with the two countries' populations passing each other at around the 102 million mark (Dillin 2001).

Even at the time, such a prediction seemed unlikely, not least because to assume constant fertility rates, especially after a decade of exceptional upheaval and economic difficulty, was to make an improbable assumption. From a dozen or so years later, the demographic outlook seems a little more positive, as fertility rates have increased. None the less, birth rates have a cyclical element. Low birth rates in the 1990s mean that two decades later there will be a smaller cohort of women having children. To that extent, demographics retain an element of predictability. However, many less predictable elements – such as quality of healthcare, lifestyles, war, immigration and emigration – also have a significant impact on population growth and decline. Contemporary Russia still has reason for concern with regard to demographic developments, both in terms of overall population levels and with regard to the age profile of that population, since the size of the working population in relation to the overall population has economic importance.

In his first 'state of the nation' address to the Russian parliament after returning to the presidency in 2012, Putin encapsulated this mixed picture with regard to demography. On the one hand, he sought to emphasize the positive, noting that the most recent indicators showed that Russia's population grew in 2012. On the other hand, he warned of the particular need to tackle the country's high death rate, singling out smoking, alcoholism and drug use as culprits and pushing the pro-natalist agenda of his regime. Russia's government has indeed acted in these areas. In 2013, Russia introduced anti-smoking regulations banning smoking in a number of public places. Measures have also been introduced to encourage larger families, including social support for young families, measures to reduce the number of abortions, and state awards – known as Orders of Parental Glory – to parents who have brought up seven or more children. The Soviet Union and then Russia had long been notorious for the prevalence of abortion as the main form of birth control, heading the global abortion rate statistics by a significant margin for many years. While contemporary Russia still remains the abortion capital of the world, in recent years numbers of abortions have decreased sharply and the use of contraceptive methods for birth control has increased. Since the 1990s, the number of abortions carried out in Russia has decreased from 4.1 million to 1.2 million per annum. This still leaves an abortion rate of around 50 per 1,000 women of childbearing age. The comparable figure for the United Kingdom is 18, and for the United States it is 20.

What do the official figures tell us about Russia's population? In 1989 the population of Russia was 147 million, in 2002 it was 145 million, and in 2010 143 million. Within these data, the share of ethnic Russians has decreased faster than the population as a whole, and the number of migrants entering the country from the collapse of the Soviet Union to 2010 was around 5 million people. In terms of population decline related to birth and death rates, then, the decline has been even worse than the overall figures indicate. Russia's population began to grow again in 2010, although the gap between birth and death rates was still negative, with immigration enabling a small increase to be posted. 2012 was the first year since 1991 when the population of Russia grew, even discounting immigration. Russia's government celebrated the return to population growth and, as governments do, claimed it as a partial validation of government policy. To return to President Putin's 2012 annual address, though, population growth depends on both birth rates and death rates. Throughout the post-Soviet period, life expectancy in Russia has been remarkably low, particularly for Russian men. By 2013, life expectancy was 76 for women and 64 for men, according to CIA estimates. Although these data show a clear improvement on recent years (the figures for 2008 were 73 and 59 respectively), they also represent particularly low life expectancy for males in a developed country, and one of the biggest gaps between male and female life expectancy in the world. Overall life expectancy in Russia briefly reached 70 in 2012, and this indicator actually saw a slight decline in 2013. In the

United States and the United Kingdom life expectancy is around a decade longer.

Why are so many Russian men dying early?

- Alcohol consumption, accompanied by the Russian pattern of drinking, has been identified in studies as a major contributory factor to low levels of male life expectancy. An anti-alcohol campaign spearheaded by Mikhail Gorbachev (Soviet leader 1985–91) in the second half of the 1980s led to a slight improvement in male mortality rates, but by 1994 twice as many Russian men between 15 and 64 died as had been the case in 1986. It is estimated that 40,000 Russians die every year from accidental alcohol poisoning. In the United States – without adjusting for the fact that the US population is nearly double that of Russia – around 300 people a year are recorded as dying from the same cause.
- Alcohol abuse contributes also to particularly high rates of death by external causes (accidents or violence) afflicting Russian men, with such causes resulting in up to 80 per cent of deaths in the 15–24 age groups in some post-Soviet years. Within this category the highest identifiable cause was suicide, followed by vehicle accidents and homicides. The male suicide rate in Russia is more than six times that for females. Alcohol poisoning *per se* came at the bottom of the list of 'external causes', but clearly alcohol abuse had a role under a number of the other headings. Since the early 2000s, death rates due to suicide and homicide have begun to decline a little, but still remain at high rates in terms of international comparison.
- Russia also has some of the highest rates of alcohol-related illnesses such as cardiovascular diseases, psychiatric disorders and liver problems. Cardiovascular diseases account for almost double the number of deaths among Russian men than do external causes. 'Binge drinking' is associated with an increased risk of cardiovascular disease. In addition, in Russia the ratio of smokers to non-smokers is almost twice as high as in Western Europe.

The demographic problems outlined above are similar to, though worse than, those experienced in a number of developed countries. However, these difficulties are compounded in Russia due to its specific features of size, ethnic mix and political culture. Where allowing an increase in immigration might be seen as an obvious solution to population decline in the abstract, in reality socio-political

Table 4.1   Tuberculosis incidence in Russia, 1960–2013, per 100,000 population

Year	Incidence per 100,000 population	Year	Incidence per 100,000 population
1960	99.5	1996	67.5
1970	72.0	2000	90.4
1975	56.8	2005	132.2
1985	47.4	2011	97.0
1990	34.2	2013	68.9

attitudes – including relatively widespread xenophobia and exaggerated security concerns – make such an option difficult politically. Furthermore, although a number of the demographic features outlined above may be similar in type to those experienced in many developed countries, they are greater in scale and differ in certain key details.

One further major health problem in Russia that we have not yet mentioned is the especially acute threat from tuberculosis and AIDS. Tuberculosis is a disease which was relatively well controlled in the Soviet era, but weaknesses in the public health system and increasing poverty have meant a resurgence, especially with a new strain known as multi-drug resistant tuberculosis (MDR TB) emerging in the 1990s. The incidence of tuberculosis peaked in the middle of the last decade and has now begun to decline (Table 4.1).

At the same time, the far more publicized spread of AIDS has constituted a growing global health threat – and of course the combination of these two threats is mutually destructive to health, as TB is the main infection to which AIDS sufferers in Russia become vulnerable. It is difficult to obtain precise figures for the number of HIV/AIDS cases in Russia. In 2008, 471,676 cases were registered; this figure increased to 703,781 by 2012. However, fear of stigma makes many unwilling to register. Estimates from those working with HIV/AIDS victims posit a figure of at least 1.2 million HIV-positive people.

Russia's health system

During the Soviet era, the state created a system of health care which entitled every citizen access to medical services, free at the point of use. Official health indicators for decades showed improvement across a range of indicators – albeit from a low base. The healthcare provided by the Soviet state was far from perfect; stories abound of poor treatment in unhygienic hospitals, and there were inevitable regional discrepancies across the vast territory of the Soviet Union. In general, the Soviet health system used techniques, equipment and treatments far below the level of developed nations. The health system suffered too from the vagaries of the centrally planned economy, with its emphasis on quantity over quality and its sometimes counterproductive use of targets. For example, targets for the number of 'bed days' provided led hospitals to keep patients in hospitals longer than necessary and to prioritize the number of beds rather than the quality of other resources. Furthermore, health spending in the Soviet Union was low as a percentage of GDP – typically around 3 per cent, compared with 10–12 per cent in the West. According to figures from the Russian Ministry of the Economy, around 6 per cent of all hospitals were financed and run by places of work, such as an industrial enterprise or collective farm. This figure related to the country as a whole, and in some regions the percentage could have been significantly higher.

As the Soviet Union headed for collapse in the late 1980s and early 1990s, so the health system severely worsened as its funding declined dramatically in real terms. Such a situation clearly had some impact on the serious downturn in health statistics noted above. Policy responses to this took a number of forms, chief among these being the introduction of health insurance funds, and the decentralization of the funding and delivery of services. Health reform legislation was passed in Russia in 1991, and then in amended form in 1993. This legislation put responsibility for all but forty of the country's hospitals in the hands of regional government and introduced a system of mandatory medical insurance to be paid by a uniform payroll tax. The health insurance fund would operate alongside central state funding. In reality, such reforms, although perhaps necessary, fell far short of what was needed to provide adequate, let alone high quality, health care coverage for the population. The World Health Organization (2000) ranked the health systems of 191 countries. Russia came in at 130, between Peru and Honduras.

The economic growth of the first decade of the twenty-first century enabled more resources to be devoted to health care. None the less, progress was slow. By the end of Putin's first term as president in 2004, the increase in national wealth due to booming oil prices was still not reflected in public funding of the health system. An official report for President Putin in 2003 found that Russia's health insurance funds received only a fifth of the amount necessary to adequately sustain the health system. Health insurance paid for by a payroll tax leaves those not in employment out of the equation, and it is often such people who are more likely to need medical services. A separate insurance fund exists for non-working people, payments into which are to be made from the federal and regional budgets.

In keeping with his long-standing emphasis on issues relating to standards of living, President Putin sought to address health care provision as a priority within the framework of the 'national projects' that were introduced at the beginning of his second term in office. National projects in the areas of health, education, housing and rural life were announced in September 2005. In relation to health care, the staffing situation has been improved by higher pay for doctors and nurses and the training of more staff. There was also an emphasis on technological solutions, with new, high-tech medical centres built, more ambulances bought, and higher levels of technological provision in hospitals.

The projects were initially put under the charge of then first deputy prime minister, Dmitrii Medvedev, who succeeded Putin as president in 2008. At the end of 2008, a government 'Healthcare Development Concept to 2020' was published, and was designed to work with the national project on health. In terms of aspirations, this health care concept targeted areas of clear need, and set specific targets; for example, reducing strokes and heart attacks by 20 per cent, and increasing average life expectancy from 66 to 75 years by 2020. The concept also set out plans for a complete move to a centralized mandatory health care insurance scheme. As the Medvedev presidency (2008–12) progressed, the national projects faded from national attention, and health care reforms tended to be announced as presidential initiatives, no doubt partly to boost regime popularity ahead of the 2011–12 election season. In 2010, President Medvedev announced a US$3.3 billion boost to health care spending focused on children, and then Prime Minister Putin promised a US$16 billion increase on health spending during 2011–12, the amount being that which an increase in the health care payroll tax from 3.1 to 5.1 per cent would bring in. This new money went into a fund, within the Compulsory Medical Insurance Fund, designed for new equipment and capital projects, as well as buying medicine and increasing doctors' pay. By 2013, the health ministry was able to report that 8,000 doctors, who had agreed to work in rural hospitals during

Table 4.2   Russian health indicators, 2013

Life expectancy, years	
Total population	69.9
Male	64.0
Female	76.0
Infant mortality, under one year old, per thousand	
Male	8.0
Female	6.3
Infant mortality, per thousand	7.2
Total health expenditure, percentage of GDP	4.0

Sources: CIA, *World Factbook* (2013); health expenditure figures from ITAR-TASS report June 2013 (www.itar-tass.com/c154/780087.html).

2011–12, had become rouble millionaires as a result of this initiative. None the less, even the Russian government acknowledges that there is plenty of scope for continued improvement in health care provision in so vast a country with a population so comparatively, in terms of developed countries, susceptible to illness and accident.

Education

The nature of educational provision within a given country varies according to economic, political and social factors. In the Soviet Union the primary task was to establish a system of mass education suitable for a modern industrial country, which at its most basic meant achieving full literacy across the population, and developing universal secondary education and mass higher education. All of this was achieved during the Soviet era. At the same time, the Soviet state sought to socialize and politicize its citizens in the ideology of Marxism–Leninism. Contemporary Russia's educational require-ments are clearly different. The Russian state's commitment to economic modernization and diversification (see Chapter 6) demands an education system of comparable international standing with the leading nations, able to produce a sufficiently and appropriately educated population to develop and sustain a modernized twenty-first-century Russia.

In the Soviet years, the state taught what it wanted its citizens to know, including compulsory lessons in Marxism–Leninism. The history curriculum was replete with uncritical praise for all that the Party had done, and studiously avoided topics such as the Stalinist terror or the ideas of 'the renegade Trotsky'. English-language text-books included accounts of poverty-stricken Londoners oppressed by the bourgeoisie. Economics and law followed narrow ideological courses, and sociology barely existed until Gorbachev embraced some of its findings to bolster his reform programme in the mid-1980s. Political reliability was not only central to curriculum content; it could also have an influence on admission to the best universities. In the Soviet period, the drive to recruit working-class children to higher education gave them priority, but such priority could always be trumped by members of the new ruling class, the Communist Party leadership, and their families.

Political bias aside, the Soviet education system represented an impressive achievement, providing universal education, and creating a literate and highly educated population with specialists capable of rivalling the world's best. In the post-Soviet era, however, the difficulties facing the public sector at large swept away much of the good from the old system. While debates about curriculum reform occupied many specialists, schools were undermined by salary arrears, equipment shortages and a lack of teachers. The teaching profession in Russia became so unattractive in the 1990s that by the end of the decade only about half of those graduating from teacher training institutions went on to teach in schools. The difficulties in attracting teachers were felt in particular in remote regions, as the Soviet practice of requiring teachers to work in designated schools on qualification was discontinued. Furthermore, there was an exodus from the classroom by teachers, as real incomes declined or wages simply were not paid, and it was reported by the education minister as late as 2001 that up to 2 million children of school age in Russia did not in fact attend school. At the tertiary level, Russian higher education became increasingly expensive and open to corruption.

When President Putin came to power in 2000, reform of the education system fitted in with his declared focus on domestic issues. In August 2001, the State Council – a body set up by Putin, with a membership made up of the heads of regions, but with only advisory status – considered the issue of education reform. In a speech to the State Council, Putin called free education 'the cornerstone' of the state system, but also talked positively of the contribution to be made by an ordered private system. The major reform announcement was that educational spending would become a national priority. The most obvious immediate beneficiaries of this change in policy were teachers, who saw their salaries doubled – but this was to a figure equivalent to a meagre US$80 to US$100 per month. A further 50 per cent pay rise followed in 2005. In a reversal of decades of Soviet practice, in 2004 the Ministry of Education proudly announced that state spending on education outstripped that on the defence industries, a significant shift away from the priorities of the Soviet era.

The reforms of 2001 included the introduction of a standard school leaving exam, on which entry to university would be based. This reform sought to make entry into higher education more egalitarian, and less prone to the corruption which beset it in the immediate post-Soviet era. Further reforms in the school system included a change in teachers' terms and conditions, so that pay was more closely related to hours taught and thus 'moonlighting' diminished. These initial education reforms of the Putin years were followed by the introduction of the national project for education, specifically aimed at creating an education system capable of supporting the development of civil society and of an economy suited to technological innovation. The aims of the project were framed on the one hand in terms of support for innovative approaches, support for the best teachers and most talented young people, and the development of regional centres of excellence. On the other hand, there was also a more universal commitment to the provision of internet connections and computers, adequate school transport, improvements in school meals, and repairs to buildings. The national projects as a whole sought to integrate the more remote towns and cities of Russia into the development process, and this included a dramatic increase in online capabilities.

Looking at the key indicators for Russia's education system between 1990 and 2010 (Table 4.3), it is apparent that the number of schools and school students fell markedly. This was primarily due to the demographic downturn of the 1990s, and its impact in terms of school provision was particularly felt in rural areas, where declining numbers meant the closure of schools at a rate disproportionate to that experienced nationally. School provision should not, however, only be judged in terms of numbers. Recent years have seen some important reforms in terms of the curriculum, with new subjects introduced to prepare pupils for the contemporary world, and a distinct separation being made between education up to Year 9 and onward to Year 11, enabling the higher two years to be spent either in advanced classes in school or undertaking vocational training in college. This latter shift largely explains the increase in the number of students and institutions in the vocational training sector – a sector that saw initial rapid decline in the 1990s as many of the old Soviet

Table 4.3   Russia's education indicators, 1990–2010

	1990	2010
Number of schools	69,667	50,128
Number of rural schools	48,214	30,326
Number of school students (thousands)	20,851	13,569
Number of vocational training institutes	4,328	5,206
Number of students in vocational training institutes (thousands)	1,867	3,133
Number of higher education institutions	514	1,577
Number of students in higher education institutions (thousands)	2,825	8,251

Source: UN Human Development Survey: Russia (2012).

industrial enterprises closed down. As well as curriculum reform, changes are also gradually being introduced in the way in which pupils are taught in school, with the old emphasis on rote learning of facts and figures supposedly giving way to the teaching of independent and creative thinking.

When President Medvedev came to power in 2008, he made it his particular business to focus attention on reform of the higher education system, even making it the subject of one of his regular video blogs on the presidential website. In the preceding years, initiatives had been developed to reduce the level of corruption involved in gaining university places; in particular, a standardized national test at the end of secondary school was introduced. A poll in 2007 found that 66 per cent of Russians considered their higher education system to be corrupt, with some families spending over a third of their income on what is supposed to be a free education. There were regular stories of university staff accepting bribes for good marks – 30 to 40 cases coming to light a year in Moscow alone – and of university authorities selling building permission for private profit or using state funds for purposes other than those intended. The low levels of pay for university lecturers no doubt contributed to the level of corruption. In 2013, the government intervened to provide a notable increase in wages for academics.

Despite these difficulties, the expansion of the university sector in Russia in recent years has been a success story. Between 1990 and 2010, the number of students in higher education in Russia increased threefold, alongside a similar trebling in the number of higher education institutions. Russia now has the highest proportion of working population with higher education in the world, and some 70 per cent of the 17–22 age group were in higher education by 2010. Around 15 per cent of students study in non-state institutions. As with data on schools – though this time from the point of view of an increase rather than a decrease – numbers do not tell the full story of university-level provision. The proliferation of higher education institutions in early twenty-first-century Russia meant that state spending per student decreased, the number of students studying by distance learning increased dramatically, and many institutions of varying quality adopted university title. In an attempt to differentiate within the sector on the basis of quality, the universities of Moscow and St Petersburg have been given the title 'national universities', seven universities – including new ones established in the Siberian and Southern Federal Districts – have been granted federal status, and the government is creating a core of thirty or more 'national research universities'. The ambitious aim is for Russia to have five or six institutions in the world's top hundred universities by 2020. This is not going to happen in terms of Russian institutions breaking into any of the internationally recognized global rankings. Only Moscow State University features in the Shanghai Jiao Tong top 100 universities, in 80th place in 2012, having fallen ten places since 2008. The only other Russian university in the top 500 in 2012 was St Petersburg – which came in the 400–500th place listings.

Judicial policy

All of Russia's recent leaders, including the last Soviet leader, Mikhail Gorbachev, have committed themselves in principle to the rule of law. Early on in his time as president, Vladimir Putin repeatedly emphasized that the law should not be applied differentially on political grounds – though his choice of phrase left something to be desired when, in an echo of the Communist Party's commitment to a 'dictatorship of the proletariat', he called for a 'dictatorship of the law'. Despite this formal commitment to the rule of law, however, cases such as the Yukos affair (Box 4.1) and the trial of opposition activist Aleksei Navalny in 2013 suggest that political control over the courts still prevails where deemed necessary. This despite the fact that when Dmitrii Medvedev became President in May 2008, he declared that 'our main objective is to achieve independence for the judicial system'.

At the fundamental level, Russia's Constitution, adopted by national referendum on 12 December 1993, forms the basic law of the Russian Federation and is a recognizably liberal democratic document. There is a fundamental commitment within it to the separation of powers and equality of citizens before the law (for more details of the Constitution, see Chapter 5). Under Boris Yeltsin's presidency (1991–9), Russia ceased to apply the death penalty, in line with the conditions for membership of the Council of Europe. Russian citizens are also able to take their cases to the European Court of Human Rights and, as of October 2011, approximately 41,300 cases pending before the Court originated in Russia, the largest number from any country. The fact that more citizens of Russia than of any other country petition the European Court of Human Rights is an indication of the failure of the Russian court system to uphold these rights.

President Medvedev (2008–12) spoke of the need to reform Russia's judiciary in order to stem the flow of cases to Strasbourg. In 2002 a much-trumpeted judicial reform package had been introduced by President Putin. Among its provisions was enabling legislation to introduce the constitutional provision of trial by jury on a nationwide basis, as previously it had only been available in limited locations. Despite the continued right of defendants in serious cases to request trial by jury, Putin declared in 2010 that jury trials were not effective and should be restricted to federal level cases in order to prevent regional trials being skewed by ethnic or geographical loyalties. The reforms of 2002 also sought to enhance the status and independence of the judiciary by improving judges' pay by 40 per cent, increasing the number of judges, and ending their lifetime tenure and immunity from prosecution. Measures were introduced to enhance the rights of suspects and create a level playing field for defence lawyers in relation to the previously overwhelmingly influential prosecutors. Trials in absentia were banned; searches, arrests and detention beyond 48 hours must now be sanctioned by courts, rather than by prosecutors; plea bargaining was introduced for offences with a prison term of less than five years; and the practice of sending criminal cases back for 'additional investigation' – that is, enabling the prosecution to patch up a poor case – was ended.

As a package of reforms, the measures introduced in 2002 and 2003 were impressive. At the very least they indicated an awareness of continuing problems and of international norms. None the less, the problems with the Russian judicial system have proved deep-rooted in terms of culture. In 2010, President Medvedev introduced a further set of judicial reforms, focused primarily on liberalizing sentencing and thereby reducing Russia's prison population, which in the early years of the twenty-first century had been second only to the United States in terms of the proportion of the population imprisoned. In 2006, Russia's prison population was 827,000; by 2012 it was 715.000. Alongside judicial reforms, Medvedev also implemented wide-ranging reforms of Russia's police. The main features of these changes were: a name change from 'militsiya' to 'politsiya'; a reduction in force numbers by 20 per cent, to be implemented by a re-certification process designed to weed out undesirable officers; a renewed emphasis on legality, impartiality and public trust; a change in uniform; and a pay rise.

Alongside these apparently liberal reforms, however, the reputation of the legal process has taken something of a hammering in Russia in recent years, with many of the cases causing concern being brought to court by the Investigative Committee, which functions under the direction of the presidency. The Investigative Committee, in its present form, was established in 2011 and has over 20,000 employees, headed by Aleksandr Bastrykin, a former university classmate of Putin's in the 1970s. Bastrykin is loyal to the president, and he and his committee have gained increasing prominence and authority since 2011. Nearly all of the controversial and politically-oriented cases that have been brought during the first year or so of Putin's third term as president have involved the Investigative Committee – for example, the cases against Aleksei Navalny and the Bolotnaya Square protesters (see Chapter 5), and the abandoning of the investigation into the death in custody of Sergei Magnitsky on the grounds of 'absence of a crime'. The removal of Deputy Prime Minister Vladislav Surkov from his post in 2013 was accompanied by what was widely seen as a strong attack on him, authored by an Investigative Committee spokesman, in the leading daily newspaper, *Izvestiya*.

In July 2013, 50 prominent lawyers and legal scholars took the opportunity of the Russian Constitution's 20th anniversary to publish an Open Letter strongly condemning the authorities for the decline in the status of the rule of law in Russia. On the back of internationally condemned trials – such as the second trial of Mikhail Khodorkovsky in 2010 (Box 4.1), the Pussy Riot trial in 2012 (Box 7.1), and in 2013 the posthumous trial of Sergei Magnitsky (Box 7.2) and the Aleksei Navalny trial (see Chapters 5 and 7) – the authors of this letter asserted that the Constitution's description of Russia as a law-based state had become essentially meaningless. They accused the state law

---

Box 4.1   The Yukos affair, Khodorkovsky and Basmanny justice

Any claim on the part of the Russian authorities to support an independent judiciary and fair legal system must be considered against the
Yukos Affair. This represented a watershed in several key elements of
Russia's recent development, from both the political and economic
perspectives. For the purposes of this chapter, however, the main focus
is its judicial aspect.

Yukos was Russia's largest private oil company, the CEO (Chief
Executive Officer) of which, Mikhail Khodorkovsky, was arrested in
October 2003 and charged with tax evasion and fraud. There are several
explanations as to why Khodorkovsky was singled out for arrest and
prosecution, especially given that Yukos was renowned for being the
first Russian company to comply with international accounting standards in terms of releasing financial data, and paid a higher proportion
of its earnings in tax than other leading oil companies. Khodorkovsky
had supported political parties financially. Political engagement went
against the spirit of the alleged agreement between Putin and Russia's
leading businessmen in 2000, that, if they kept out of politics, the state
would not revisit the legality of the privatizations of the 1990s, in
which lay the root source of their wealth. Khodorkovsky was also a
strong critic of corruption in the Russian government.

Aside from the politics, some argue that Yukos's intention to create
the country's largest oil company, by merging with Sibneft, cut across
the ambitions of other companies with state influence. Or that Yukos
showed a willingness to disrupt the state's oversight of pipeline policy,

⯮

---

enforcement bodies and security services of fabricating cases against
opponents of the regime, and the courts of giving credence to such
actions by displaying bias and arriving at 'obviously unjust guilty
verdicts'.

Such a low opinion of the state of justice in contemporary Russia is
not restricted to legal professionals. Opinion polls in 2012 showed that
only 5 per cent of Russia's population considered the country's judiciary to be fully independent of the presidential administration, and
64 per cent considered it either completely or significantly dependent.
In August 2013, an opinion poll found that nearly 60 per cent of
Russians would only consider using the court system to obtain justice
as a last resort. Despite the fact that the same percentage ranked a fair
trial as the most important individual right, way ahead of freedom of
speech or conscience, they did not trust Russia's court system to
provide it. It still remains the case in Russia that anyone investigated

viewed by the administration as a critical economic and foreign policy tool.

Whatever the precise weight of the different elements, the Parliamentary Assembly of the Council of Europe summed up the impression of many, particularly in the West, when suggesting that the arrest of Khodorkovsky went beyond the pursuit of criminal justice to include elements such as weakening an outspoken political opponent, intimidating other wealthy individuals, and regaining control of economic assets.

Khodorkovsky's trial gave rise to the phrase 'Basmanny justice', after the Basmanny district court in Moscow where it took place, as a description of a Russian judicial system where the state can rely on, or lean on if necessary, the judiciary to deliver the desired verdict. Besides the bigger question of why Yukos was singled out, Khodorkosky's lawyers allege a whole series of procedural and due process violations during the case. Mikhail Khodorkovsky was found guilty and sentenced to nine years' imprisonment. In 2007, further charges were brought against him, and as a result he was sentenced to remain in prison until 2014. President Putin signed an amnesty ordering Khodorkosky's release in December 2013.

Even as Khodorkovsky's trial was continuing, the Russian state began to break up and sell Yukos to recover some of the alleged tax debts. In December 2004, the little known Baikalfinansgrup bought Yuganskneftegaz, Yukos's prime asset, for an amount reported to be significantly below market value, and swiftly sold it on to the state-owned company, Rosneft.

and charged labours under a presumption of guilt rather than innocence. According to official data, 99 per cent of cases in Russian courts result in the conviction of the accused, though an independent website providing data on Russia's judicial system suggests that there are even fewer acquittals, at the level of one in every 500 cases. Anyone attending a Russian court case will be immediately struck by the fact that defendants – whether dangerous or not – give their evidence from inside a cage in the courtroom, as if to emphasize the fact that they are almost certainly to be found guilty.

5

Politics and Government

It is not unreasonable to ask: what precisely was the point of Russia's apparent choice in favour of a democratic political system in the early 1990s? A quarter of a century later there has still been no democratic change of government. Those heady days saw the Communist regime brought down with remarkable speed. The rhetoric of democracy held sway, Russia adopted a democratic constitution, new parties sprang up and some flourished, elections were hard fought, and unpredictable results occurred – and yet all of this has ended up in a political system over which, if all goes according to plan until his third presidential term ends in 2018, Vladimir Putin will have been the dominant figure for 18 years. That is as long as Leonid Brezhnev ruled the Soviet Union (1964–82). Brezhnev died in 1982 at the age of 75. Assuming Putin serves out his third term, he will be 65 years old at its end, and constitutionally allowed to stand for a further six-year period as president. To put it mildly, such dominance by a single figure and single regime – whatever their qualities and faults – sits very uneasily with the idea of a modern democracy.

I use the verb 'ended up' in relation to Russia's political system with reluctant deliberation. For a long period after the Soviet collapse, the talk among analysts and politicians alike was of democratic transition; democracy could not be imposed overnight, it had to be developed – institutionally, culturally, behaviourally – until it became the norm, the 'only game in town' in political terms. The late American political scientist Samuel Huntington proposed a 'two turnover test' for democratic consolidation in post-authoritarian regimes. If power peacefully changed hands by democratic process twice – say, from ruling regime to opposition and back again – then the transition process could be said to be over and democracy consolidated (Huntington 1991). In Russia President Yeltsin came to power in 1991, was re-elected in 1996, and nominated his preferred successor, Vladimir Putin, in 1999. Putin won two successive elections in 2000 and 2004. Having reached the constitutional limit of two successive presidential terms, Putin nominated his preferred successor, Dmitrii Medvedev, who was duly elected president in 2008 and nominated Putin as his prime minister. Then in September 2011, Medvedev and Putin jointly revealed that all along the plan had been for Putin to return to the presidency in the 2012 election, which he duly did, nominating Medvedev in turn as his prime minister.

For many observers, at some point in this procession of nominated successors duly taking power, the notion that a process of democratic transition was actively being pursued by Russia's rulers fell by the wayside. For the more sceptical, the presidential election of 1996, which saw some of Russia's richest men rally behind Boris Yeltsin to move him in six months from an opinion poll rating of 8 per cent to a second round victory with 54 per cent of the vote, marked the end of genuine transition. For others the key moment was Yeltsin's early resignation in 1999, which meant an early election, which his chosen successor, Vladimir Putin, was able to easily win from the position of incumbent acting president. For more optimistic – or naïve – observers, however, it was a dozen years later that the final nail was hammered in transition's coffin. Putin's stepping down from the presidency in accordance with the constitution in 2008, and the election of a younger and more liberal-sounding president in the form of Medvedev, had raised hopes that, although glacial in terms of speed, some form of democratic transition was still being implemented by Russia's rulers. However, the 'castling' manoeuvre of 2012 – when President Medvedev became prime minister, and Prime Minister Putin became president – left little traction for this notion of creeping democratization to hold any further. With Putin back as president from 2012 onwards, a democratic change of regime appears further away than ever. If a quarter of a century has passed without one democratic turnover, it can safely be assumed that Huntington's two turnover test remains a long way from being passed by contemporary Russia.

It must be noted, however, that there is something else, apart from longevity, which Brezhnev and Putin have shared politically, and that is relative popularity. Over the past decade or so Brezhnev has often been cited by opinion polls as the most popular Russian or Soviet leader of the past century, whereas Putin has retained ratings of, for the most part, over 50 per cent throughout his time in power. Pro-Putin observers, and indeed the regime itself, might cite such popularity as evidence, alongside election results, that the Russian people have the leader that they want. Many would readily admit that the niceties of democratic procedure are not fully entrenched, and that the concept of genuine opposition remains problematic in the Russian political system. They would argue in turn that Russia remains unsuited to direct borrowing from Western systems, and requires its own form of democracy, with an emphasis on national unity and clear leadership.

Whether one accepts this case or not, it represents further confirmation that the process of democratic transition, as commonly understood, is in abeyance in contemporary Russia. While the majority of the population appear to accept the *status quo*, the mass demonstrations in Moscow around the 2011–12 election period marked a renewed willingness by anti-Putin forces to engage in direct political action. The relatively hard-line response by the authorities, which has seen a number of demonstrators tried on charges of rioting, shows a recognition by the Putin regime of the potential significance of such action.

This chapter sets out the details of how Russia's political system functions today. It covers the formal institutional and constitutional powers, which still remain within the democratic pale, structurally if not functionally. The development of presidency, government, parliament and other key institutions is traced from the late Soviet period until today, as is the fluctuating situation with regard to political parties, opposition and regional governance. At the same time, though, central to the analysis set out here – and, indeed, to understanding the politics and government of contemporary Russia – is the realization that formal powers do not necessarily indicate how Russian politics really works. Equally, some would say more, important are the system's informal features such as personal relationships, the use of the judicial system for political purposes, the force of half-spoken threats and persuasion, and the existence of influential networks encompassing business, politics, regional interests, the security services, the media and so on. Of course, the existence of such factors is scarcely the preserve of Russian politics alone. However, their influence and co-existence alongside a sometimes genuine, sometimes nominal, adherence to formal procedures and institutions represents a central feature of contemporary Russia's political life.

The development of Russia's political system

The Soviet behavioural legacy

The collapse of the Communist political system in Russia in the period 1989–91 was the end of what had become widely known as the command-administrative system. This was politics by central *diktat*. Power was concentrated at the centre among the senior ranks of the Communist Party, and the function of other elements of the system – parliaments, central government, republican, regional and local authorities – was to put central instructions into practice. Nor was the exercise of power restrained by legality, since laws were only arbitrarily applied, and elements of the legal code, such as the notion of 'anti-Soviet activities', were so broadly interpreted that they were frequently taken to mean any activities of which the authorities disapproved.

Command-administrative politics were largely non-political politics. That is to say, what was missing in this political system were information flows, and the free interchange of ideas and alternatives for society. The atmosphere was one of instinctive secrecy and obsessive official control over information presented in the media or through the arts and literature. Soviet Russia was largely cut off from foreign influences, both benign and damaging. The use of a particular language of political discourse, the language of Marxism–Leninism, ruled out certain alternative directions of development, including calls for the introduction of market mechanisms into the economy. It also deified other practices, such as the leading role of the Communist Party, which at its worst became the belief that the Communist Party collectively was never wrong. There was no role for political opposition, let alone any possibility of opposition one day becoming government. The lack of opposition and the lack of an independent system of police and courts meant that a chronic problem for the system was accountability.

This was broadly how Soviet politics operated in the period before Mikhail Gorbachev's abortive attempts to reform and purify the system between 1985 and 1991. It was an environment that encouraged habits of command and elitism, and of seeing politics not as the comparison of alternatives and a search for compromise but as a means for the political destruction of opponents. Clearly, it would be difficult for those acculturated by such 'non-political politics' to adapt to democratic modes of political behaviour, such as respect for opponents, adherence to constitutional norms, and – above all – commitment to implementing the will of the people. In the immediate post-Soviet period, these modes of political behaviour were hard to find as the political leadership of the new Russian state, within the institutions of the presidency and the parliament, literally fought for power. By October 1993, military action trumped democratic debate in the struggle to agree a constitutional arrangement for the emergent Russian state (see Chapter 2).

The struggle for a Constitution

The need for a new constitution for Russia after the collapse of the Soviet Union was clear on three counts – institutional, ideological and legal:

- At the institutional level, the operative constitution in Russia in 1992–3 was the 1978 Constitution of the RSFSR (Russian Soviet Federative Socialist Republic) – the old name for Russia in its Communist-era existence as one of fifteen republics in the Soviet Union. This 1978 Constitution was therefore predicated on the existence of an institutional framework which had disappeared in 1991 along with the Soviet state. It assumed implicitly the existence of a one-party state. The Communist Party of the Soviet Union was the institution that had held the Soviet state together. Once this had gone then decision-making processes reverted back to the formal procedures of a constitution that had been written for another political age, and even then had never borne much relation to the way the state was really governed. In particular, the means by which the centre controlled the regions – a relationship known in Russia as the 'power vertical' – virtually disappeared along with the Party.
- At the ideological level, the old constitution adhered to communist ideology in its Marxist–Leninist form, whereas the Russian Federation after 1991 saw itself more as a Western-type liberal state. This makes a fundamental difference to the underlying concept of any constitution. In a liberal state, the rights of the individual are supreme. Under Marxist–Leninist ideology, the individual came second to the rights of and obligations to the workers as a collective in the form of the state.
- At the legal level, the need for a new constitution was evident if one considers what constitutions are for. A constitution is supposed

to be the fundamental law of a state, containing concepts that, if not unchangeable, are certainly meant to have a depth of durability. The constitution of the United States, for example, has only been amended around twenty-seven times since its adoption over two centuries ago, in 1787. By 1992, the old Constitution of the RSFSR had been amended more than 300 times in fourteen years. It could scarcely be seen as a fundamental law.

Virtually all politicians in Russia accepted the need for a new constitution after the collapse of the Soviet Union. Despite this, it took two years from the end of the USSR for the new Constitution to come into existence. The primary cause of this delay was the power struggle between President Yeltsin and the parliament in 1992–3. Having abandoned Marxism–Leninism and chosen a democratic path, the Russian Federation and its political elite had to decide on their preferred form of democracy. The two key issues to be resolved were the relationship between president and parliament, and the relationship between the centre and the regions. These issues are central elements of the 'rules of the game' and therefore of the Constitution.

The failure to decide between presidentialism and parliamentarism held up agreement over a new constitution. Participants in this dispute between president and parliament couched their arguments largely in terms of which system better suited the nascent democracy of Russia in the immediate post-Soviet era. However, the dispute had as much to do with the past and present as with democratic guarantees for the future. It was a power struggle between parliament and the president fought in terms of not only the relative democratic legitimacy of these two institutions, but also ultimately the extent to which they could command the use of force.

The Russian word 'soviet' literally means 'council' or, at the highest levels, 'parliament'. As its name suggests, the Soviet Union throughout its existence had claimed to be run by a series of workers' councils, which culminated with a central Supreme Soviet where, in theory, state power lay. In practice, power lay with the Communist Party, which dominated the soviets and reduced them to virtual rubber-stamping bodies throughout most of the twentieth century. Only after Gorbachev's reforms in the late 1980s did some real power begin to return to the soviets, and particularly to the Russian soviet, or parliament. Therefore, at the collapse of the Soviet Union, the Russian parliament enjoyed more power than it had known before. Many members were understandably reluctant to see this long-denied power swiftly removed again and given to the president, particularly since the parliament had been reasonably democratically elected in 1990.

The president, on the other hand, could lay claim to a still more recent mandate. Boris Yeltsin had been chosen as Russia's first ever democratically elected leader in June 1991. Not only had he won the election, but he had won it overwhelmingly. Yeltsin had received a majority over all the other candidates combined, thereby negating the need for the second round of votes provided for in electoral rules. He believed, with some justification from opinion polls, that the people favoured a presidential system. However, the presidency itself was a new institution, introduced with some haste as a tool in the power struggle between Yeltsin and Gorbachev, Russia and the Soviet Union, in 1991. It had no history or tradition on which to draw, and there was no established consensus with regard to the role and power of the president.

As if to demonstrate its inadequacy as a fundamental law, the old Constitution offered no clear way out of the dispute between president and parliament. The obvious solution would have been a general election or binding referendum. However, only parliament had the constitutional right to implement such a course of action, and was unwilling to exercise this right and dissolve itself mid-term. President Yeltsin wanted to dissolve parliament but was constitutionally barred from doing so. The impasse held up policy-making and the enactment of a new Constitution until September 1993, when Yeltsin unilaterally, and acting outside his formal powers, dissolved parliament. Some parliamentary deputies refused to accept this dissolution and remained under armed siege in the parliament building until, provoked by attempts by armed parliamentary supporters to seize the central television building in Moscow, President Yeltsin ordered a military attack on the parliament building in early October 1993, which left over a hundred defenders of the parliament dead.

Having won the military struggle in Moscow, President Yeltsin put a heavily presidential Constitution before the Russian people in a referendum on 12 December 1993, the same day as a general election of deputies to the Federal Assembly. The 1993 election therefore chose members of a parliament whose existence would depend on the result of the constitutional referendum. To critics, even the very process by which Russia adopted its new democratic constitution was not entirely democratic. Referendum and election happened simultaneously, making it difficult for anyone running for election to parliament to urge a vote against the Constitution that would create the very parliament in which they were seeking a seat.

In addition to a democratic deficit in terms of procedure, the actual voting on the Constitution did not indicate the wholehearted support of the Russian people for their new system of government. To be binding, the referendum on the Constitution had to attract a turnout of over 50 per cent of the electorate. In the event, the Constitution was adopted by 58 per cent of the vote, with a 54 per cent turnout. To put it another way, the Russian Constitution was adopted on the basis of the votes of under one in three of the Russian electorate, amid accusations from many quarters about falsification in the course of the referendum.

Russia's Constitution

The 1993 Russian Constitution was drawn up against the background of the power struggle between president and parliament, and near civil war on the streets of Moscow. More importantly, it was drawn up by the winning side in this dispute – the presidency. The resulting Constitution consequently provides for a strong presidency and a comparatively weak parliament. Under this Constitution, Russia has an executive (president, presidential administration and government) almost wholly independent of parliament. The legislature (parliament) consists of upper and lower chambers, the Federation Council and the State Duma, respectively, known collectively as the Federal Assembly. The document also establishes a constitutionally independent judiciary, a Constitutional Court and a Supreme Court. Other sections of the Constitution define the Russian Federation as a democratic, law-based state where a range of human rights are observed.

The difficulties surrounding the adoption of the Constitution mean that the method by which constitutional amendments are introduced has considerable political significance. The procedure is quite elaborate. Two-thirds of each chamber of parliament and two-thirds of regional legislatures must approve changes. It is this procedure that was used in 2008 to introduce amendments extending the presidential and parliamentary terms to six years and five years, respectively, and requiring the government to present an annual report to parliament. In the case of changes to chapters 1, 2 and 9, which are the sections containing the basic principles of the Constitution (democracy, rule of law, the structure of the federation, as well as bans on official ideology and on the establishment of a state religion), individual rights and the procedure for constitutional amendment, there is an additional need for the convening of a Constitutional Assembly and, if this assembly so decides, a national referendum in which at least half the electorate must participate.

The executive

The presidency

The formal powers of the presidency in the Russian Federation enable him, or her, to rule with relatively little reference to the parliament. The president ultimately appoints the government and decides on the size and personnel of the influential presidential administration. It is the presidential administration which usually prepares the decrees – binding throughout the Russian Federation – issued by the president, though, as we note later, the number of such decrees has decreased as the number of laws passed by parliament has increased. From 2012 onwards, the president serves for a six-year term, as opposed to the previous term of four years.

The presidential administration

There is a fluidity within the presidential administration as the president can freely set up and close down different executive bodies, for

---

Box 5.1   The powers of the president of the Russian Federation

The president:

- is head of state;
- is supreme commander in chief of the armed forces;
- issues decrees, the implementation of which is mandatory throughout Russia;
- directs foreign policy;
- nominates the prime minister;
- appoints, dismisses and has the right to chair the government;
- forms the presidential administration and the Security Council;
- dissolves the State Duma (according to constitutional procedures).

Box 5.2 The presidential administration, 2013

Leadership of the administration
Head of administration, 2 first deputy heads, 3 deputy heads, 9 presidential aides

Other key officials
Including presidential press secretary, head of presidential protocol, 10 presidential advisers, 8 presidential representatives in the regions, presidential representatives in the upper and lower houses of parliament and the Constitutional Court

Branches of the administration
Including the State-Legal Directorate and the Directorate for the Civil Service

Source: http://state.kremlin.ru/administration.

---

example, between 1996 and 1998 a Defence Council existed, created by President Yeltsin to rival the Security Council. During his first two terms in office, President Putin sought to reduce the size of his administration, but it is once again increasing in number during his third term. The current structure of the presidential administration is set out in Box 5.2. Alongside this presidential administration, and under the president within the executive branch of power, there exist five other institutions or types of institution, namely: the government, the Security Council, the State Council, Presidential Commissions, and Presidential Councils. In addition, the Public Chamber, although not part of the executive, is made up initially of presidential nominees and so is dealt with in this section.

The government

Russia's government is headed by the prime minister, who is appointed by the president with the approval of the lower chamber of parliament, the State Duma. The president has the right to preside over meetings of the government and to dismiss the prime minister and government. For most of the post-Soviet era, Russia's government has focused on domestic policy, chiefly economic affairs, under a technocratic prime minister. However, during Putin's second spell as prime minister, between 2008 and 2012 while Medvedev was President of Russia, the responsibilities of the government in relation to the president increased somewhat in practice, though there was no formal change in the institutional balance (see below, 'Power relations between president, prime minister and parliament'). The structure of the government is set out in Box 5.3.

The Security Council

After the government, potentially the most important body in the executive branch is the Security Council, which is identified specifically in the Constitution. Formally, this council has sweeping powers to oversee social, political and economic threats to security and it serves as an inter-agency body, bringing together key political actors and the 'power ministries' of defence, foreign affairs, the emergency ministry, the security service and the foreign intelligence service. The Security Council exercises its power under the president, and so at times has been influential and at times peripheral, according to the president's wishes.

In recent years the Security Council has been quietly significant, providing a forum where the key players in the Russian state meet regularly to discuss key issues. For example, during the short war with Georgia in August 2008, the Security Council was the key forum where decisions were made. Its membership under President Putin in 2013 included 12 permanent members, among whom were the prime minister, defence minister, foreign minister, minister of internal affairs, the speakers of both chambers of parliament, and the heads of the presidential administration, the Federal Security Service, and the Foreign Intelligence Service. There were a further 17 ordinary members, including the presidential representatives in Russia's federal districts, the prosecutor general, the justice minister, the head of the general staff, the mayor of Moscow and the governor of St Petersburg.

In short, the Security Council brings together for regular meetings, under the president and separate from meetings of the government, all of the key players in Russia's politico-security nexus. During Putin's third term as president, the permanent members of the Security Council have been meeting three or four times a month. It is little wonder that some have described Russia's Security Council as bearing some resemblance to the Soviet Politburo in terms of being

---

Box 5.3   The Russian government, 2013

Prime Minister

1 First Deputy Prime Minister, 6 Deputy Prime Ministers

21 Ministers
(for Agriculture, Communications and Media, Culture, Defence,
Development of the Far East, Economic Development, Education and
Science, Emergency Situations, Energy, Finance, Foreign Affairs,
Health, Industry and Trade, Internal Affairs, Justice, Labour and
Social Protection, Natural Resources and Ecology, Regional
Development, Sport, Transport)

Source: http://government.ru/en/gov/.

---

the real 'cabinet' of the country. Indeed, during the mid-1990s, when President Yeltsin was incapacitated by illness, a power struggle developed between the Prime Minister and the Secretary of the Security Council over the respective authority of the government and the Security Council, since, as the official website of the Security Council acknowledges, 'national security is a very broad term'.

The State Council

The State Council of the Russian Federation is an advisory body, chaired by the president as head of state and made up of the heads of all of Russia's federal regions. Unlike the Security Council, there is no constitutional mandate for its existence. The State Council was established by President Putin in 2000, partly as a sop to regional leaders after their right to sit in the upper chamber of parliament, the Federation Council, was removed. The use of the title State Council is a deliberate reference to the imperial State Councils, which advised the Tsars in pre-revolutionary Russia. In the twenty-first century, the State Council meets at least four times a year, sometimes more, and sometimes in joint session with the Security Council. Its business is typically a major theme of national importance, usually put forward by the president.

In establishing the State Council in 2000, President Putin created a major state body that was not mentioned in the Constitution.

President Yeltsin had done this at a lower level, by creating a Defence Council within the presidential administration, but the State Council represented – in terms of symbolism and informal power at least – a more significant innovation, in that it brought together the executive heads of all the regions in the Russian Federation, under the chairmanship of their head of state, the president of Russia.

Presidential Commissions and Presidential Councils

The final bodies that go to make up the executive *per se* are the Presidential Commissions and Presidential Councils, which are essentially part of the presidential administration. The difference between the two is that commissions are oriented to specific tasks – for example, the Commission for Rehabilitation of the Victims of Political Repression – and councils are concerned more generally with particular areas of activity – for example, the Council for Co-ordination with Religious Organizations. In 2013, there were 14 Presidential Commissions and 16 Presidential Councils.

The Public Chamber

The extra-constitutional, rather than explicitly unconstitutional, creation of state institutions by the president, which was seen in the case of the State Council in 2000, was repeated in 2005 with the establishment of the Public Chamber. This institution is not part of the executive *per se*, as it is supposed to sit outside of government structures in order to engage the wider public in governance. The Public Chamber's remit is to ensure co-operation between citizens and the organs of state power at both federal and regional level, including analysing draft legislation and monitoring the performance of federal and regional bodies. In essence, it brings together representatives of civil society into a formal structure. As explored in detail in Chapter 7, from the mid-1990s onwards, Russia's leadership had become increasingly concerned about the development of civil society. One aspect of such concern was the fear, particularly within the security services, that non-governmental organizations (NGOs) were being too easily funded from abroad, and so becoming a means for undermining Russia's security, either through their open activities or by serving as a front for espionage.

Since the Yeltsin years, Russia's government had been putting the bodies that make up civil society on a more formal footing, with ever tighter laws being passed concerning the registration of religious organizations, political parties and NGOs, and imposing extra requirements on such bodies receiving funds from abroad (see Chapter 7). Alongside such developments, the notion of adopting a Russian model of democracy, rather than being dictated to by the West, came increasingly to the fore in Russia during the first decade of this century. Within this discourse there was support for establishing a strong indigenous Russian civil society, rather than allowing free rein to foreign NGOs. This approach differs from Western attitudes to civil society, in that it smacks of the state creating civil society, and is therefore seen as something of a contradiction in terms.

The creation of the Public Chamber seemed to tick all the boxes in relation to these policy strands. It brought civil society into a state-led structure, whilst emphasizing support for Russian NGOs and in theory encouraging them to exert appropriate pressure on the state. However, many aspects of the Public Chamber's regulatory framework suggest that it is as much about promoting the ruling elite's positions as about criticizing them. The rules by which the Public Chamber is formed reflect this tension between being state-led and yet independent of the state. The Chamber has 126 members. The first 42 of these are nominated by the president – and would normally not include politicians or businessmen. The next 42 are nominated by NGOs. These 84 together then select the final 42 members of the Public Chamber. There are also regional-level public chambers. At first, the Public Chamber was empowered only to assess draft legislation at the request of the president, but in 2009 a law was passed mandating the State Duma to send all bills to the Public Chamber for assessment. This quasi-oversight function carries with it little substantive power, since the recommendations of the Public Chamber can simply be ignored by president and parliament. However, the relatively diverse make-up of the Public Chamber has helped it to at least provide a voice questioning the state in some specific cases – for example, defending the use of jury trials and seeking action against absenteeism among Duma deputies.

From the point of view of the institutional structure of Russia's political life, both the State Council and the Public Chamber can be seen as shadowing institutions that have already been established constitutionally. The State Council can be seen as a shadow executive, and the Public Chamber as a shadow legislature. Neither has anything but advisory powers, but none the less they have a presence on the political scene, the regime asks for their opinion on key issues, and the decisions and resolutions of both are reported as having some weight in policy discourse. In short, when the state creates institutions such as these, they find a role, and that role diminishes to some extent the constitutionally established bodies of the executive and the legislature.

The legislature

Russia's parliament, or Federal Assembly, is made up of two chambers – the State Duma and the Federation Council. The lower chamber, the State Duma, consists of 450 members. Russia's first State Duma met in 1906. When the Bolsheviks came to power in 1917, one of their first actions was to abolish the newly elected State Duma. The revival of the name, State Duma, for Russia's new parliament in 1993 symbolized continuity with pre-Communist Russia. The upper chamber, the Federation Council, consists of two representatives from each subject (region) of the Russian Federation, irrespective of the size or population of that region. Its make-up emphasizes the federal idea of Russia.

The State Duma

The State Duma was last elected in 2011, for a five-year term, by means of proportional representation under the party list system. Parties were required to receive at least 7 per cent of the national vote in order to gain their proportion of seats in the parliament. Electoral procedures for the State Duma are not set out in the Constitution, but are established by federal law. Consequently, it is a relatively straightforward matter for the ruling regime to change the electoral laws. Before the 2007 election, the Duma was formed by an unusual combination of proportional representation and 'first-past-the-post' systems, whereby half of the deputies gained their seats under a party list system and the remaining 225 deputies were selected on a constituency basis, and may or may not have had a party affiliation. The abolition of the constituency element of the Duma in favour of an entirely party-based proportional representation system during Putin's second term as president (2004–8) was part of a process designed to strengthen the role of political parties and to encourage smaller parties to amalgamate. The threshold to be passed in order to gain seats was raised from 5 per cent to 7 per cent for the 2007 election, and the Law on Political Parties of 2001 had already introduced requirements in terms of size of membership and geographical spread before parties could run in elections.

Further changes were introduced for the 2011 Duma elections. Most importantly, the term for which the Duma would be elected increased from four to five years. There were also some minor changes to the threshold required for representation, with parties receiving between 5 and 6 per cent being entitled to one token seat in the Duma, and this token doubling to two seats should a party receive between 6 and 7 per cent. As it happened, such an occurrence did not arise in the elections of 2011. Still more changes are in line for the Duma election scheduled for 2016, with the regime proposing a return to the previous system, whereby half of the 450 seats are elected through a party list and half on the basis of single-mandate constituencies, and a planned reduction to 5 per cent for the threshold required in the party list half of the ballot.

In addition to its legislative function, the State Duma has to confirm the appointment of Russia's prime minister following presidential nomination, as well as confirm and dismiss the head of the Central Bank and the Commissioner for Human Rights. The State Duma also has particular powers that may come to the fore in times of political crisis, as it is here that confidence proceedings in relation to the government, and impeachment proceedings in relation to the president, take place.

The Federation Council

The upper chamber of Russia's parliament, the Federation Council, represents Russia's 83 regions, with each having two seats. These seats are filled by a representative of the regional legislature and a representative of the regional executive, known informally as senators. The upper chamber has employed three different methods for selecting its members since its foundation in 1993. Its first convocation consisted of members elected on a regional basis at the 1993 election. From 1995 until 2000, deputies gained their seats in the upper chamber on an *ex officio* basis; these seats were taken by the heads of, respectively, a region's legislature and executive. In the latter case, this would be the governor or president of a region, or, in the case of the 'city regions' of Moscow and St Petersburg, the mayor. When Putin came to power in 2000, he put forward proposals, accepted by the Federation Council, that ended the filling of the upper house on this *ex officio* basis. Instead, as the terms of office of each region's head came to an end, they were replaced in the upper house by representatives of the regional legislature and executive, rather than by the heads of the legislatures and executives themselves. By way of compensation, the heads of Russia's then 89 regions were given membership of the advisory State Council.

Further changes to the process for choosing members of the Federation Council have been made as the method by which the heads of regions are chosen has been amended (see below, 'Relations between the centre and the regions'). The representative chosen by regional legislatures has now to be elected from among that legislature's deputies, whereas previously any elected official in the region could be nominated by the legislature. The Federation Council representative selected by the regional executive now, in the case of elected governors, is chosen from one of three people nominated by a gubernatorial candidate ahead of the regional election. In the case of an appointed governor, procedure for the selection of the Federation Council representative continues to consist of direct appointment by the regional head.

The legislative role of the Federation Council is supplemented by particular authority in relation to matters concerning the internal borders between subjects of the Russian Federation. This obligation, with regard to the fundamental nature of the Russian state, extends also to the requirement that any declaration of martial law or a state of emergency, and any decision to use the armed forces beyond Russia's borders, must be approved by the Federation Council. The upper chamber also has responsibility for the appointment of judges to Russia's three highest courts (the Constitutional Court, the Supreme Court and the Court of Arbitration) and of the Procurator-General.

Power relations between president, prime minister and parliament

In terms of international comparison, the Russian parliament's powers in relation to the president are weak and, should differences between the two institutions prove irreconcilable, the last word almost always rests with the president. For example, the Constitution allows parliamentary involvement in government formation on one issue only – that of the appointment of the prime minister. The president nominates a candidate whose appointment must be confirmed by the State Duma. However, should the Duma not confirm the candidate, then the president, after three rejections of his nominee, dissolves the Duma.

There are three other levers of influence with which a legislature might exert its influence over the executive branch of power:

- First, through its legislative power; that is, by means of passing laws or blocking bills. Under the terms of the Constitution, a law passed by parliament outranks a presidential decree, even though the latter has the force of law pending any legislative act that supersedes it. In the early period of the post-Communist transition in Russia there was a legislative gap, which was filled to some extent by presidential decrees, drawn up and signed in their thousands. If the parliament passes a law it is submitted to the president, who either signs it or sends it back to the parliament. If the parliament then passes the law a second time, unaltered, the president is constitutionally obliged to sign it. Presidents Putin and Medvedev have both shown a clear preference for passing laws through parliament rather than issuing presidential decrees. This is largely due to the fact that the political make-up of the parliaments elected since December 1999, and particularly since 2003, have made it increasingly easy for the president to be sure of support in parliament.
- Second, the Duma might pass a vote of no confidence in the government. To force the president to take action, such a vote has to be carried by a majority of the 450 members of the State Duma twice in three months. Even then the president may decide to either dismiss the government or dissolve the Duma.
- Third, the final sanction the legislature might apply against the executive is the impeachment of the president. Under the Russian Constitution, this procedure is not easy. The only grounds allowed are those of treason or 'some other grave crime', and the process can only be completed with the agreement of the Supreme Court, the Constitutional Court and a two-thirds majority of both legislative chambers. Although half-hearted impeachment procedures were begun by the Communist Party of the Russian Federation against Boris Yeltsin over his decision to go to war against Chechnya in the 1990s, there was never any serious prospect that the stringent conditions for impeachment might be met.

In addition to these potential levers of influence over the executive in the hands of the parliament, a constitutional amendment of 2008 requires the government to submit an annual report of its activities to parliament, including the answers to questions put by the State Duma.

Listing these ways in which the parliament might in theory hold the executive account is not by any means to suggest that it is likely to do so in the near future. By a combination of factors – including legislation on elections and political parties, the use of administrative resources to electoral benefit, media bias in favour of the ruling regime, corruption amongst parliamentary deputies, and the fact that Putin and Medvedev have enjoyed genuine popularity among the Russian population – Russia's parliament in the twenty-first century has been for the most part unquestioningly supportive of the executive branch of power. It would take a serious crisis or a split in the executive branch to upset this equilibrium.

The Putin–Medvedev 'tandem', 2008–12

In short, then, the Russian Constitution is strongly presidential in comparison with other constitutions within the democratic pale. However, presidential authority appeared to be diluted somewhat during the presidency of Dmitrii Medvedev. The Medvedev–Putin leadership of Russia between 2008 and 2012 was widely referred to as a 'tandem' leadership, with the consensus of observers inside and outside Russia being that Putin – although in the formally subservient position of prime minister to which he was appointed by President Medvedev – held the upper hand in terms of authority. This situation represents a fine example of the balance between formal and informal power in contemporary Russia's political system.

In formal terms, between 2008 and 2012, everything happened as required by Russia's Constitution. Vladimir Putin had served his constitutional limit of two consecutive presidential terms between 2000 and 2008. He therefore could not stand again for the presidency in 2008, and so supported the successful candidacy of Dmitrii Medvedev, who then appointed Putin as his prime minister. As the constitutional limit specifies two *consecutive* terms, Putin was free to stand again for the presidency in 2012, and duly did so, with Medvedev not seeking re-election. On regaining the presidency in 2012, Putin appointed Medvedev as prime minister. Furthermore, during the period of the tandem leadership (2008–12), although President Medvedev had the formal power to dismiss his prime minister and government at will, Prime Minister Putin also led the

Box 5.4 Russia's prime ministers since 1992	
Viktor Chernomyrdin	December 1992–March 1998
Sergei Kirienko	March 1998–August 1998
(Chernomyrdin nominated unsuccessfully August–September 1998)	
Yevgeny Primakov	September 1998–May 1999
Sergei Stepashin	May 1999–August 1999
Vladimir Putin	August 1999–March 2000
(Putin was acting president from 31 December 1999)	
Mikhail Kasyanov	May 2000–February 2004
Mikhail Fradkov	March 2004–September 2007
Viktor Zubkov	September 2007–May 2008
Vladimir Putin	May 2008–May 2012
Dmitrii Medvedev	May 2012–

United Russia party, which had a clear majority of seats in the State Duma and, through its domination of around 90 per cent of regional legislatures, in the Federation Council. This combination of power in the executive, the legislature and the regions is not one envisaged in the Constitution, and it demonstrates that although Russia's Constitution is heavily weighted in favour of presidential power, such power is not boundless.

So far, so constitutional – even if a little contrived. In informal terms, however, in the period 2008 to 2012, Putin also wielded far greater influence than previous, or subsequent, prime ministers of the Russian Federation. Medvedev effectively owed his position to Putin's endorsement. Before the 2008 presidential election, it was President Putin who selected Medvedev to receive the regime's backing as president. The personal relationship between the two men was always one where Medvedev was the junior figure and Putin his boss and mentor. Furthermore, Putin, as a once and future president, had immense experience and influence which naturally played a part in enhancing the power of his office as prime minister. Medvedev, although appearing to put his slightly more liberal stamp on policy in certain limited areas (for example, law and order reform), represented a continuation of the Putin regime by other means, and willingly stood down after one term as president in order to allow Putin's return to the presidency.

Relations between the centre and the regions

When the Soviet Union broke up in 1991, many observers worried that Russia itself would soon follow suit, and some of its regions would break away. This did not happen, but the price paid for the maintenance of Russia's territorial integrity included war in Chechnya (see Chapter 3) and a lengthy period, throughout the Yeltsin presidency (1991–9), when the federal government's grip on the regions was ill-defined and weak. In particular, regions that had a distinct ethnic identity, like Chechnya and Tatarstan, or regions with a degree of economic clout, were especially likely to act independently. In the mid-1990s, there was even talk of a 'Siberian federation', in which an amalgamation of regions east of the Ural mountains would break away from Moscow's control.

Yeltsin's solution to the problem of holding Russia together was to allow a great deal of flexibility; the centre signed a series of bespoke 'bilateral' treaties with more than a quarter of Russia's regions, setting out in each case what the relationship between the Kremlin and the region in question should be. This led to a situation of 'asymmetrical federalism', and the constitutional equality of all regions in their relations with the centre went by the board. When Vladimir Putin came to power in 2000, he made it a priority to strengthen the centre's control over the regions. To do this, he established seven federal districts, covering all of Russia's regions and each headed by a presidential representative. The first task of these presidential plenipotentiaries was to oversee the process of bringing into conformity with federal law the estimated 70,000 regional laws that contradicted it. Gradually, the Putin regime began to rein in some of the autonomy enjoyed by many regions. None the less, he wanted to go still further.

In the early years of the 1990s, Yeltsin had appointed the heads of Russia's regions himself, before this arrangement was replaced by the direct election of regional heads in the mid-1990s. In 2005, using the Beslan school massacre (see Chapter 3) as a justification, President Putin re-established the presidential appointment of regional heads. Such appointments had to be ratified by regional legislatures, but given their domination by the United Russia party, this was pretty much a formality. Presidential appointment strengthened what is known as the 'power vertical' in Russia, helping to ensure that Moscow's remit ran across Russia's vast territory.

Towards the end of his presidency, in December 2011, Dmitrii Medvedev announced a return to elected governors. Such elections would take place when the five-year term of the leader of a federal subject (usually the governor of a region) expired, with the first such elections taking place in five regions in October 2012. In the last months under which the previous system of presidential appointment remained operative, the president had replaced and re-appointed a number of governors in order to start the clock anew on their five-year terms. The electoral process had also been hedged around a little, with candidates being allowed to stand only with approval (verified by signature) of a requisite percentage of elected officials from the region's municipalities, and subject to 'consultation' with the president over the appropriateness of nominated candidates. In March 2013, even this democratically diluted process was reined in still further when the Duma passed a law allowing individual regions to decide for themselves whether their leader should be elected by the new procedures, or directly appointed by the president, as before.

Although the system for choosing regional leaders – that is, the heads of the regional executives – has swung between appointment and election, the legislatures of Russia's regions have consistently been elected. The increased central control over regional legislatures has been facilitated by the embedding of the pro-Putin United Russia party across Russia's regions. United Russia has enjoyed striking electoral success, for similar reasons – ranging from popularity to malpractice – as at the federal level (see below, 'Electoral politics'). The organization of regional elections from Moscow has been helped with the introduction, since 2006, of unified voting days. Before this date, Russia's regions had held their elections on different days; since then, all regional elections have been held on the same days – initially two dates a year, one in the spring and one in autumn, and, since 2013, the second Sunday in September.

Electoral politics

Electoral politics in contemporary Russia are beset with predictability and allegations of malpractice. For the past decade or so, few people have had any doubt that the Putin regime's candidate (be it Putin himself in 2000, 2004 and 2012, or Medvedev in 2008) would win the presidential election, and that United Russia would emerge from parliamentary and regional elections as the dominant party. In the case of the presidential elections, so assured of success were Putin and Medvedev that they scarcely bothered campaigning – leaving such tiresome matters as television debates to the lesser candidates.

Of course, it would be remiss not to note from the outset of our discussion here, that a significant reason for the predictability of elections in Russia has been the popularity of the ruling regime. Most observers would concur, for example, that between 2000 and 2012, Putin and Medvedev were genuinely the most popular candidates in their respective presidential elections – although many would want to nuance that acknowledgement with a discussion about media bias and restrictions on the political space allowed to opposition groups. Alongside regime popularity, however, electoral manipulation has been cited as a reason for electoral success throughout the post-Soviet period, as noted in our discussion of the constitutional referendum in December 1993. In recent years, such allegations have come particularly to the fore, as the regime has stopped welcoming Western electoral observers, opposition parties have walked out of parliament in protest at electoral malpractice, and tens of thousands of people joined demonstrations in Moscow in 2011–12 demanding fair elections.

The electoral system and electoral manipulation

Control of an electoral system by a regime is always a matter of degree. Elections the world over can be 'manipulated' by a number of techniques, both legitimate and illegitimate. The sort of electoral control that might be deemed more legitimate relates to matters such as how elections are organized, who is allowed to stand for office, what the rules are for gaining representation, and when elections take place. More illegitimate control might include such elements as unfair campaigns (for example, denying media access to opposition candidates), undue pressure on voters or electoral officials to achieve the 'correct' results, and straightforward voting or counting fraud. In recent years Russia has seen the full range of such approaches used, resulting in the situation where the ruling regime is all but guaranteed victory in elections.

As set out above in our discussion of the State Duma, Russia's electoral system has changed several times in the recent past, and is set to change again before the next Duma election in 2016. There is a degree of legitimacy when an elected government changes electoral laws through constitutional procedures. At the same time, however, any such legitimacy is undermined when – as appears to be the case in Russia – the motivation for such changes springs from a desire to limit the electoral chances of the opposition. During the first decade of this century and beyond, Russian legislation on political parties and on the criteria for standing in elections had the effect of limiting the chances for the opposition to participate in the electoral process. Rules governing party registration were tightened so much that between 2004 and 2008 the number of parties fell from 46 to 7. At the same time, the introduction of a high threshold – 7 per cent of the vote – before representation could be secured, reduced still further the number of parties capable of gaining seats, and therefore, in a self-reinforcing process, likely to receive votes.

The rules under which individuals could stand in the presidential election became sufficiently tight that potentially dangerous candidates – such as former prime minister Mikhail Kasyanov in 2008 – were prevented from standing, on the grounds that they had breached election rules. In Kasyanov's case, the electoral commission ruled that too high a proportion of the signatures on the nominating petitions required were forged. It is impossible to judge from outside whether the signatures were forged or not. However, the fact that electoral commission chief Vladimir Churov told a newspaper that his first rule is 'Mr Putin is always right' made many observers sceptical of his impartiality in this and other cases (Kolesnikov 2007).

As well as the management of elections by means of rule changes, more serious allegations of regular voting malpractice have become common in Russian elections. Allegations of practices such as 'carousel voting' (groups of voters being bussed from polling station to polling station to cast multiple votes), ballot stuffing, the creation of fictional polling stations, and counting fraud – made easier to hide by the introduction of electronic vote counting – reached such a peak during the Moscow city elections in 2010 that the three opposition parties in parliament walked out and demanded, without success, that the elections be re-run. Reports of similar malpractice in the Duma election of 2011 contributed to the mass demonstrations in Moscow in the winter and spring of 2011–12, which worried the Putin regime sufficiently to spur it into a subsequent combination of concession and clampdown.

The switch, in 2005, to presidential appointment rather than election of regional heads led many to claim that regional leaders who failed to deliver an appropriate vote in their region when federal elections came round might fear for their position. The means by which such a vote might be achieved include use of what is known as 'administrative resource'. In other words, regional leaders may use their position to influence the election by, for example, leaning on businessmen to fund favoured candidates, mobilizing state-funded employees to vote the 'right' way, hindering the campaign of opposition candidates by such means as instigating tax inspections or safety audits, or – in extremis – falsifying voting returns. In 2011, the Duma election result recorded from Chechnya saw 99.5 per cent of votes go to United Russia.

On top of the use of the administrative resource, most national broadcast media are owned by the state or by state-friendly companies, and the same goes for regional broadcast companies. When Western electoral observers were welcome in Russia they found, in 2007 for example, that United Russia received as much airtime on state-funded television as all of the other parties put together. To point to these factors is not to deny the popularity of United Russia, or of Dmitrii Medvedev and Vladimir Putin. It does perhaps though partly explain this popularity, in that people's perceptions of political actors are shaped by what they know of them.

The management of elections, however, requires more nuance than might at first be thought. In a country where the regime asserts its democratic credentials, elections represent that regime's primary tool for legitimating its rule. Crude electoral fraud and 99.5 per cent votes actually undermine legitimacy. A really astute electoral process in a managed democracy requires balancing the amount of plurality, openness and opposition support against the *sine qua non* that the regime should retain power. The difficulty of this task goes some way to explaining the constant modifications to electoral procedures in Russia. Current signs indicate that a loosening up of party registration requirements will allow more parties to stand in the 2016 Duma election. This looks like a liberal move in a pluralist direction. It could also be interpreted as a belated realization by the regime that under the 2011 system, where only three or four parties were seen as having any chance of entering the Duma, opposition voters were effectively directed to concentrate their votes. If a larger number of opposition parties were allowed, then the opposition vote might be more fractured, and United Russia could win even with a lower level of support.

Election results and political parties

While acknowledging the democratically flawed nature of many aspects of contemporary Russia's political life, nevertheless, when it comes to assessing the broad political mood in Russia, the results of elections to the lower chamber of the Russian parliament (Table 5.1) provide a basic indication of the strength of the various streams of political thought among the Russian people. The clear winner in the 2011 parliamentary election was United Russia, the party whose political position is, simply put, to support the policies of Vladimir Putin. These policies can be summed up as the modernization of the country – developing its infrastructure, diversifying the economy, and producing an upturn in all indicators of social well-being – at the same time as supporting socio-political stability, national unity, and Russia's international status as an independently-acting power, balancing its national interest with appropriate global integration. United Russia's leaders style themselves as pragmatic managers rather than politicians.

The United Russia party is the latest, most successful and longest-lasting of a constant phenomenon in post-Soviet Russia, the 'party of power'. This notion turns on its head the situation common in developed democracies where the country's leader is in power because he or she has the support of their political party. With a 'party of power' the situation is reversed, and the party is in power because it has the support of the president. This is partly a result of the institutional situation in Russia in the 1990s, where a strong presidency was established before a party system was in place. It is partly too a result of a political culture which is used to following a single leader and to allowing position and power to trump political convictions.

The phenomenon was exemplified clearly in the crucial Duma election of 1999. This election took place just before the end of Yeltsin's second term in office. It was clear that he would be stepping down, but it was unclear who would be succeeding him. The election of 1999 therefore had an element of unpredictability not seen in Russian elections since then. Putin was an emerging figure, having recently become prime minister, but Moscow mayor Yurii Luzhkov looked a possible president too. The December 1999 election result saw Putin's preferred party, Unity, finish second to the Communists, but only seven seats ahead of Luzhkov's party, Fatherland–All Russia. The 'regime vote' had been split between those backing Luzhkov and those backing Putin. By the end of January 2000, Yeltsin had resigned, and

United Russia, led by Dmitrii Medvedev, is the dominant party in Russian politics.

Illustration 5.1   A United Russia rally next to the Kremlin

Putin had become acting president and clear favourite to be elected president in March. As a result, over thirty Fatherland–All Russia Duma deputies simply left the party and joined Unity instead. What mattered was not the party platform on which they had been elected, but whether they were in the same party as the next president, Putin. In other words, in a fine example of the 'party of power' principle at work, Unity became the most powerful party because it had the support of the president, and not the other way round.

The notion of parties being created from above, by the political elite, rather than developing from below, by popular initiative, is one that has been favoured by the executive in Russia under all three post-Soviet presidents. Yeltsin supported the creation of centre-right and centre-left parties, Our Home Is Russia and the Bloc of Ivan Rybkin, respectively. Neither exists today. Putin oversaw the amalgamation of

Table 5.1   Percentage of votes on the party list ballot for the Russian Duma, December 1999, December 2003, December 2007, December 2011

Party	1999	2003	2007	2011
United Russia *	——	37.6	64.3	49.3
Unity	23.3	——	——	
Fatherland–All Russia	13.3	——	——	
Communist Party of the Russian Federation	24.3	12.6	11.6	19.2
Liberal Democratic Party of Russia	6.0	11.5	8.1	11.7
Rodina ('Motherland')	——	9.0	——	
A Just Russia **	——	——	7.7	13.2
Russian Democratic Party 'Yabloko'	5.9	4.3	1.6	3.4
Union of Right Forces	8.5	4.0	1.0	
Agrarian Party of Russia	——	3.6	2.3	
Patriots of Russia	——	——	——	1.0
Right Cause	——	——	——	0.6

*   United Russia was formed by an amalgamation of, primarily, Unity and Fatherland–All Russia.
** A Just Russia was formed partly out of the Rodina ('Motherland') party.

Note: In the elections of 1999 and 2003, the party list ballot elected only half (225) of the deputies in the Duma. The rest were elected from single-mandate constituencies.

Unity and Fatherland–All Russia into United Russia. He also backed the creation of a centre-left party, A Just Russia, in an apparent move to take some of the left-leaning vote away from the Communists. A Just Russia has established itself as a social democratic party with the third-largest faction in the Duma. Although occasionally taking an oppositionist stance, it is dogged by the assumption that it remains essentially loyal to the Putin regime. Medvedev sought to see the gap on the liberal reformist right of the party spectrum filled by the creation of the Right Cause party, which flopped in the 2011 election. As noted above, managing electoral processes from above is no straightforward matter.

The two parties in the current Duma that were not formed with the backing of the Kremlin are the left-wing and nationalist Communist Party of the Russian Federation (CPRF) and the right-wing and nationalist Liberal Democratic Party of Russia (LDPR). The facts that these parties have consistently gained seats in Russia's parliament for over two decades, and that their leaders in 2013 – Gennady Zyuganov and Vladimir Zhirinovsky – have been in post for the same length of time, have led critical observers to label them 'semi-opposition'. Such critics see these parties' existence, and apparent acquiescence to the regime's way of running things, as more useful than threatening to President Putin, allowing him to point to the presence of opposition forces in Russia's political institutions in order to bolster the assertion that Russia is a functioning democracy.

After the collapse of the Soviet Union in 1991, the previously monolithic Communist Party virtually disintegrated and was briefly banned from the territory of the Russian Federation. By the time of the 1993 Duma elections, however, a Communist Party of the Russian Federation had re-emerged, and by the 1995 Duma election had turned into the largest party in terms of membership and votes received. Its leader, Gennadii Zyuganov, became the closest challenger to Boris Yeltsin in the presidential election of 1996, and forced the only second-round run-off in the history of Russian presidential elections. It is a measure of the lack of vitality in Russian politics, and an indicator of the virtual impossibility of anyone from outside of the regime becoming president, that in the 2012 presidential election, Zyuganov, still the leader of the CPRF, remained Vladimir Putin's closest challenger (Table 5.2). The Communists have consistently been the main challenger to the regime in electoral terms, and have carved out a position as a constant feature of Russian political life.

At their revolutionary peak, in the decades before and after their seizure of power in 1917, the Communist Party represented, above all, the young industrial workers inhabiting and building the cities of the new Russia, and took an avowedly internationalist political stance. By the 1990s, the Communists could be characterized fairly accurately as the party of the elderly and the rural. They became the conservative option for those who had lost out in the upheavals of the 1990s, and they embraced Russian/Soviet nationalism. As the economy of the country improved, and the ruling regime became more popular and a little more nationalist and anti-Western, the Communists experienced a relative decline in the elections of 2003 and 2007 – in which they none the less finished second. However, as the 2011 election showed, they have to some extent revived their support-base, drawing in younger members, focusing more on social equality, and continuing to offer a voting option to the increasing number of Russians dissatisfied with the Putin regime.

Table 5.2   Presidential election results in Russia, 2000–12 (only candidates polling over 5 per cent in at least one election)

Candidate	2000	2004	2008	2012
Vladimir Putin	52.9	71.3	—	63.6
Dmitrii Medvedev	—	—	70.3	—
Gennady Zyuganov (Communist)	29.2	—	17.7	17.2
Vladimir Zhirinovsky (Liberal Democratic Party of Russia)	2.7	—	9.3	6.2
Mikhail Prokhorov (Independent)	—	—	—	8.0
Nikolai Kharitonov (Communist)	—	13.7	—	—
Grigory Yavlinsky (Yabloko)	5.8	—	—	—

For some time in the 1990s, the more alarmist observers predicted the emergence of an extreme nationalist regime in Russia. Such fears of fascism did not spring from nowhere. In 1993, in post-Soviet Russia's first democratic elections, the right-wing – and misleadingly named – Liberal Democratic Party of Russia, led by Vladimir Zhirinovsky, gained almost a quarter of the popular vote. The Liberal Democratic Party's vote has fluctuated in subsequent elections (Table 5.1) but remains significant, though the sense of apprehension and fear surrounding its surprise appeal in 1993 has dissipated a little as Zhirinovsky has become to some extent a licensed maverick in the political establishment, expected to give the outrageous quote, occasionally insult – or even assault – opponents, but in the end essentially loyal to the current political settlement in Russia.

Informal and contentious politics

From its outset, this chapter has noted that informal politics are central to political life in contemporary Russia. It is possible to set out the development of the formal political system and to detail the constitutional rules of the game, to delineate the executive institutions and to discuss election results – to have done all of this and yet still to have missed something of the heart of Russia's political system. The domination of the ruling regime in Russia encompasses, but is by no means limited to, the formal constitutional and institutional procedures. Within and beyond this formal aspect of politics are informal power structures – a web constructed around patron–client groups, business interests, common backgrounds, the security services, kleptocratic tendencies, a gate-keeping function to Russia's elite, mutually held inside knowledge, and the will to power.

The essential corollary to this world of the elite insider is the existence of the excluded, of political forces which are allowed no place in either these informal structures or in the formal political life that they control. These are the people who are forced into the contentious politics of the street, of protest and of direct action – political groups who are refused registration, campaigners whose causes clash with elite interests, and former insiders who find themselves, voluntarily or otherwise, on the other side of the metaphorical barricade.

Much of the substance of Russia's informal and contentious politics is covered elsewhere in this book; for example, the connections between business and the political elite in Chapter 6, and the politics of campaign groups and civil society in Chapter 7. None the less, an account of politics in contemporary Russia would be incomplete without some overview of the major features of, and actors in, this aspect of political life. Among those analysts who follow Russian politics closely, a favourite pastime is to discern the alliances and connections within the political elite, and their respective power in different spheres of activity. Three particular aspects of this realm of political life justify the designation 'informal'. First, the relative power of individuals does not necessarily match their formal political position. Second, a good proportion of the key players involved are either not politicians at all, or they move in and out of the world of formal politics. Third, personal connections, often built up over many years and stemming from common backgrounds and interests, play a significant role.

The most obvious example of a mismatch between formal and informal power came during the Putin–Medvedev tandem years (2008–12), when President Medvedev was formally the head of state, but it is widely believed that Putin, though formally his subordinate, remained in control. This obvious example, however, is too elevated to serve as a typical case. Within the ruling regime, there exist many interconnections where business, politics, and even family interests overlap. For example, a central figure in attempts by analysts to discern activities in the informal sphere of Russian politics is Igor Sechin, a close Putin ally, who was deputy prime minister during 2008–12 and has for several years been the CEO of state-owned oil company, Rosneft. Sechin's closeness to Putin meant that as Prime Minister Putin's deputy during the Medvedev presidency, he was regarded by some as exercising more political power than the president. Relative power cannot easily be measured. However, Sechin, even out of government and with no formal political position since 2012, seems to remain a figure of considerable influence, not just in his position as CEO of Rosneft, but also more widely within his network of like-minded political actors.

Within the Putin regime a number of figures – including, but by no means limited to, those listed below – go back a long way with the president:

- Sergei Ivanov, Head of the Presidential Administration (and formerly first deputy prime minister and defence minister), served with Putin in the Leningrad KGB during the 1970s;
- Vladimir Yakunin, Head of Russian Railways and former government minister, reportedly formed a dacha co-operative in the 1990s along with Putin and several others who went on to hold important government or business posts;
- Aleksandr Bastrykin, head of the increasingly influential Investigative Committee of Russia (see Chapter 4), was apparently a university classmate of Putin in the mid-1970s; and
- Dmitrii Medvedev himself has worked with Putin since 1990, when they both served under Mayor Sobchak in St Petersburg.

Such long-standing connections are far from unusual in Russian politics, and they lead to various factions in political life being identified and designated by their common origin – the most well-known being the *siloviki*, the term used to denote those with a background in the security services who have risen to influential positions during the Putin years. By their nature, the precise make-up and influence of these informal groups proves difficult to pin down, as membership shifts and loyalties overlap. Plenty of stories exist in Russian politics of mutual antipathies, corruption, plotting, threats of investigation by the security services or the Investigative Committee, and so on. When Defence Minister Anatoly Serdyukov was sacked in 2012, allegations abounded not only of corruption but also of rifts with his father-in-law, former prime minister and long-term Putin associate, Viktor Zubkov. Indeed, scarcely a personnel change takes place without some political journalist explaining how it indicates the rise or fall of one faction or another. No doubt much of such analysis amounts to little more than gossip. However, taken as a whole, informal links and agreements continue to play a role in contemporary Russian politics which is both significant and – by its nature – not transparent.

The flip-side of informal politics consists of those political actors who do not engage in formal political life because they are denied access to it, or believe it to be so stacked against them as to be unfit for their purpose. There are many minor parties and political groups in Russia who seek to change the political system. Political actors who openly challenge the regime have been met with a range of responses from harassment to co-option. Although some might try to register in elections, in many cases a combination of official obstruction and simple lack of public support either prevents registration or undermines their electoral performance if allowed to register. Groups such as the Party of People's Freedom (PARNAS), the Left Front, and the Solidarity Movement have turned instead to demonstrations on the streets. Again, though, laws on demonstrations have often been applied to prevent such action, and unsanctioned demonstrations have been broken up by the police.

In the winter and spring of 2011–12, large demonstrations, tens of thousands in number, took place in Moscow under the slogans 'For Fair Elections' and 'March of the Millions'. These demonstrations received international attention, and opinion polls at the time showed a roughly even split among the Russian population with regard to whether they supported the demonstrations or not. The response of the Putin regime was multi-faceted. On the one hand, concessionary promises were made, for example, with regard to relaxing party registration laws and re-introducing gubernatorial elections. As noted above, these have been diluted to some extent in their implementation. On the other hand, more direct attacks on the opposition forces were brought into play. Attempts were made, with some success, to influence public opinion by TV documentaries and news items creating a negative picture of the protest movement's leaders. More forcefully, direct legal action was taken against key players in the protest movement and a number of lesser known protesters. Among the latter, 27 people were arrested and accused of rioting and violence against the police during the 'March of the Millions' in May 2012. Convictions would lead to many years in prison. The houses of key opposition leaders were searched and the leader of the Left Front, Sergei Udaltsov, charged with conspiracy to provoke mass unrest. The most prominent opposition leader, Aleksei Navalny, was charged with offences unrelated to his political actions (see Chapter 7). In July

2013, he was found guilty and sentenced to five years in prison, but unusually – and following international condemnation and street protests in Moscow – he was released the next day pending his appeal.

Informal 'contentious' politics encompass a wide-range of political opinion. In 2012 a number of opposition groups elected a 45-member Co-ordination Council, with representatives from left, liberal and nationalist groups, in order to work together against the ruling regime. In the West, it is liberal oppositionists who receive most media attention. They campaign under the banner of democracy and freedom, and so have ready allies among Western politicians and NGOs. They are also often savvy media performers, with a sprinkling of well-known names, such as former world chess champion Garry Kasparov. Far less attention is given to the potent nationalist senti-ments in Russian informal politics. Opinion polls show that a sizeable minority, around 15 per cent, strongly support the slogan 'Russia for the Russians', and a majority are sympathetic to its intent. The rheto-ric of the Putin regime has been consistently strong against the activ-ities of the far-right in Russia, and such rhetoric has been accompanied by action. According to data from the Russian anti-racism group, SOVA, hate crimes peaked in 2008, when 116 people were killed and 449 injured in Russia. The corresponding figures for 2012 were 19 and 187, a reduction to some extent achieved by consis-tent state action against neo-Nazi groups. None the less, ultra-nation-alist movements in Russia, most of which have no desire to work alongside liberals and leftists, continue to exist, attract members, and engage in their own, often violent, form of contentious politics.

6

The Economy

The need for economic transformation runs through Russia's modern history like the thread on a banknote. From the abolition of serfdom in 1861, through the Stolypin agricultural reforms just over a hundred years ago, on to nationalization by the Bolsheviks and the great upheaval of rapid industrialization under Stalin – Russia's social and political life has been shaped by, and has shaped, economic requirements. Likewise, contemporary Russia is emerging from one such fundamental economic transformation, and seeking to engage in another. It is emerging from a transition process to dismantle the centrally planned economic system of the Soviet years and replace it with a market economy. It is seeking to engage in the modernization and diversification of Russia's economy, in an effort to reduce reliance on raw materials and energy exports, and to develop a more diversified and technologically advanced economy.

The two words, diversification and modernization, feature prominently in official statements setting out the main tasks of contemporary Russia's economic development. However, these aims are easier to identify than to achieve, especially since Russia's current economic well-being remains heavily dependent on energy resources. How to channel energy revenue into a modernization programme, at the same time as meeting the usual set of demands (security, health, education, welfare and so on) facing a twenty-first-century state, represents a major economic challenge for Russia today. What is more, it is a challenge complicated by factors at home and abroad. The global economic downturn of recent years has particularly affected Russia's main trading partner, the European Union, which in turn affects Russian economic growth, the amount of foreign investment going into Russia, and the financial flows that contribute to

128

modernization. At home, Russia's economy is undermined by corruption and a degree of legal uncertainty, which both puts off foreign investors and causes uncertainty in the domestic business community. Despite the transition from central planning to the market, the Russian state still plays a significant economic role beyond the legitimate direction of economic policy. The state holds stakes in a number of major companies and appears able to intervene with relative ease in management decisions and ownership disputes, motivated either by factors that it deems to be in the national interest, or by less elevated reasons of personal gain.

This chapter begins by considering the most recent transformation in Russia's economy; namely, the transition from the centrally planned, state-dominated economic system of the Soviet era to the capitalist, market-based economy that we see today. It sets out the basic tasks required in such a transition, and considers their impact on Russia. The 1990s were a time of economic hardship for most Russians, but they also saw the rise of the oligarchs, a super-rich and politically engaged sub-set of the broader 'new Russians' phenomenon. These years make up the economic and political background for the rise of Vladimir Putin, in whose first two terms as president (2000–8), the economy grew, Russians as a whole became more prosperous, and the political campaign against the oligarchs was won by the regime – resulting in state direction of strategic branches of the economy and a variety of fates (co-option, exile, imprisonment) for individual oligarchs. These years of relative economic success came to an end with the onset of the global financial crisis in 2008, and set the scene for the final part of this chapter, which considers in detail contemporary economic performance and policy priorities as the aims of modernization and diversification come to the fore.

The Soviet planning system

The Soviet Union's economic system was based on the notion of 'command planning'. There was state or collective ownership of almost all economic resources, with minor exceptions such as private plots that enabled small-scale agricultural production for personal use. State planning authorities made production decisions centrally, with economic units (factories, farms and so on) given production targets, usually for quantity (gross output). Planners also set prices for all goods and services and made distribution decisions, with factories and farms instructed what to do with their output. Stemming partly from ideological reasons, and partly from the vested interests of powerful groups within the Soviet state, heavy industry – particularly defence manufacturing – received preference over the production of consumer goods.

The economic theorists, from Marx onwards, who had supported a planned form of political economy, had hoped that it would have a number of advantages. Rational economic planning would prevent the waste caused by cyclical variations in the market economy, such as mass unemployment and machines sitting idle during recessions. Resources would no longer be frittered away for useless purposes such as advertising. Elimination of private ownership would mean the end of the 'exploitation of man by man' as unscrupulous capitalists appropriated surplus value to themselves. Planning would also ensure equitable distribution: 'from each according to his ability, to each according to his needs' would be the formula for distribution in a communist economy. Since their decisions would be able to take all factors into account, planners would be able to ensure that the full costs of economic activity, including so-called 'externalities' such as pollution, would be taken into account in making economic decisions. There would also be important motivational effects: since people were working for the good of each other, rather than for the benefit of private individuals, they would work harder. Abolition of commercial secrecy and a more rational organization of production would lead to greater efficiency. For all these reasons, socialism would supposedly prove itself to be an economic system superior to capitalism.

The reality of the planned economy represented an enormous contrast to these hopes. Certainly, there were some benefits for the country and individuals. Prices for basic goods were low and stable, and basic services were provided free of charge. The plan proved a successful means of industrializing the Soviet Union rapidly in the first place – albeit at great human cost – since it enabled resources to be concentrated in the areas of priority to the state. However, the systemic problems of command planning eventually proved terminal (see Box 6.1).

The Soviet economy had achieved impressive growth rates as it industrialized in the 1930s, or in the reconstruction period after the Second World War, but such growth was from a low base and was achieved by putting resources into industrialization and reconstruction. By the 1970s, growth needed to be sought from innovation and technological advance, both of which, as we have seen, were hampered by the centralized plans of the Soviet system. According to some estimates, 'the long-run context shows that from 1928 until 1973 the Soviet economy was on a path that would catch up with the United States one day … However, in 1973, half way through the Brezhnev period, the process of catching up came to an abrupt end' (Harrison, 2002: 45). The situation might well have been even worse were it not for the development of oil production, particularly in Siberia, in the 1960s and 1970s. More oil became available for hard currency export, enabling in turn the import of food and industrial technology, and effectively subsidizing an inefficient domestic industrial base.

The increased resources put into consumption meant that living standards for many Soviet citizens did improve a little in the late 1960s and early 1970s. However, the absence of genuine structural reform of an inefficient economic system meant that the transition to a more intensive type of economic growth did not happen. Low fertility and increases in the mortality rate caused by difficulties in the Soviet health system, as well as rising alcoholism, meant that population growth was minimal. Easily accessible sources of raw materials had largely been exhausted. Collectivized agriculture frequently failed to produce enough food to feed the population, and grain had to be imported from elsewhere. Attempts to keep up with the United States militarily drained resources from civilian research and development, and diverted skilled workers into unproductive employment. By the time of Brezhnev's death in 1982, economic growth had virtually ceased.

On coming to power as General Secretary of the Soviet Communist Party in 1985, Mikhail Gorbachev became aware quite rapidly that piecemeal reform of the planned economy would not be enough to solve economic difficulties, and that more radical steps would be necessary. Some measures were taken – for example, workers' co-operatives and so-called individual labour activity were legalized, creating a private sector in some areas of the economy. Gorbachev's policy was also to reduce the amount of planning which went on, thus giving managers more autonomy to take necessary decisions. Arms limitation agreements, it was hoped, would reduce the burden of military expenditure.

However, real structural reform and marketization of the economy did not occur in the 1985–91 period. For all their talk of restructuring the economy, and a plethora of alternative reform proposals, the Gorbachev years saw mere tinkering and talking in relation to the great economic problems facing the Soviet Union:

Box 6.1   The problems of economic planning

- There was a constant problem of shortages; if one part of the plan failed to be achieved, knock-on effects followed. For much of the Soviet period, consumers had to suffer empty shops and queues for the most basic necessities, and those with the lowest prices, as a fact of everyday life.
- The plan, though designed ostensibly to foster continuing growth, was too static a conception of economic activity. A very difficult issue for planners to confront was how to manage change. For economic units to alter processes or improve products takes time and is disruptive in the short term, which threatens plan fulfilment and consequent bonuses. There was little incentive to innovate arising out of the possibility of large profits accruing to individuals who think up something new and so the economy had an inclination towards stagnation.
- Quality took second place to quantity. Since it was the most measurable attribute, quantity of output tended to be the key target in plans. However, quantity is only one of a number of desirable features of production. Others include quality, range, style and so on. Too often plans were formally fulfilled, but at levels of quality too low for the output to be of much use to its eventual recipients.
- There was a propensity to waste, as economic units had little incentive to economize on inputs of raw materials and labour. Hungarian economist János Kornai developed a concept central to understanding planned economies, namely, the 'soft budget constraint' (Kornai, 1992). Essentially, state enterprises drew on state resources and so

⟶

- The huge, monopolistic industrial monoliths, which dominated the economy, continued to operate in familiar ways, and continued to be subsidized by the state.
- There were so-called 'price reforms' under Gorbachev, but prices were still controlled.
- The refusal to allow unemployment meant that the labour market remained unreformed.
- No real competition was created, because the government failed to address issues of bankruptcy, or to create the conditions whereby non-state economic actors could enter markets and compete with state industry and agriculture.
- Accumulated savings which Soviet citizens had been unable to spend represented 'repressed inflation', and, in combination with the growing state budget deficit, meant that an inflationary surge was inevitable should real reform take place.

notions of costs, profit and loss, and bankruptcy were alien to them. In fact, not only did they have little incentive to economize on inputs, they had every incentive to maximize them.

- In the last instance, economic units were judged on achieving their targets, however many inputs they used to do so. This contributed to the fact that, in the view of some economists, much Soviet industry, far from adding value, was actually value-destroying, with the raw material inputs worth more than the final product.

- Soviet industry could also be seen as value-destroying, because of irrational pricing structures. Energy prices, for example, were very low in Communist countries compared to world market prices, which meant that much industry was highly energy-inefficient.

- International trade as a whole was neglected in planned economies. This was damaging because trade allows new technologies to spread rapidly, and also because of what economists term 'gains from trade', which arise out of specialization suiting the particular strengths of individual economies.

- Trade in a state planning system tended to be more narrowly functional. The Soviet Union's export of oil in the 1970s arguably kept its economy afloat, funding the import of food and some technology production when the domestic economy was insufficient.

- The gains that Communist economies had hoped to make as a result of increased worker motivation never arose. The economic system was imposed by force, income distribution was never in fact egalitarian, and a low priority was put on meeting the needs of ordinary citizens. As the East European joke had it: 'Capitalism is the exploitation of man by man. Socialism is the reverse.'

Overall, the Gorbachev period destroyed the effectiveness of the planned economy without replacing it with operative market mechanisms. Economic units were given greater freedom, but the continuation of soft budget constraints meant that no means of market discipline developed. When the Soviet Union collapsed and Yeltsin came to power in an independent Russia, he proved himself willing to back real reform to address the economic crisis, rather than merely to vacillate.

From planning to the market, 1992–8

The economic team created by Yeltsin was headed by the acting prime minister, Yegor Gaidar, and contained a significant number of younger, highly pro-market ministers, such as Anatoly Chubais, who

---

Box 6.2   What was needed to turn a planned economy into a market economy?

After the collapse of communism, the countries of Eastern Europe and the former Soviet Union were attempting something without historical precedent in seeking to move from a system of command planning to a free market economy. There was no template to work from. This represented a transition far more fundamental than merely privatizing a few nationalized industries. Soviet ideology had seen capitalism and private ownership as an exploitative evil. Post-Soviet reforms involved changing the nation's entire economic mindset.

In terms of specific reforms, the following were required:

Ownership changes and de-monopolization were required to create the competition central to market efficiency. In practice, state ownership had often been the effective equivalent of no ownership. Managers and workers stood to gain little from committed work or forward thinking, and knew that loss-making enterprises would be bailed out by state subsidies, a situation referred to by the eminent Hungarian economist János Kornai as the 'soft budget constraint' (Kornai, 1992).

Privatization was the process by which ownership changes and de-monopolization would be achieved. To privatize whole industries was a major undertaking in a system that had not previously been a market economy. Questions arose as to how much the industries were worth, how their sale would be organized, and who were to be the beneficiaries of that sale. Russia's industries belonged to 'the people' in the form of the state, and so the Russian people should somehow benefit from the sale of what were theoretically their assets. This in turn raised questions as to whether foreign ownership should be allowed.   ⬛▶

---

was in charge of privatization. Many of them had knowledge of economics outside Russia, and were convinced that only market mechanisms could solve the deep economic problems facing the country.

Nevertheless, Yeltsin's economic team was also very aware that, however essential the policy of marketization seemed to them, it would be a far from easy path to follow. Difficulties would come in the detail of the reforms and in their social impact. A common phrase used in the early 1990s to sum up the marketization of formerly centrally planned economies was 'shock therapy'. The therapy came in the treatment of what was deemed to be a terminally failing economic system, incompatible both with a globalizing world economy and with the new democratic polity being ushered in. The

Bankruptcy and unemployment, virtually unheard of in the Communist economic system, needed to be allowed, since market competition means that loss-making enterprises are ultimately forced out of business. Russia's economic geography included a large number of company towns, where virtually all employment – as well as maintenance of housing stock, food supplies, holiday facilities, social services and so on – was dependent on a single employer. Closing down industries in such places would raise questions over the towns' survival.

Price reform meant allowing the market rather than the state to set prices. The rational allocation of resources in competitive markets arises through the interaction of supply, demand and price. Economic reform required removing subsidies and increasing prices for many basics of life, such as staple foodstuffs, domestic heating and rents.

Monetary stabilization. The rouble as a currency was not one in which citizens had much confidence, and it failed to act as a store of value in the way that harder currencies did.

The state budget. Russia inherited public expenditure commitments far beyond levels that could be financed by taxation. Large budget deficits had to be reduced by cutting state spending and increasing tax revenue.

Foreign trade and payments. In order to facilitate trade and foreign investment, integration with world markets became increasingly important for post-Soviet Russia.

The infrastructure of the market economy. Developed market economies operate with sophisticated capital markets able to finance potentially profitable projects. The banking system was entirely undeveloped in Russia in 1992, and the legal basis for the operation of free markets (for example, contract enforcement and debt recovery) did not exist. New, and complex, legislation was required.

shock came in the inevitable hardships caused by inflation, unemployment, the closure of uncompetitive industries, the cutting of social welfare and so on. As the 1990s progressed, the familiar – and heartfelt – comment to be heard was that Russia's economic reforms were all shock and no therapy. The population as a whole experienced great socio-economic hardship. There was a reduction in state subsidies for social goods such as housing, transport and energy; inflation wiped out personal savings; unemployment rose; and wages went unpaid for months at a time in the state sector.

None the less, dealing with the substance of the economic reforms, clearly some 'therapy' was taking place alongside the 'shock'. The immediate freeing of prices, which led to initial rapid inflation, was designed to shift to a more rational price structure. In January 1992, 90 per cent of all retail prices were freed from the previous system, where the state determined the price of goods. The effectiveness of all other market reforms was predicated on this. Markets cannot be efficient without a system of prices determined by the interaction of supply and demand. In addition, there was a massive amount of 'spare' money in the system – that is, money which had been saved by citizens in a situation where its value was undermined by the lack of access to goods. Freeing up prices absorbed much of this monetary overhang.

In order to combat subsequent inflationary pressures, and to create a stable currency and real money, monetary policy remained at the forefront of policy decisions. By 1995, this had been sufficiently successful for it to become possible to fix the rouble to a band of values against the dollar, in what became known as 'the rouble corridor'. Governments continued to attempt to ensure as stable a currency as possible, to control inflation, to increase domestic and international confidence in the state of the Russian economy, and to enable business to begin to make future plans with some degree of certainty. In parallel, there was a process of opening up the Russian economy to the outside world, and by 1998 Russia was significantly more integrated into the world economy than in 1992. This still did not represent free trade in key areas, with price distortions supported in some sectors by export quotas, high export duties, and import subsidies and controls.

A third strand of the reforms was the attempt to reduce the economic role of the state. Privatization took place in the mid-1990s, initially via the distribution to all Russian citizens of vouchers that could be redeemed for shares in newly privatized companies. Subsequently, it took place via auctions, and the highly controversial 'loans for shares' policy, where certain banks and industrial combines acquired shares in companies at prices far below their true market value in return for loans to the government. The voucher privatization scheme was intended as an innovative way to solve the problem of selling off state-owned assets. By giving vouchers to all citizens, the question of the fair distribution of property among the population was addressed. In addition, it was hoped that voucher privatization would create, at a stroke, a nation of shareholders with a vested interest in the success of the economy. In addition to privatization by voucher, this stage of the process also involved giving shares in enterprises to their workers and managers.

Laudable though this approach might seem in theory, the results were not quite as anticipated in terms of a wide base of share ownership. Many small shareholders were persuaded to offload their shares to enterprise managers, either voluntarily or pressured by economic circumstances or managerial arm-twisting. In their turn, some such enterprises were sold on to Russia's larger business empires or, less often, to foreign investors. In thousands of cases too, the ability of shareholders to control companies was curtailed by the government retaining a controlling interest, having declared the need to do so because of the strategic importance of an enterprise to national security.

A related aspect of the attempt to change Russia's economic structure was the creation of a legal and regulatory framework for a market economy. Some aspects of this proved much more straightforward than others. The privatization programme, for example, was conducted largely by presidential decree. Bankruptcy laws were adopted with little major resistance, whereas laws on private ownership of land, foreign investment and taxation codes, to name just three, provoked notable disagreements between government and parliament. It would be misleading, however, to represent privatization in Russia as neatly governed by legal process. Alongside the creation of laws, there developed a culture of lawlessness in which corruption, violence and turf-wars marked a scramble for control of industry and resources. Russia gained the epithet 'the Wild East' due to the prevalence of criminal activities, including many killings, in the business sphere during the 1990s.

The results of these reform approaches were painful for both the Russian economy and the people. As Table 6.1 shows, Russia experienced dramatic and sustained economic problems in the 1992–8 period. According to official statistics, national output fell every year except 1997. By mid-1999, gross domestic product (GDP) was little over half its 1990 level, though these official figures may overstate the true decline in GDP since official figures have difficulty in reflecting the amount of informal economic activity outside officially monitored channels – for example, households growing their own food.

In parallel with this rapid decline, the economy fundamentally changed its character in several important respects during the 1990s. Figure 6.1 shows how, in a very short period of time, Russia moved from being an economy dominated by industry to one where services predominated. Such a de-industrialization was a process experienced by many developed countries, perhaps two decades earlier than was the case with Russia.

Table 6.1   Russia's economic indicators, 1992–8

	1992	1993	1994	1995	1996	1997	1998
GDP, % change year on year	−14.5	−8.7	−12.6	−4.2	−3.6	1.4	−5.3
Industrial production, % change year on year	−18.2	−14.2	−20.9	−3.0	−4.5	2.0	−5.2
Fixed investments, % change year on year	−40.0	−12.0	−27.0	−13.0	−18.0	−5.0	−12.0
Unemployment, % of work force	4.9	5.5	7.5	8.2	9.3	9.0	11.8
Inflation, %	2520	842	224	131	22	11	84

Source: Official Russian data.

This relative decline in industry and agriculture (see Box 6.3) was in part a consequence of Russia's increasing openness to the world economy. The sectors of the economy that were hit hardest by recession were in most cases subject to particularly strong foreign competition, such as clothing, agriculture and food processing, or industries such as electricity production or construction, demand for which directly reflects levels of output and investment. Similarly, the industries that struggled least – oil and gas, basic metals and various other natural resources – were ones in which Russia is highly competitive on world markets.

The rise in the importance of service industries – both business and consumer – has remained fairly constant since the early years of this century, and in 2012 the service sector accounted for just over 60 per cent of GDP. This shift to services reflected a fundamental change in the nature of the economy. In a planned economy relatively closed off to the outside world, there was little need for accountants, management consultants, market researchers, advertisers, investment bankers and all the other job categories that help make a competitive market economy function. The relative neglect of consumers in the planned economy meant that there was an insufficient supply of, for example, plumbers, electricians, travel agents, automobile dealers, and many of the other providers of goods on which individuals might want to spend any surplus earnings. This restructuring also had an important

Figure 6.1   The structure of Russia's GDP, 1990 and 2003

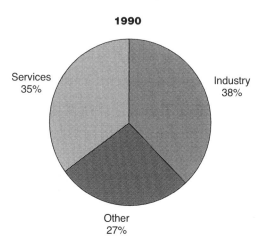

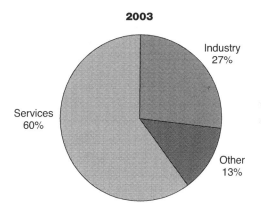

Source: Official Russian data.

regional aspect. Regions that were relatively successful tended to be either resource-rich or metropolitan centres with good international transport connections, able to act as entry points for international trade. Regions whose economy declined particularly seriously were often those especially vulnerable to competition from imported goods, or agricultural republics that were already under-industrialized.

The crash of 1998

On 17 August 1998, the Russian government devalued the rouble and announced that it would no longer be able to pay much of its domestic debt and was imposing a moratorium on payment of much of its foreign debt. Prices rose rapidly, and, not for the first time in the 1990s, citizens who had deposited money in Russian banks saw their savings wiped out. The 35-year-old prime minister, Sergei Kirienko, who had only been in post a few months, was dismissed by President Yeltsin.

At root the 1998 crisis was a standard currency crisis, albeit one that was exacerbated by the state's inability to reach a stable balance between income and expenditure. Russia's policy of achieving stability through a fixed – within certain limits – exchange rate backfired since the rouble was overvalued. Government overspending meant that a large amount of debt accrued. Coupled with significant capital flight out of the country and an economy that was not growing – along with international unease following the Asian financial crisis of 1997 – the situation proved unsustainable. From a level of 6 roubles to the US dollar, the currency collapsed to 25 roubles to the US dollar.

This macroeconomic explanation is given more depth by bringing in developments – or rather the lack of them – at the micro level. Using the exchange rate as the principal means of stabilization enabled the government for too long to avoid the necessary structural reforms and budget cutbacks. The subsidization of uncompetitive enterprises that had been a feature of the Soviet system, had to a large extent continued. Furthermore, as in the Soviet era, such subsidization had been facilitated by oil revenues. The collapse of oil prices during the Asian crisis of 1997–8 exposed the shaky state of Russia's public finances.

The 1998 financial crisis, however, seemed to act as a cleansing storm on the Russian economy. Two outcomes in particular proved to have positive longer-term effects. First, government policy after the crash was firmly oriented towards macroeconomic stability. The growth in exports following the August crash resulted in a rapid increase in money supply, and in normal economic circumstances unsustainably high levels of inflation would be expected to follow. However, the fact that Russia's industrial economy before then had been based more on barter and US dollars than on roubles meant that the growth in rouble supply was absorbed in the development of a financial sector, and the concomitant release of bank credits, which in turn boosted consumption. The second outcome worked in tandem with this growth in credits. The 1998 crisis meant that the cost of imported goods became too high for many to afford, and so domestically produced goods were more in demand, prompting an increase in output and competitiveness among Russia's producers.

Economic progress, 1999–2008

In the nine years following the August 1998 financial crisis, Russia's economy saw strong growth. This coincided, from 2000 onwards, with the presidency of Vladimir Putin. In this section we assess the reasons for the impressive economic performance of these years, question to what extent that performance was a result of government policies, and analyse the impact of rising GDP on the underlying economic structure of Russia. To sum up before engaging with the details, economic growth in the period 1999 to 2008 was based overwhelmingly on high global prices for Russia's chief export goods – oil, gas and metals – and on the attendant increase in production volumes by Russian firms. The Putin regime's economic policies contributed to some extent, particularly during his first term, but increasing state control in key areas held back production growth, hindered foreign direct investment, and failed to promote sufficiently the innovation and diversification necessary to move the economy away from over-reliance on raw materials.

When President Putin came to power in 2000 he declared that:

> It will take us approximately fifteen years and an 8 per cent annual growth of our GDP to reach the per capita GDP level of present-day Portugal and Spain, which are not among the world's industrialized leaders. If during the same fifteen years we manage to annually increase our GDP by 10 per cent, we will then catch up with Britain or France. (Putin, 2000: 213)

It is important to note that President Putin was talking about taking fifteen years to catch up with where Portugal and Spain were at the turn of the millennium. And if things went really well, then by 2015, Russia might reach the per capita GDP levels attained by Britain or France in 2000.

Between 1999 and 2008, virtually all of the key economic indicators showed positive trends (see Table 6.2). Real GDP in Russia grew by an average of 7.6 per cent per year. The strongest growth came in the export-driven industries, particularly in the oil sector, where high global oil prices proved crucial. In 1998, oil was priced just above US$10 a barrel; by early 2008 it was nudging US$160. Growth in this sector, however, is not the whole story, with the service and industrial sectors also growing, assisted by the knock-on effects of the oil price boom. Oil price rises were followed by increases in the price of gas and metals. Overall, during these boom years, the energy sector earned almost two-thirds of Russia's export income, which in turn made up about 40 per cent of public-sector revenue, and 30 per cent of national income.

In short, then, between 1999 and the onset of the international economic crisis in 2008, the Russian economy flourished in terms of most key indicators. It demonstrated a level of macroeconomic stability the country had not known for many years, evidenced and facilitated by impressive GDP growth, increased investment, a balanced budget and a current accounts surplus. Real wages, and disposable incomes, were well above levels found before the 1998 financial crisis, with the number of people living below the official poverty line having fallen by around 55 per cent between its peak after the 1998 financial crisis and late 2007, when 15.7 per cent were officially in poverty. A growth in consumer credit also increased both spending power and demand. Unemployment declined from 13 per cent in 1998, to just over 5 per cent in the first quarter of 2008 (though by the end of 2008, as the global financial crisis began to kick in, unemployment was nudging 8 per cent). The federal budget was in surplus every year from 2000 onwards, facilitating the establishment of a stabilization fund to meet budget needs in years when external factors, particularly low oil prices, might otherwise cause a shortfall. The stabilization fund amounted to over 10 per cent of GDP by 2008, when it was split into the Reserve Fund and the National Welfare Fund. As noted later in this chapter, Russia's persistence in building up such funds during the years of relative plenty, driven to a large extent by Aleksei Kudrin (Finance Minister, 2000–11), was to prove significant during the difficulties in the international economy from 2008 onwards.

During Putin's first term (2000–4) in particular, important economic reforms proceeded apace. Legislation was introduced to regulate and clarify activity in areas such as labour, bureaucratic oversight, customs codes and land ownership (see Box 6.3). Tax reforms saw the introduction of the lowest level of income tax in Europe, at 13 per cent, with the intention of drawing many Russians out of the shadow economy and making them taxpayers. Investment

Table 6.2 Russia's economic indicators, 1999–2008

	1999	2000	2001	2002	2003	2004	2005	2006	2007	2008
GDP, % change year on year	6.4	10	5.1	4.7	7.3	7.2	6.4	7.4	8.5	5.2
Industrial production, % change year on year	11.0	11.9	2.9	3.1	8.9	7.3	4.0	3.9	6.8	0.6
Fixed investments, % change year on year	5.3	17.4	10	2.8	12.5	11.7	10.7	13.5	21.1	9.8
Unemployment, %	12.4	9.9	8.7	9.0	8.7	7.6	7.7	6.9	6.1	7.8
Inflation, %	36.5	20.2	18.6	15.1	12.0	11.7	10.9	9.0	11.9	13.3

Source: Official Russian data.

Box 6.3 Agriculture in Russia

Agriculture can seem totemic in Russian life. The image of the Russian peasant, either in a Tolstoyan idyll or – more often – suffering under serfdom or forced collectivization, suffuses many pictures of what Russia is. In economic terms, though attention is most often focused on energy and innovation, agriculture still matters greatly to contemporary Russia. 'Food security' (the ability of a country to provide food for itself) has risen up the security agenda in contemporary Russia, major agricultural reforms have taken place in the twenty-first century, and the Russian state devotes substantial resources to the development of farming.

In the Soviet era, all agricultural land was owned by the state, and farmed in state or collective farms. As the privatization process rushed ahead in the 1990s, the question of land ownership proved particularly problematic, partly due to the emblematic connection between the people and the soil, reflected in an unease about land being sold to private owners. In the years since 1991, reform efforts concentrated on the lowering of state subsidies, the liberalization of prices, and the gradual encouragement of private farming and land ownership.

The right of private citizens to own land was established in the Constitution of 1993, but for years the Duma refused to pass a law enabling this right. Finally, in 2001 and 2002, laws enabling the sale of, respectively, urban and agricultural land were accepted, with the latter law forbidding the sale of rural land to foreigners, though allowing foreign owners to have land on a long-term lease. A little over 90 per cent of Russia's vast territory, however, remains in the ownership of the state in its various national, regional and municipal forms, and the federal government continues to seek further privatization.

As with other areas of the economy, the 1990s was largely a decade of decline in the Russian agricultural sector, with 1998 being a particular low point. In this year, there was a low harvest, with production of many key crops (grain, potatoes, vegetables in general and sugar beet) being less than half that in 1992. Over a similar period, meat production and livestock numbers also declined by more than half. Overall, between 1990 and 1998, agricultural production fell by 44 per cent in real terms. Russia came to rely increasingly on imports in the 1990s, particularly imports from the United States – becoming, for example, the top foreign market for US poultry exports. Food prices began to rise

⫸

grew even faster than GDP for much of the 1999–2008 period, at around 11 per cent in 2004–5, though as a percentage of GDP, investment in Russia remained lower than in many developed economies, let alone in those seeking to catch up. During the boom years of high oil prices, both Russia's current account and its foreign exchange beyond the means of the poorest sectors of society, and both the United States and the European Union sent substantial food aid to Russia in 1999 and 2000.

After the 1998 financial crash, the Russian agricultural sector began to recover and within ten years, in 2008, Russia enjoyed the biggest grain harvest it had ever known, 112.5 million tons. Between 2007 and 2012, the Russian government implemented a five-year National Project for agriculture, spending a total of US$23.5 billion over that period. Although results for 2008 were impressive, the impact of the global financial crisis, subsequent economic slowdown from the end of that year onwards, and a poor harvest in 2010–11 meant that the goals set for this National Project proved over-optimistic, with only the meat production target met by 2012.

The missing of targets aside, the agricultural sector developed so that by 2012 the value of agricultural exports reached an all-time high of US$16.6 billion, and, in terms of food security, Russia produced virtually all of the grain that it consumed in 2012. Apparently impressive monetary figures for 2012, however, are not unconnected with the fact that, following the poor harvest in 2010–11, Russia put in place a ban on grain exports and thereby contributed to a rise in global agricultural prices. In agriculture more than most sectors, seasonal factors impinge. Impressive figures for 2012 were followed by another poor harvest and a subsequent need to import more grain in 2013.

A new phase of the State Programme to Develop Agriculture, running through to 2020, is anticipated to cost the state US$72.4 billion over eight years. Its main priorities focus on the infrastructure of the agricultural market, including exports, and the modernization of related industries. Since the turn of the century, larger corporate farms – some of the biggest being foreign-owned – have begun to develop in Russia, while smaller family farms have declined. In terms of the value of output, these larger farms now make up around half of all agricultural output. This to some extent begins to address the long-standing problem of a poorly paid agricultural workforce seeing life in the cities as a more attractive option, particularly for younger people. None the less, agricultural wages remain among the lowest in Russia. Problems also persist with the under-use of land. The government is seeking to attract more foreign investment into agriculture, and to increase the crop hectarage by cultivating unused land, much of it currently state-owned.

reserves grew impressively. By mid-2008, Russia had currency reserves of almost $500 billion. In 2006 Russia paid off in full, and early, the debts inherited from the Soviet Union owed to the Paris Club (a group of creditor governments from the major industrial nations). This payment amounted to US$22 billion, and represented the largest early payment of debts in the history of the Paris Club. Russia had total foreign debts of US$133 billion when Putin became president in 2000. By 2008 that figure was down to US$37 billion.

None the less, despite the clear progress made by the Russian economy since the financial collapse of 1998, there was still plenty of room for further improvement, even before the international economic crisis of 2008 onwards hit. As one observer put it in the early twenty-first century, with reference to the attractiveness of Russia for foreign investors, on a scale running from 'dreadful' to 'excellent', improvement thus far had been from 'very bad' to merely 'bad'. Perhaps this should not be surprising, given the extent of the tasks necessary to transform a failing centrally planned economy into a successful market economy (see Box 6.2).

The success of the Russian economy during the period 1999–2008 was fundamentally based on rising global energy – specifically oil – prices, and the ability of Russian firms to capitalize on these by increasing output. In early 1999, *The Economist* magazine suggested that Russia's economic state was so bad that instead of being in the club of the world's leading industrialized nations, it would perhaps be more at home with other war-ridden, poor, debt-encumbered and failing states such as Somalia, Sudan and the Congo. Even allowing for the slightly tongue-in-cheek nature of this comment, to many observers the country was a basket-case in economic terms at the end of the last millennium. And yet, within a matter of years, Russia was booming and critics accused it of throwing its economic weight around like a global bully. What is clear is that this sudden transformation did not stem from a deep-rooted transformation or structural reform of the economy. It was too swift for that. Indeed, even Russia's leadership consistently acknowledged that the good times stemmed initially from high oil prices, and that the benefits that they offered should not be squandered. To this end, the Russian state paid off debts, salted money away for when the downturn came, and began to make plans to diversify the economy and reduce its reliance on the production of raw materials.

Crisis and reform ... again, 2008–13

The international economic crisis that arrived in the second half of 2008 had a significant impact on Russia. As Table 6.3 shows, the following year, 2009, saw a notable decline in GDP, with a record fall

Table 6.3   Russia's economic indicators, 2009–12

	2009	2010	2011	2012
GDP, % change year on year	−7.8	4.5	4.3	3.4
Industrial production, % change year on year	−9.3	8.2	4.7	2.6
Fixed investments, % change year on year	−16.2	6.0	8.3	6.7
Unemployment, %	7.8	8.2	7.2	5.3
Inflation, %	8.8	8.8	6.1	5.1

Source: Official Russian data.

of 8 per cent in aggregate output, as a combination of factors came together to hit the Russian economy. The price of oil fell, domestic consumption declined, and there was a marked drop in investment, as the difficulties in international financial markets made credit more elusive and more expensive.

There is no doubting the exceptional severity of Russia's recession in 2009. None the less, the Russian economy returned to a pattern of steady growth fairly rapidly. That it was able to do so was in no small measure due to the existence of the Reserve Fund and the National Welfare Fund, built up during the boom years. These funds provided the basis for a stimulus package that did not increase Russia's indebtedness too substantially. A gradual rise in oil prices also helped to get the economy back on a growth track by 2010. However, as Tables 6.2 and 6.3 demonstrate, growth since the economic crisis of 2008–9 has been at a far lower level than during the preceding decade. Although annual growth rates of around 4 to 5 per cent over these years would be considered robust in many Western economies, they can also be seen as indicative of structural challenges facing the Russian economy over the next few years. An expert report detailing necessary revisions of Russia's economic 'Strategy 2020', argued in 2011 that higher growth rates would only be achieved with reforms that demonstrated a genuine commitment to tackle corruption and created a legal system that could be relied upon to apply the law impartially and protect property rights. Some leading experts on Russia's economy believe that such a commitment remains unlikely, because the country's ruling elite maintains a vested interest, both politically and financially, in the *status quo* (Hanson and Teague, 2013).

Let us return then to where this chapter began. The Russian economy has completed its post-Soviet transition from a centrally

Illustration 6.1   The Moscow International Business Centre

Under construction on the banks of the Moscow River, this business complex symbolizes the shifting focus of Russia's economy as it modernizes.

planned 'command' system. As an emergent market economy, it has grown on the back of high oil prices and energy exports with sufficient success not to be brought to its knees by the international financial crisis. Russia is now seeking to modernize and diversify its economy so as to reduce vulnerability to oil prices and export fluctuations. However, growth has been slower than expected in recent years. It was not until late 2012 that Russia's output returned to its pre-crisis 2008 levels. Growth in the domestic economy remains hindered by the fact that demand on the part of the Russian consumer is skewed towards imports.

It is one thing to correctly identify the existing vulnerabilities of the Russian economy, but quite another to fix them. In other words, you can punch modernization and diversification into the satnav, but the journey treks through the rough terrain of current conditions. Several obstacles stand in the way of prospects for the successful modernization and diversification of contemporary Russia's economy, notably: the dangers of the 'resource curse'; vulnerability to external, particularly European, shocks; and barriers to doing business in Russia.

Whilst Russia of course has reason to be very thankful for its energy riches, the problems known collectively as the 'resource curse' figure large in forecasts and action plans. An over-reliance on energy resources can bring with it a number of problems:

- First, as oil prices fall, the Russian economy slows down. Oil and gas together represent more than half of the total value of Russia's exports, and unsurprisingly Russia's GDP growth broadly tends to track oil prices. According to former Finance Minister, Alexei Kudrin, this relationship has grown more, rather than less, significant in recent years. Kudrin calculates that for Russia's federal budget to balance, oil prices were required to be twice as high in 2012 as had been necessary in 2007.
- Second, energy revenues can lull policy-makers and public alike into a false feeling of security, diminishing the urgency for, and commitment to, necessary social and economic reforms. The relative popularity of the Putin regime appears to owe some of its longevity to an increase in social spending in recent years. Russia's longer-term economic interests might well be better served by resources being used to diversify and modernize the economy, rather than spent on welfare and the military.
- Third, the political and economic elite in particular engage in the practice known as 'rent-seeking', enriching themselves through control of the profitable energy sector. Such behaviour then further reduces the chances of peaceful political reform, as those in a position to carry out such reforms have too much to lose and are tainted by collusion in corrupt practices.
- Fourth, energy production itself begins to decline as necessary investment is not forthcoming. Rent-seeking reduces resources for domestic investment, while foreign investors are put off by fears of lack of control and corrupt practices. International oil giants, BP and Shell, have both had their troubles in recent years as they have sought, with varying degrees of success, to gain a place in the lucrative Russian energy market.

As well as seeking diversification away from over-dependence on energy resources, Russia's economy might also benefit from geographical diversification. More than half of Russia's exports are to the European Union, and similarly about half of its imports are from the EU. Such has been the case, with the occasional exception, for many years. One such exception, however, is particularly illustrative. In 2009, as the countries of the EU were embroiled in financial crisis, Russia's exports to the EU as a whole fell, and unusually made up less than half of Russia's exports that year. This aberration illustrates how Russia's economy carries a particular vulnerability to economic downturns in Europe. Some experts estimate that for each percentage point that GDP falls in the Euro area countries of the EU, Russia's GDP falls by more than one percentage point. Again, as with energy, Russia clearly has reason to make the most of the comparative advantages which come from geographical proximity to, and compatible trading requirements with, its European neighbours. At the same time, though, such a relationship carries dangers outside of Russia's control. Future diversification requires a geographic as well as a sectoral aspect. As detailed in Chapter 8, Russia is seeking to further develop economic links with Asia, and particularly with China. Such development, however, takes time and, as with combating the resource curse, requires commitment to see it through.

Barriers to doing business in Russia represent the last of the obstacles to diversification and modernization identified above. While such barriers should not be overstated, there exists a consensus among many observers – abroad, in Russia, and even within Russian policy-making circles – that for the economy to develop and grow faster requires a more flexible environment, allowing new companies to flourish, and property rights to be secure. In 2013, the World Bank's Ease of Doing Business index, assessing a range of indicators connected to the robustness of legal frameworks and the complexity and cost of regulatory requirements, placed Russia 112th out of 185 countries. Russia's economic development remains hampered by bureaucracy and corruption, which inhibits domestic entrepreneurs and discourages foreign investors.

None of this is news to Russians and their government. It manifestly represents, however, a complex of issues difficult to shift. Despite years of rhetoric by Presidents Medvedev and Putin, and some high profile cases involving government ministries (for example, the defence ministry and the agriculture ministry), the suspicion remains that anti-corruption drives show the legal process being used as a political tool, rather than demonstrating a genuine commitment to cleaning up the system. These suspicions are only strengthened by cases, such as those in 2013, against opposition activist Aleksei Navalny, and – in an extraordinary attempt at posthumous prosecution – the late Sergei Magnitsky (see Chapters 5 and 7). Even with clear political will, the removal of these barriers to doing business would prove difficult. In a country where such a commitment remains in doubt and the ruling elite appears to vest its interests in the continuation of a graft-ridden business environment, these barriers may prove immovable for many years to come

7

Rights, Freedoms and Civil Society

Western perceptions of contemporary Russia very often begin with the question of human rights and freedoms. Cases such as the prosecution of Pussy Riot or Sergei Magnitsky, tighter regulations on non-governmental organizations (NGOs), and the trial of opposition activists, these make up the headline images of Russia in the Western world today. When Western leaders meet with Russia's president, reference is almost invariably made to the latest such events. There seems little doubt that Russia's reputation in regard to rights, freedoms and the flourishing of civil society has declined under President Putin, and particularly so since Putin's return to office for a third term in 2012.

Unsurprisingly, Russia's leadership, and indeed many Russians, dispute the criticism of their country's record in a number of ways. Russia's foreign ministry has produced critical reports on human rights in the United States and the European Union, in an attempt to show that its critics do not themselves have unblemished rights records. Russian officials also argue the merits of each specific case, often responding to criticism from abroad by maintaining that the matter in question is being dealt with in a legally correct manner without political interference. To defend its rights record in this manner is in keeping with Russia's own formal commitments – in its Constitution, as a member of the Council of Europe, and as a signatory to major international human rights declarations – to an international consensus on human rights. At the same time, though, there exists in the Russian discourse a defence of its rights record that stems from an assertion of state sovereignty and civilizational identity. While President Putin has acknowledged that human rights trump national sovereignty, he has also warned against the use of human rights as an excuse by some countries to violate the sovereignty of others. Beyond official statements, a strong stream of national-patriotic and Orthodox discourse in Russia rejects the very notion of rights as widely understood in the West, arguing instead that Russia's traditions mandate a less individually-oriented concept of rights and bridling at what is seen as the aggressive and alien promotion of rights focused around sexuality and gender issues.

This chapter considers contemporary Russia's record on rights, freedoms and civil society from both a critical and a cultural perspective. A brief overview of the Soviet legacy provides essential background, as this legacy understandably creates a heightened sensitivity to the question of rights and freedoms within Russia. The chapter then assesses both the formal legal situation, in terms of the Russian state's official and constitutional commitments to human rights, and the informal lived experience of its citizens in relation to these rights in Russia today. Consideration of civil society similarly raises questions of the relative role of the state and of citizens, and the right of people to collectively and legally act independently of the state. Specific examples enable us to illustrate developments in contemporary Russia, and to consider too the counter-arguments made against critics of Russia's rights record. To this end, the chapter covers in some detail freedom of worship, the war in Chechnya, the Pussy Riot and Magnitsky cases, securitization in Russian life, rights in the military and in prisons, the development of civil society both independently of and at the instigation of the Putin regime, and the legislation of Putin's third term, including increased fines for unauthorized demonstrations and regulations requiring foreign-funded NGOs to register as 'foreign agents'.

The Soviet legacy

The Soviet Union had a developed legal system, backed by a Constitution outlining the rights and obligations of its citizens. After the founding Constitutions of Soviet Russia (1918) and the Soviet Union (1924), the USSR had two further constitutions, the Stalin Constitution of 1936 and the Brezhnev Constitution of 1977. As Mark Sandle puts it, 'the basic ethos was that the rights of the individual were state based, and were then delegated to the individual from the state' (Sandle, 1998: 402). In practice, this meant that the authorities appeared to be above the law in those cases in which they had a particular stake. Such cases, usually of political importance, would be decided not on judicial grounds alone, but as a result of what became known as 'telephone law', whereby the political authorities would instruct the judicial authorities as to the desired verdict and the sentence. Moving forward to contemporary Russia, as the Khodorkovsky case demonstrates (Box 4.1 on page 92), at the highest level such 'telephone law' still exists in the sense that the authorities are able to get a court verdict in their favour in circumstances where this is deemed essential.

In the Soviet years, however, the denial of rights and freedoms went way beyond the mere application of 'telephone law' in select cases. Building on the oppression of 'class enemies' under Lenin from the revolution of 1917 onwards, the Stalin era saw a dictatorship that brought about the state-induced deaths of millions of its own citizens through execution, famine, displacement and forced labour. Driven by a combination of factors – an ideology that subordinated individuals to its supposedly greater cause, a desire on the part of the state to control all aspects of citizens' lives, the self-preservation instincts common to any authoritarian regime – the Soviet state had little time for individual rights and freedoms, and no space at all for the existence of civil society. At the same time, though, the Soviet Union's understanding of rights and freedoms emphasized social rights, in the form of equal access to social goods such as health care, education, housing and so on, and at times did so more successfully than many Western countries.

From the mid-1950s onwards, the Soviet Union became a little more benign in the treatment of its citizenry as a whole, but this was only in comparison to the brutal dictatorship of the Stalin years. Until almost the end of the Soviet era, citizens were not allowed to travel freely, only the most trusted could travel abroad, communication with foreigners was monitored, all media were controlled by the state, their content decided by the state, and no organization legally existed outside the purview of the state. Such restrictions on basic rights and freedoms applied to all citizens. When it came to Soviet citizens who were unwilling to abide by state-imposed norms or, even worse, actively opposed the state, then the infringement of rights went still further. Those who refused to participate in the rituals and requirements of the state – for example, religious believers who persisted in attending churches and refused to join Communist organizations –

might find their lives blighted by being unable to go to university, progress in their profession, or gain adequate housing. Those who moved to overt opposition and became known dissidents might be subject to arrest, exile or psychiatric treatment.

Among dissidents of the later Soviet decades, a distinction could be made between 'politicals', who sought the end of the Soviet regime, and 'legalists', whose demands amounted to merely the correct observance of the procedures laid down in Soviet legislation. In 1975, the Soviet government signed the Helsinki Final Act, which committed it to respect fundamental rights and freedoms, such as freedom of conscience and belief, and the Moscow Helsinki Group was established to monitor and insist on – too often in vain – the observation of the Soviet state's legal and international obligations. The legalists' insistence that the state act in accordance with its own laws represented, as it continues to do today, a difficult stance for the state to refute. When Mikhail Gorbachev came to power in 1985, he called for, and began to create, a 'law-based state', which he described as essential to the stability of the Soviet Union. However, the ideological, institutional and constitutional confusion of the Soviet endgame did not allow for the clear development of this concept, let alone its embodiment in the behaviour of the authorities.

Gorbachev had been working towards the enactment of a new Soviet Constitution. With the Soviet Union no longer existing after 1991, the task became the development of a new Russian Constitution. As noted in Chapter 2, arguments over the nature of the Constitution and questions of how and by whom Russia should be ruled eventually led to military action on the streets of Moscow in October 1993, and the forcible dissolution of parliament by troops loyal to President Yeltsin. It is to discussion of the rights and freedoms contained in the 1993 Russian Constitution, still serving as the fundamental law of the Russian Federation, that we now turn.

Constitutional rights in contemporary Russia

The Russian Constitution was adopted by national referendum on 12 December 1993. A constitution can perform a variety of functions, setting out the rules of the game for political engagement, the institutional arrangement of power, the 'mission statement' of a state, the division between central and devolved powers, the limits of the state and so on. In different chapters of this book we deal with different aspects of constitutional provision (in particular, Chapter 5 covers the institutional arrangement of power). Here, though, we are concerned with what the Russian Constitution says about individual rights and freedoms, and the supremacy of law.

Before tackling this topic in any detail, it is worth pointing out that, to many people, the Russian Constitution's position on the supremacy of law was compromised before the Constitution was ever adopted because of the circumstances surrounding its adoption. We outlined in Chapters 2 and 5 the events that led to armed conflict in Moscow between supporters of the president and the parliament in 1993. The key point for our purposes here is that the dissolution of the parliament by the president in September 1993 was not allowed under the Constitution then in force. In other words, whatever the current Russian Constitution says about the supremacy of the law, it was adopted on the back of a fundamentally unconstitutional act, namely the dissolution of the parliament by the president.

There is, of course, a counter-argument to this view, which is that the Constitution still in force in September 1993 was void of real authority and served as a barrier to the democratic development of Russia. It was the 1978 Constitution of the Soviet-era Russian republic, and had been amended so many times that it could scarcely be called a fundamental law any more. Though this argument is correct so far as it goes, the fact remains that, from a legal-technical point of view, the dissolution of parliament in 1993 was not lawful.

Despite its provenance, the Russian Constitution provides an apparently firm foundation for the provision of human rights. We have noted that, under the Soviet system, individual rights were subsumed by the needs of the state. This Marxist–Leninist conceptualization of rights is replaced in the current Constitution by a liberal approach, with Article 2 declaring that 'the individual and his rights and freedoms are the supreme value'. An entire section of the Russian Constitution is then devoted to 'human and civil rights and freedoms', which are guaranteed within 'the generally recognized principles and norms of international law'.

Among the rights and freedoms to be guaranteed by the Russian Constitution are all those which might be expected in a liberal democracy, including:

- equality before the law;
- inviolability of the home and the person;
- the presumption of innocence;

- freedom of conscience;
- freedom of thought and speech; and
- the right of association.

There are also a number of rights and freedoms that carry specific echoes of the Soviet era. Some of these involve statements of rights that were often infringed during the Communist years, such as the right to travel and to live where one chooses, the right to privacy of communication, and the right to own property. Others involve guarantees reminiscent of the broad social welfare provisions claimed by the Soviet state; for example, guaranteed provision of pensions, certain social security benefits, housing and education; the right to a decent environment; and the constitutional statement that 'the development of physical culture and sport … are encouraged'.

It is clear, then, that the Russian Constitution provides a substantial legal underpinning of the rights and freedoms to be enjoyed by the citizens of the Russian Federation. The Constitution is the fundamental law of the state, and all other laws must be in accordance with it. As we shall see, though, the mere statement of something in a constitution does not in itself mean the application of that provision. A key question to ask is whether the legal guarantees of the current Russian Constitution have resulted in a change of behaviour on the part of the state. Does the state now act in accordance with the view that individual rights take precedence? Does the old view that the state is more important still hold sway? In some ways, the location and nature of power in today's Russia is too complex to give a clear answer to these questions. A more nuanced view is required, along the lines that in any given situation the precedence to be given to the rights of the individual or to the requirements of the state depends on the specifics of the case. In fact, the situation is even more complicated than that, as the state and the individual do not represent the only two actors involved; the interests of businessmen, powerful individuals, and influential organizations all come into play. The cases of Pussy Riot and of Sergei Magnitsky, covered in detail later in this chapter, clearly demonstrate the reality of this more complex picture. It is doubtful whether the Pussy Riot trial would have progressed as it did without the involvement of the Russian Orthodox Church. Similarly, the Sergei Magnitsky case – as with the Khodorkovsky case covered in Box 4.1 – can scarcely be assessed without an awareness of the business and financial interests of those implicated.

We must also bear in mind that the provisions of the Constitution are broad-ranging, and many of them require a detailed outworking in law before they can be applied. An example of this is provided in our consideration of freedom of worship. Similarly the Russian Constitution declares that potential conscripts into the military have the right of alternative service. Despite this, the lack of a law defining how such alternative service might be undertaken meant that, until such a law was finally passed in 2002, this provision was very difficult for private citizens to enforce. The lack of such 'enabling legislation' hampered several areas of constitutional provision in the years after 1993, and was all but inevitable given the radicality, and associated legal complexity, of the changes that the 1993 Constitution introduced in terms of content and approach. A good example is the right to strike, which is enshrined in the Constitution. As in other countries – for example Germany and the United States – where this right is explicitly set out in the legal code rather than assumed under broader rights such as freedom of association, the details of how the right is to be implemented require further legislation. The difficulty then arises that not all enabling legislation actually seems to enable. Expert analysis in Russia claims that the official procedures required before a strike is legal would take well over a month to complete. Similarly, the 1997 religion law, which is discussed below, introduces provisions that appear to directly contradict those contained in Russia's Constitution with regard to the rights of religious associations.

Freedom of worship

According to the Russian Constitution of 1993, freedom of worship is guaranteed in the Russian Federation. To enshrine this right in the country's fundamental law marked a clear break with the past, and particularly with the Soviet era, when persecution of religious believers had been continuous and widespread. The situation for religious believers in the Soviet Union had begun to improve under Gorbachev's leadership, particularly from 1988 onwards. This was the year that marked the millennium of Christianity in Russia, and it was officially celebrated across the country, with the atheist Communist leadership even sanctioning the production of postage stamps marking the occasion.

In 1990, the Soviet Union introduced a Law on Freedom of Conscience and Religious Associations, which declared the fundamental right of freedom of conscience, the equality before the law of believers and non-believers, and the right to freely choose, hold and disseminate religious or non-religious convictions. As is apparent in a number of areas related to freedoms and democracy (for example, see the question of media freedom covered in Chapter 8), the period of the 1990s was freer and more open than the situation that applies in Russia today. Old laws and practices had been swept away, and there was a sense of intoxication with new freedoms.

What did these new freedoms mean for religious believers? At the most basic level, believers of all faiths could begin to attend church (or mosque, synagogue, temple, and so on) more freely and openly than before. They were able to obtain religious literature (particularly Bibles) with increasing ease, religious groups were able to engage in charitable work and in the expression of their faith, and there was more contact with fellow believers abroad. This latter point meant a growth in overt evangelistic activity by different religious groups on the streets or through the media.

In short the official recognition of religious freedom brought a surge of religious activity across a range of faiths. The Russian Orthodox Church, which still sees itself as the carrier of the faith of the Russian people, was by no means excluded from such activity. Indeed, it enjoyed the full range of rights, and began to enjoy financial benefits from the state, the return of property confiscated by the Communist regime earlier in the twentieth century, and an increasingly prominent position alongside the state machinery. For example, the Patriarch of Russia began to participate in state ceremonies, such as the inauguration of the president, and the Russian Orthodox Church once again had official links with the Russian armed forces.

As the 1990s progressed, however, there was something of a backlash against this burst of religiosity. In particular, nationalist, anti-Western elements within federal and regional government, and within the hierarchy of the Russian Orthodox Church, began to object to the activities of what they termed 'non-Russian religious sects and cults'. Several streams of thought came together in this view. There was an element of the idea, found increasingly in other policy areas as the 1990s progressed, that Russia should not simply accept what the West had to offer, but should build on its own traditions and civilization to find its own Russian path. There was also a fear expressed, particularly in the Orthodox Church, that the Russian people might be 'led astray'. The argument was that, after decades of atheistic propaganda, the Russian people might slake their spiritual thirst on whatever was put before them, without having the depth of knowledge necessary to discern between the various faiths on offer. The existence of certain extreme cults in Russia backed up this fear, but also led to many denominations and faiths being branded as cults because they were not Russian Orthodoxy nor one of the other long-standing traditional faiths in Russia, such as Islam, Buddhism and Judaism. Confessions that had existed since at least the early years of the twentieth century in Russia and persisted throughout decades of Communist persecution (such as the Baptists or the Pentecostals) found themselves referred to in Russian Orthodox publications as cults, and accused of being 'Western' faiths, even in cases where the leadership was entirely Russian. These fears surrounding the growth of religious freedom found an echo among a good proportion of the Russian population, and gradually regional leaders began to promulgate laws that restricted the activities of 'non-Russian' religious groups and, in doing so, often ran counter to the provisions of the Russian Constitution.

In 1997, after a couple of failed attempts, the Russian parliament finally passed a law on religion which President Yeltsin signed. The provisions of the 1997 law 'On Freedom of Conscience and Religious Associations' were a step backwards from the 1990 Soviet-era law in terms of religious freedom, and they also appeared to contradict the Russian Constitution. In its preamble, the 1997 law singled out Russian Orthodoxy as making a 'special contribution' to Russia, and then gave respect to those faiths that form 'an inseparable part of the historical heritage of Russia's peoples', naming specifically Christianity, Islam, Buddhism and Judaism. According to the Constitution of Russia, no faith is to be preferred by the secular state. While the 1997 law's preamble makes no specific provision for preferable treatment to be given to the religions there named, the singling out of Russian Orthodoxy as the foremost faith of Russia reflects the general attitude of the authorities. Under President Medvedev (2008–12), the 'traditional faiths' – with the ambiguity removed of listing both Christianity and a specific sub-set of Christianity, Russian Orthodoxy – became the formal basis for religious education in school. Since 2010, school pupils have had to choose one of six courses on the cultures of Orthodoxy, Islam, Judaism, Buddhism, world religions or secular ethics.

The most substantive part of the 1997 law with regard to the practice of religious freedom came in the differentiation it makes between different types of religious association. According to the Constitution, all religious associations are equal before the law. The 1997 religion law, however, declared that religious associations fall into two categories – they are either religious organizations, which are registered and have the full rights of a legal personage, or they are religious groups which are not registered and do not have those rights. Religious groups are therefore, among other restrictions, not able to own property, establish and maintain buildings, employ people, or issue invitations to foreign citizens. In order to facilitate registration, many smaller groups had to place themselves within larger 'umbrella organizations', because belonging to a centralized religious association made registration easier. Furthermore, the passing of the 1997 law on religion appears to have been seen, particularly by regional authorities and certain elements in the Orthodox Church, as authorization of the harassment of non-Orthodox groups. In the early twenty-first century, the Roman Catholic church in particular seemed to have problems with visas for its clergy. In a number of such cases, lawyers operating on behalf of church groups appealed successfully against the actions of officials. None the less, it is clear that a group that has been denied registration will have less of a case in law than does a registered association.

The situation has deteriorated further in recent years through the mis-application to selected religious groups of the 2002 law 'On Fighting Extremist Activity'. This law bans religious hatred and violence, in a manner not dissimilar to laws in a number of European countries, including the United Kingdom. However, it has increasingly been applied selectively to some religions, the Jehovah's Witnesses in particular. As part of its efforts to combat extremism, Russia maintains a Federal List of Extremist Materials, and distributing any item on this list is illegal throughout Russia. More than 1,300 works appear on this list, many of which are peaceable religious texts deemed extremist by local courts after 'expert analysis' at the behest of prosecutors or the FSB (Federal Security Service).

Overall, the current picture of religious freedom across Russia is decidedly mixed. For the most part, most of the time, most religious groups can meet and worship freely. However, particular regions continue to single out particular 'non-traditional' faiths for harassment, using legal provisions not originally intended to deal with religion in order to prosecute believers. The 2004 law 'On Meetings, Rallies, Demonstrations, Marches and Pickets' has, for example, been used in some regions to prosecute selected religious groups for holding meetings without telling the authorities, whereas courts in

Box 7.1   Pussy Riot

In February 2012, the all-female radical punk band Pussy Riot tres-
passed on the sanctuary in Moscow's Cathedral of Christ the Saviour.
Wearing their trademark primary-coloured balaclavas, they briefly
performed an expletive-laden song protesting against the links between
the Russian Orthodox Church and the Putin regime. Soon afterwards, a
video of their performance was posted online. Three members of the
band were subsequently arrested and eventually, in August, sentenced
to two years in corrective labour colonies. One of their number,
Yekaterina Samutsevicha, was released early, in October 2012. The
other two, Nadezhda Tolokonnikova and Maria Alyokhina, were
released in December 2013 as part of an amnesty to celebrate the twentieth anniversary of Russia's constitution.

The case of Pussy Riot reveals differing attitudes towards rights and
freedoms in contemporary Russia. To many observers, the trial of the
Pussy Riot members – two of whom are young mothers – represented
a gross overreaction to their actions. Even if it is accepted that their
behaviour warranted prosecution, their pre-trial detention, their
sentence, and many legally dubious elements of their trial were widely
seen as politically motivated, an attack on free speech, and a warning
to opponents of the regime that they face increasingly tough measures
in the Russian courts. To many others, however, Pussy Riot's actions
were seen as having overstepped the line of what is acceptable.
According to opinion polls, their trespass and their performance were
construed negatively by most Russians, with three-quarters believing
their sentence to be either just right or not long enough. The Supreme
Church Council of the Russian Orthodox Church called the faithful to
prayer, on 22 April 2012, in defence of the faith and of desecrated sanc-
tuaries. The Patriarch spoke against the idea that blasphemy and deri-
sion of the sacred should be put forward as a lawful expression of
human freedom that must be protected in today's society.   ⫸

other regions have ruled that religious worship lies outside the law's
scope. As well as creating a confusing inconsistency, the application
of laws on extremism, demonstrations and terrorism to religious
affairs also brings the FSB increasingly into the oversight and control
of religion. In 2013, the introduction of new regulations on the
foreign funding of NGOs, which again is not supposed to apply to
religious groups, saw hundreds of such groups being checked up on
by the authorities. While contemporary Russia is clearly a very long
way from the blanket state-led, anti-religious persecution of the
Soviet years, there remains a somewhat arbitrary harassment of
particular non-traditional religions, applied sporadically by some

Such a polarization of opinion on the Pussy Riot case stems from a number of overlapping factors:

- broadly speaking, though by no means without exception, Western observers thought the treatment of Pussy Riot harsh, while Russian observers were far more likely to consider it justified;
- Western powers (including the United States and the European Union) expressed concern over the case, Amnesty International called the women 'prisoners of conscience', and a number of Western popular musicians called for the release of the imprisoned Pussy Riot members;
- the involvement of the Russian Orthodox Church in the case emphasized the idea that Russian values were at stake and under threat;
- the effectiveness of the strong and outspoken support for Pussy Riot in the West was ambiguous, in that, as well as highlighting the plight of the prisoners, it strengthened the notion that they were somehow identified with Western ideas set against Russian tradition – the trial could therefore be seen as encapsulating a 'culture war' over values in what is still a largely conservative and patriotic country;
- the Putin regime denied that it had any direct involvement in the case, and insisted that the legal process was taking its course independently, though whether this was so or not, pro-Pussy Riot agitation from the West was always more likely to stiffen the resolve of the Russian authorities than to ameliorate the fate of the prisoners;
- the case can be read from a political perspective rather than a cultural one, with the rise in overt opposition to the Putin regime in Moscow during the 2011–12 election season creating a febrile atmosphere in which Pussy Riot provided the regime with a convenient example to punish in order to discourage others;
- the justification that Pussy Riot themselves provided for their actions included a rejection of the patriarchal, sexist, homophobic, xenophobic, traditionalist and fundamentalist attitudes that their accusers were said to be displaying.

regional judicial structures and law enforcers. It is too early to talk of the firm establishment of freedom of worship on Russia.

Freedom of speech and assembly

From our analysis of freedom of religion, we can discern a pattern in relation to rights and freedoms in Russia that is familiar from other areas of discussion in this book. The pendulum of reform swung out wide in the early to mid-1990s, and then began to swing back. For example, despite some progress in democratization in the 1990s,

Rebuilt in the 1990s, following the demolition of its predecessor in the Soviet era, the cathedral became widely known in 2012 as the location for Pussy Riot's brief 'punk prayer' performance.

Illustration 7.1   The Cathedral of Christ the Saviour, Moscow

there was no full transition to a normative Western liberal democratic system, let alone the consolidation of such a system. In the twenty-first century, Russia has swung away from democracy, although again not undergoing a full reversion to the situation existing in the Soviet years.

Looking at human rights in general, with particular reference to Russia's place in the international sphere, we can note that Russia is a signatory to the six core UN Human Rights treaties. It has also accepted the human rights obligations of the Council of Europe. None the less, despite these binding assertions, which take precedence over Russian law, problems have existed in relation to Russia's human rights record for most of this century, and indications during the early years of Putin's third term (2012–18) are that the direction of travel is towards deterioration rather than amelioration. The main areas of concern in recent years have included the fundamental human rights of freedom of speech and freedom of assembly; individual rights within the 'closed institutions' of the military, and the Russian prison system; and the area that had most international attention in the first decade of the twenty-first century, the conduct of military action in Chechnya. (Wider questions of freedom of speech with regard to press freedom are dealt with in detail in Chapter 8.)

We shall deal with these issues in order. First, freedom of speech. The several freedom of speech cases that gained international attention around the turn of the twenty-first century tended to be related to national security. Perhaps the most noteworthy of these were the separate cases of environmental activists Aleksandr Nikitin and Grigory Pasko, who were both charged with espionage after revealing details of the environmental impact of Russia's nuclear naval facilities. They were investigated by the FSB and charged, but although they both served time in prison, both men were also at different times acquitted by Russian civil courts. More recent freedom of speech cases, however, appear to have less to do with national security and to be more politically motivated. In 2012, the Pussy Riot case garnered much international attention. As Box 7.1 details, the conviction of three members of Pussy Riot represented a complex case for analysis, bringing into the debate a range of issues around the limits of free speech in relation to religious offence and perceptions of acceptable behaviour. In legal terms, the Pussy Riot conviction was for hooliganism. None the less, the lyrics of the song performed, which included the refrain 'Mother of God, chase Putin away', suggest that issues around freedom of speech also played a part in the case.

Other cases that may be seen in some way to be a denial of freedom of speech stem from the rise in opposition activity in Russia from late 2011 onwards, including mass demonstrations against the Putin regime on the streets of Moscow, particularly in the period December 2011 to May 2012. Following this upsurge in anti-Putin protests, a number of prominent oppositionists have found themselves facing legal proceedings. Sergei Udaltsov, a left-wing leader of the opposition movement, was placed under house arrest in 2013, after having been accused of accepting money from the Georgian security services in a meeting that was secretly filmed. Udaltsov's defenders see this as a sting operation to incriminate him. Another prominent participant in the anti-Putin protests, Leonid Razvozzhayev, attempted to apply for asylum in Ukraine. Shortly afterwards, he turned up in police custody in Moscow. Razvozzhayev alleges that he was kidnapped and tortured by the Russian security forces, and brought back over the border to Russia. Once back in Moscow, he was charged with stealing 500 fur hats fifteen years ago.

In the Soviet era, the maxim 'show me the man, and I will show you the offence' was used to indicate that if the authorities wanted to put someone in prison, they would charge him with any offence to fit their purpose. The most prominent opponent of the Putin regime around the time of the upsurge in protests from 2011 onwards has been Aleksei Navalny. In 2013, Navalny went on trial accused of the theft of timber in 2009 – a guilty verdict would put him in prison, though, of course, not ostensibly for his political activities. In July 2013, Navalny was found guilty and sentenced to five years in prison, but unusually – and following international condemnation and street protests in Moscow – he was released the next day pending his appeal. Navalny and his supporters insist that the charges are trumped up and stem entirely from a desire on the part of the regime to silence him and to punish him for his opposition, including his popularizing of the epithet 'the party of crooks and thieves' to refer to Russia's dominant political party, United Russia. His release pending appeal enabled him to stand in the election for the post of mayor of Moscow in September 2013, where he came second with 27 per cent of the vote. The pro-Putin candidate, Sergei Sobyanin, won with just over 51 per cent, sneaking over the 50 per cent threshold required to avoid a run-off.

As well as these cases related to freedom of speech, following on from the demonstrations of 2011–12, the Russian authorities also began to make changes to the law on freedom of assembly. The anti-Putin demonstration on Moscow's Bolotnaya Square on 6 May 2012, the eve of President Putin's third term inauguration, resulted in clashes between the police and some demonstrators. Almost thirty demonstrators were subsequently charged with rioting as a direct result of this. Furthermore, a new law on assembly was swiftly passed, taking less than three weeks to get through parliament and onto the statute book, which increased the fines for violating the law from US$165 to US$9,700, as well as tightening laws on the responsibilities of organizers and permissible locations for protests. However, when Russia's Constitutional Court heard appeals against the enhanced legislation on assemblies, it ruled that the new fines were set too high and struck down other elements, including those relating to organizers and locations. The Constitutional Court did not find that the State Duma had violated parliamentary procedure in adopting the law so hastily, but this finding was a split decision, with a minority of judges believing that the Duma had indeed done so.

Even without the new legislation on demonstrations, however, the Russian state's obligation to allow freedom of assembly has been rather patchily applied in recent years. On the one hand, a good number of protest rallies have taken place with permission granted according to the law, including the massive rallies of tens of thousands in Moscow in December 2011. On the other hand, from 2009 onwards, an opposition campaign called Strategy 31 – after Article 31 of the Russian Constitution that guarantees freedom of assembly – organized rallies on the 31st day of any month with sufficient days in it, and suffered a mixed record in terms of getting approval. Many of these rallies took place without permission, as organizers and authorities argued over location. The organizers asserted that their rights had been denied, and the authorities countered that Strategy 31 had rejected city centre locations for the rally in order to claim denial of rights. When demonstrations took place without approval, a number of their participants were arrested.

In terms of international comparison, laws on demonstrations, the refusal to sanction demonstrations or to require them to be held in a designated location, and the arrest or mistreatment of protesters on legal or illegal demonstrations are by no means the sole preserve of the Russian state. Such occurrences can be found in more democratic and less democratic states than Russia. Russian officials, stung by criticism over human rights questions, increasingly have responded by alleging similar faults in Western countries. From the human rights perspective, of course, it is the individual and his or her rights that matter, and the existence or not of rights abuses elsewhere represents little mitigation.

Rights in the military and in prisons

Allegations of human rights abuses in the Russian military and prisons relate largely to the poor conditions in these institutions. Lack of resources in the military led, in the first post-Soviet decade and beyond, to poor standards of nutrition, substandard accommodation and frequent training accidents due to ill-maintained equipment and insufficient expertise among the troops. These difficulties were caused largely by lack of funding, and have been addressed to some degree by increases in military expenditure in recent years. However, the 'tradition' of systematic bullying of conscripts entrenched in the Russian armed forces had less to do with funding. The informal system, known as *dedovshchina*, saw a cycle of victimization of new conscripts by longer-serving conscripts that repeated itself with each new call-up. *Dedovshchina* led to deaths, protests and the desire to avoid being drafted into the armed forces under Russia's system of universal conscription. In 2008, the period of conscription was reduced from two years to one, partly in an attempt to break the cycle of bullying based on a hierarchy of conscripts, and partly to edge Russia a little nearer to having professional armed forces. None the less, the number of reported cases of bullying has continued to increase. Although this increase may to some extent be due to a greater willingness on the part of the armed forces to tackle the problem by encouraging victims to come forward, evidence also exists of violence arising from heightened ethnic tension within the Russian armed forces, particularly involving conscripts from the Caucasus. Official figures for 2010 indicate that thousands of conscripts are still abused each year, and dozens are either seriously injured or killed. In 2010 alone, over fifty officers were imprisoned for engaging in such abuse.

In 2011, Russia had the second-highest prison population per capita rate in the world, at about 550 per 100,000 population, with the US prison population being the highest, far higher than any other country at almost 750 per 100,000 population. Russia's prison population has declined noticeably in recent years, following a deliberate policy of reduction instigated during the Medvedev presidency (2008–12). By the end of 2012, there were 715,000 inmates in Russia's prisons, bringing the international comparison figure down to just below 500 per 100,000 population. Conditions in the Russian prison system, however, do not appear to be improving in line with the slight decline in prison population figures, with 4,121 prisoners dying in prison in 2012, a slight per capita increase on 2010. Overcrowding and violence remain rife in Russia's prisons, and the death rate is increased by disease, notably a virulent drug-resistant strain of tuberculosis (see Chapter 4). There are also allegations of torture and ill-treatment in custody. The most high profile of these, the death of Sergei Magnitsky (Box 7.2), created an international outcry and led to significant international tension between Russia and the US in particular (see Chapter 9). However, the Magnitsky case is not the only example of alleged ill-treatment. In 2012, a number of

Box 7.2 Sergei Magnitsky

Sergei Magnitsky, a 37-year-old lawyer and father of two, died in Moscow's Matrosskaya Tishina detention centre in November 2009, of apparent toxic shock and heart failure. Magnitsky was in pre-trial detention on charges – strongly denied – of organizing a tax evasion scheme with the UK-based businessman whom he represented, William Browder. Browder himself had been denied entry into Russia since 2005, following a dispute with interior ministry officials over his Hermitage Capital fund.

An initial investigation in Russia found that prison officials had neglected Magnitsky's medical problems, and led to twenty prison officials being fired. Magnitsky's boss at the law firm, Firestone Duncan, charged that the case had deeper ramifications than the Russian inquiry covered. Magnitsky's employers and supporters asserted that he had been arrested as part of a cover-up of a massive theft from Hermitage Capital and from the Russian state by Russian officials, and that he had been severely mistreated in prison in an attempt to persuade him to change his story.

The case gained international notoriety as accusation and counter-accusation came from each side. Magnitsky's supporters produced a series of online videos, under the title 'Russian Untouchables', setting out their accusations of a complex fraud involving around US$230 million, and alleging cover-ups and corruption within the Russian law enforcement structures.

Eventually, in 2012, the United States Congress passed a bill banning those accused of involvement in the case from visiting the United States or using the US banking system. Pressure for similar visa and banking restrictions grew in Europe. In Russia, the authorities took the highly unusual step of continuing with the prosecution of Sergei Magnitsky posthumously, and, in July 2013, he was found guilty. The Russian parliament also passed a law at the end of 2012, widely seen as retaliation for the Magnitsky bill, which amongst other things banned inter-country adoptions of children between Russia and the United States.

In 2013, Russia's request to have William Browder's name included on Interpol's international search list was rejected after an Interpol committee decided that Russia's case against Browder was of a predominantly political nature – a decision that Russian critics considered political itself.

cases of ill-treatment of prisoners came to light in Tatarstan, leading to the resignation of the republic's interior minister, the trial of eight former police officers, and a number of protests against police brutality across Russia. In September 2013, Pussy Riot member Nadezhda Tolokonnikova (see Box 7.1) wrote an open letter and declared a hunger strike to protest the torturous conditions suffered by women prisoners in the labour colony where she was incarcerated.

Chechnya and human rights

Before the increasing focus on political rights at the beginning of the Putin's third term, perhaps the biggest single human rights issue with which the West was concerned in relation to Russia was the conduct of war in Chechnya in 1994–6 and again from 1999 to 2000, and during the subsequent security operations in the following years. In these wars, Russian armed forces attempted to subdue separatist guer-rillas by the wholesale 'invasion' of Chechnya. (Though this was not technically an invasion, as Chechnya remains officially part of the Russian Federation.) Critics of Russian action argue that, in waging war in Chechnya, Russia targeted civilians, mistreated prisoners, sacrificed its own conscript soldiers, harassed independent media, and denied access to international bodies such as the International Red Cross and the Organization for Security and Co-operation in Europe (OSCE).

As a result of Russia's conduct of its wars in Chechnya:

- the European Union limited the funds earmarked for the promotion of democracy in Russia and transferred uncommitted funds to humanitarian assistance for refugees from the conflict area;
- the Parliamentary Assembly of the Council of Europe temporarily stripped Russia of its voting rights (2000–1), and declared 'totally unacceptable' the failure of the Council of Europe's Committee of Ministers to denounce Moscow's conduct of the Chechen war; and
- President Putin was widely criticized by the international commu-nity for his conduct of the war, and US President Clinton even used a speech to the State Duma in Moscow to urge a re-think of policy in Chechnya.

Despite all these actions by the international community, support for Russian action in Chechnya remained relatively solid amongst the Russian population, albeit with some notable exceptions – such as the Committee of Soldiers' Mothers. This is partly due to the fact that media coverage of the war largely supported the Russian position. It has also resulted from widespread anger and horror at terrorist attacks within Russia.

After the terrorist attacks by Al-Qaeda on New York and Washington on 11 September 2001, President Putin, and indeed the Chechen rebels, increasingly sought to 'internationalize' the discourse around the Chechen conflict. For Putin, the conflict in Chechnya was part of the global war on terrorism, and this interpretation was to some extent accepted by many Western governments. President Medvedev formally announced an end to counter-terrorism operations in Chechnya in March 2009. Since the end of the Chechen conflict, allegations of human rights abuses in Chechnya have been focused on the regime overseen by Chechen President, Ramzan Kadyrov. Under Kadyrov, Chechen separatism is off the agenda, and the republic remains officially loyal to the Putin regime – in the Russian general election of 2011, in the sort of result familiar to authoritarian electoral processes, the United Russia party received 99.5 per cent of the vote on a turnout of 99.5 per cent. The NGO Human Rights Watch has accused Chechen authorities of adopting a policy of punishing the families of insurgents and of violating the rights of women who refuse to wear headscarves in public.

A weak state and securitization

A key to understanding rights and freedoms in contemporary Russia is knowledge of the historical background. This applies not only to an awareness that authoritarianism and even totalitarianism dominated Soviet society during the twentieth century, but also to a knowledge of more recent post-Soviet history. In particular, we have noted a shift from the beginning of the Putin presidency in 2000 towards more state control, and a rolling back of previous advances in terms of democracy and certain aspects of rights and freedoms. An adequate understanding of the Russian government's policies in these areas requires recognition of the 'weak state hypothesis'.

A consensus began to develop at the end of the Yeltsin era among observers of contemporary Russia that the central political issue to be dealt with was the weakness of the Russian state. As an explanatory framework for what happened in Russia in the 1990s, stalled state-building explained much. The essence of the problem was the heavily presidential nature of the Russian state under Yeltsin and its role in hindering the development of democratic institutions and behaviour, thus creating a weak, personalized state, where money and connections bought influence. The super-rich oligarchs had, with a degree of ruthlessness, garnered both wealth and political influence. At the same time, under Yeltsin, the Russian state could not collect taxes, pay wages, keep order on the streets, rule its regions, provide adequate health and education services, and perform many other functions of a state.

When Putin came to power in 2000, a degree of consensus existed among observers and the new regime alike; the state-strengthening agenda headed the list of tasks facing the Russian government at the turn of the millennium. The policies of Vladimir Putin with regard to state strengthening included bringing all regional laws into line with federal legislation, reforming the tax system with a 13 per cent rate of income tax applicable to all, and undermining the influence of the oligarchs. These are policies that addressed in a straightforward manner the widely acknowledged problems Russia was facing at the end of the Yeltsin era. Switch the discourse a little, however, and a focus on Putin's approach can bring a different interpretation. The strengthening of the state under Putin meant that a president who had formerly been in the Soviet security services, along with many key officials from a similar security background, was engaged in a process of centralizing power and ensuring that the writ of the state ran across country. It was easy, even while acknowledging the need for state-strengthening, to come to the conclusion that Putin's aim was for Russia to become more authoritarian. To add more fuel to the fire, Putin's two key phrases with regard to state-strengthening echoed the Communist past. In place of the Marxist 'dictatorship of the proletariat' promised by Lenin, Putin promised a 'dictatorship of the law'. And instead of Stalin's infamous declaration during his rural terror campaign of the 1930s that he would 'liquidate the Kulaks as a class', Putin said that he would get rid of 'the oligarchs as a class'.

As we have seen, with regard to the rule of law, the record in terms of high profile cases is mixed. Courts make decisions based on legal rather than political considerations in less high profile cases, and the Constitutional Court has struck down some of the Duma's less liberal legislation. But this is a hit and miss affair. In some cases, such as the jailing of Pussy Riot members, legal procedures have been far from ideal. Similarly, with regard to the liquidation of the oligarchs as a class, again the picture was mixed. The three best known oligarchs – Vladimir Gusinsky, Boris Berezovsky and Mikhail Khodorkovsky – either moved into exile, in the first two cases, or into prison, in the latter case (see Box 4.1). Boris Berezovsky died in exile in Britain in

2013. Whatever the motivation for their removal from influence by the Russian regime, their vast media holdings largely ended up in the hands of the state, and their role as a source of funding and support for groups opposing the Putin regime was diminished.

Whatever the interpretation put on these developments, it can be argued that since 2000 there has been a process of 'securitization' going on in Russian life, in two senses. First, in the technical, political science sense of 'securitization', policy decisions have been made for avowed reasons of state security. This is not a phenomenon unique to Russia, and indeed the 'war on terror' has been a justification for policy decisions the world over since 2001. In the Russian case, decisions such as halting the direct election of regional leaders in 2005, harassing certain religious groups for possession of extremist literature, and limiting the media and electoral space of opposition voices have all been justified by reference to state security. Policy decisions across a range of areas have been justified by reference to, for example, 'food security', 'energy security', and even – in the religious sphere – 'spiritual security'.

Second, the term 'securitization' can be used to refer to the increasing role of the security services in Russia since 2000. Indeed, it could be argued that such a process began under Yeltsin, as three of his last four prime ministers all had backgrounds in the security services. Certainly there has been for some time a group of influential figures in Russian politics known as the *siloviki*, which is the Russian term for men with career experience in the armed force ministries and security services. While there may be arguments over the precise make-up and role of this group, the term has come to be used to signify those who prefer state control and lean towards authoritarian over democratic means. They do not dominate Russian politics unchallenged – and indeed former President Medvedev himself does not really fit into this group – but they are undoubtedly a powerful influence. Aside from, or perhaps alongside, the *siloviki* as a political force, the presence of the FSB (the domestic successor to the KGB) in Russian life has also become more pronounced, with media, NGO and business circles among others regularly reporting that an awareness of potential FSB attitudes to their activities has influenced their behaviour. While being some way from the KGB-dominated state of the Soviet years, again the pendulum has swung back from the weakened and demoralized state of Russia's security services in the 1990s.

Civil society in Russia

The term 'civil society' commonly refers to those non-governmental groups and organizations that operate in public life and express the particular interests of their members. So, for example, charitable organizations, campaign groups, independent trade unions, faith-based communities and so on would fit into this category. A healthy civil society is a sign of a consolidated democratic system where people are free to organize and campaign. As recent research by Elena Chebankova sets out, Russia today does have, behind its some-what rigid formal socio-political structures, a complex society where the diverse interests of distinct groups create 'a kind of pluralism' (2013: 1). In contemporary Russia, however, the development of civil society has been hampered by several factors. We conclude this chapter by considering four such factors: the Soviet collapse, the state's desire to control civil society, the co-opting of civil society by the state, and entanglement of Russian policy on civil society with questions of security and anti-Westernism.

First, the Soviet collapse undermined a potential base for civil society that had been emerging in the late Soviet period, as the underground dissident groups of the Brezhnev years developed, encouraged by Gorbachev's *glasnost* policies, into openly operating informal organizations independent of the Communist Party of the Soviet Union. The chaos and hardship of the Soviet endgame undercut such progress. Research by Marc Morjé Howard (2003) found that, of all the post-Communist countries, Russia had the weakest civil society in the 1990s, and the desperate economic straits in which most Russians found themselves in those years left little energy and motivation for doing much beyond devoting oneself to earning a living.

The second factor to consider is the state's desire to retain the means by which it might control civil society, should it deem the need to have arisen. The concept of 'snatch-squad control' offers a useful analogy for explaining how this works. The analogy is straightforward. When policing a crowd, a snatch squad may identify particular individuals, move in, arrest them, and leave the vast majority of the crowd alone. In this way, the crowd is controlled by the example of the power that the police can deploy if so minded. In Russia, beginning with the religion law of 1997, and progressing through laws on social organizations, political parties, extremists, migration, foreigners, the media, information security and NGOs, there are sufficient regulations in most cases for the state to move with a legal basis against groups or individuals that might be considered in some sense a threat. In particular, the minutiae of registration regulations and the ill-defined catch-all nature of some provisions – for example, the law on extremism's ban on 'the propaganda of exclusiveness, superiority, or inferiority' – mean that, for groups making up civil society, transgressions of the law, witting or not, are relatively straightforward to allege or identify.

As well as seeking to control civil society by a system of registration in the gift of the state, the Putin regime has also sought to co-opt and create its own movements within the space occupied by civil society. A fine example of this is the development of the pro-Putin political youth organization, *Nashi* (the Russian word meaning 'Ours'). *Nashi* was established, with support from the state, in the wake of the 'Orange revolution' in Ukraine in 2004, where street protests against flawed elections led to the results being annulled and overturned in a re-run. Although Russia's socio-political circumstances differed markedly from those in Ukraine, the Putin regime feared that such street activism might become a threat in Russia. *Nashi* provided both a genuine educational and social group for young people supportive of the regime and interested in civil engagement, and also – on occasion – a force that could be mobilized effectively to counter oppositionist street politics. From the perspective of developing civil society, the case of *Nashi* is problematic. It could be argued that *Nashi*, and other groups backed by the state, represent a Russian form of civil society, where the role of the state removes a degree of independence, but none the less distinct groups and movements remain, with a voice, a legal identity and some influence. However, from the perspective of developing democracy, the creation of state-supported groups that in turn support the state, while having some validity, does not in itself equate to a flourishing of civil society. While it is common for NGOs across the world to co-operate with, and receive money from, governments, the criticism often levelled at Russia is that groups that want to operate more independently of the Russian state, or to receive money from abroad, are less able to flourish.

The final factor to consider, in relation to hindering the development of civil society in Russia, is the fact that Russian policy on civil society has become caught up in questions of security and anti-Westernism. For some time now, the FSB has considered many NGOs to be tools of foreign influence. The Russian state under the

Putin regime has wished to develop a native civil society, not one shaped externally. Such thinking influenced changes to the laws affecting NGOs in 2006, resulting in more stringent and intrusive registration requirements, particularly with regard to groups based abroad. In 2012, regulations were tightened still further, when a law was passed requiring that all NGOs receiving funding from abroad must register as 'foreign agents' if they were engaged in 'political activity', rather broadly defined. In Russian, as in English, the term 'foreign agents' carries overtones of a lack of patriotism at best, and of treason at worst. At the same time as placing such an imposition, which comes with significantly increased monitoring from the FSB, on NGOs in receipt of overseas funding, President Putin also announced a significant increase in domestic funding for NGOs. Developments like this continue to raise questions as to the viability of a civil society in Russia independent of the state. They also impose yet more regulations with which NGOs must comply, thereby making it easier for the state to charge its less favoured NGOs with non-compliance.

So, the situation in civil society to some extent mirrors that in other spheres of Russian socio-political life. Great strides were made in the 1990s towards the democratization of Russia, and yet the ideological commitment of the regime to democracy remains uncertain. There was freedom for all sorts of groups to establish themselves in the 1990s – albeit that those with Western support, particularly financial, flourished most readily – but now there is greater control and an increasing percentage of religious organizations, political parties and other elements of civil society are having action taken against them on the basis of ever tighter laws governing civil society. The Russian regime sought, first of all, a manageable state, declaring that this was necessary to facilitate further moves towards a deeper democratic society. Developments in recent years demonstrate that the state's emphasis remains on the management of society, and ever closer management at that, ostensibly to defend the interests of Russia. Such a position has widespread support in Russia. The consideration of rights and freedoms from the perspective of geopolitical competition, rather than from a perspective of their essential qualities, has long muddied analytical and empirical waters and seems likely to do so for many years to come.

8

Culture and Media

In September 2012, Working Title Films released an innovative and engaging film version of the great Russian author Leo Tolstoy's classic nineteenth-century novel, *Anna Karenina*, with British actress and Hollywood star Keira Knightley playing the eponymous heroine. The Russian release came an unusually long time afterwards, in January 2013. Veteran Russian film producer, Sergei Solovyov, was quoted as saying, of film distributors in Russia, 'the idea of trying to peddle a movie about Anna Karenina horrifies them: No one in the younger generation knows who she is.' This vignette from contemporary culture encapsulates some of the themes pertinent to our consideration of culture and media in Russia. The notion that no one knows one of Russia's, indeed the world's, greatest literary classics any more is certainly exaggerated; after all, Tolstoy's works are still on the curriculum in Russian schools. However, the last two or three decades have seen an opening up of Russia to a more global cultural experience. The ideologically driven censorship and travel bans of the Soviet years have disappeared, and cultural globalization has spread, along with the development of the internet and social media.

This chapter explores the balance between globalization and the preservation – indeed promotion – of Russia's own national identity in the twenty-first century through such means as culture, sport and national celebrations. Not only has Russian national identity been nurtured, it had to be re-discovered to some extent after the collapse of a Soviet Union formally wedded to internationalism and an omnipresent Marxism–Leninism. As well as looking at culture, broadly defined, this chapter also considers developments in the media, including social media, in recent years. Since the 1990s, control of the media by the state has tightened, though it remains far from the rigid and all-encompassing censorship of the Soviet years. We consider here questions of media ownership, the deaths of some prominent journalists, and how such issues relate to freedom of speech in Russia today.

Russian national identity

There are few countries in the world where the concept of a 'national idea' is quite as strong as it is in Russia. Nor perhaps are there many countries where arguments are so fierce over precisely what makes up this idea, and how important it is. In order to understand a little about how Russians live, it is essential to know something of the shared experiences and narratives that shape national consciousness, as well as the story that Russia's rulers tell about their country today. A glance at the titles of a number of books written in recent years reveals that there are elements commonly acknowledged as essential to Russia that go beyond political and socio-economic questions to touch something deeper. *Russia and Soul*, *The Agony of the Russian Idea*, *Russian Messianism*, *Russia in Search of Itself* – all of these are academic books published from a range of disciplines that have in common an awareness of distinctive elements of the Russian identity.

The 'Russian Idea' is central to Russia's national identity. At its broadest, it encompasses the sense that there is a destiny and identity inherent within Russia that is not Western, that has different cultural roots and different core values. It is the idea – or perhaps more accurately, the myth – that Russians are less materialistic, less individualistic, and less shallow than their Western counterparts, and instead have a greater commitment to spiritual values, egalitarianism, community, and the deeper mysteries of faith and eschatology. The empirical evidence for such claims is weak, but their strength comes in their widespread acceptance. Russians go to places of worship and get involved in the collective institutions of civil society far less than do – in this order – Americans, Western Europeans, and even the inhabitants of other post-Communist states. None the less, such hard data as church attendance figures and engagement in civil society do not measure a more elusive inner sense and self-perception. Indeed, an authentically Russian response might be to deem as typically Western and materialist any attempt to measure the inchoate depth of such concepts as community, togetherness, spirituality and national identity.

It is perhaps difficult to talk about a vague 'Russian Idea' without falling into clichés and generalizations. As Dale Pesmen points out in her book *Russia and Soul*:

> Some Russians and others dismiss Russian soul as a hackneyed notion irrelevant to tough millennial post-Soviets. Some mourn it, implying that whatever it was died. Some figure good riddance. In all these cases, Russian soul's vitality is assumed to have disappeared. Russian soul was certainly a myth, notion, image, consoling fiction, trope of romantic national self-definition, and what romantic foreigners came to Russia for. (Pesmen, 2000)

Pesman's research notes that many Russians themselves are aware of the myth-like elements of the Russian Idea, and talk of it in self-mocking, satirical terms. And yet, as noted in many places in this book, there is a reality to the generalizations that finds outlet in political debate, policy formation, international relations and so on.

James Billington identifies three forces that give Russian culture its distinctiveness (Billington, 2004):

- *A traditional religious base*. During the 1990s – with the loss of the certainties of communism – the Russian state, and arguably its people, sought to define a national idea. Indeed a state-sponsored competition was held, with a prize awarded to the essayist who best summed up what it meant to be Russian. Almost without fail, writers and politicians – atheists and believers alike – settled on Russian Orthodoxy as a key locus of Russian identity. Russian Orthodoxy celebrates the mystery of faith, ahead of the intellectual explanations of Western Protestants. It promotes a community of believers ahead of the hierarchies of Roman Catholicism. Politicians of the left, right and centre frequently seek to portray themselves as supporters of Orthodoxy, since nothing else better serves to identify them with Russia, its uniqueness, its history and its people.

  Religion in Russia, however, is not just about nationalism and Orthodoxy, or even about nationalism and Islam. There is a tradition of an openness among the Russian people to spirituality, as opposed to organized and doctrinally precise religion. Russian peasant faith often drew from diverse sources, including Asiatic shamanism and paganism. Within such a setting, superstitions, premonitions, curses, blessings and ecstatic experiences all had a place. As too did the figure of the 'Holy Man' or 'Holy Fool', archetypically a bearded, somewhat wild, mystical figure who might live apart from society and be called upon as an adviser and healer. Grigory Rasputin, the womanizing Siberian monk who wielded significant influence in the court of the last Tsar, is a version of this figure. Such spiritual and mystical elements of life do not by any means belong solely to Russia's past; they remain part of the experience of many Russian citizens today. In 2012, a book recounting the recent and contemporary spiritual experiences of a Russian Orthodox monk sold in the millions in Russia (*Nesvyatye svyatye*, translated into English under the title *Everyday Saints and other stories* (Shevkunov 2012)).

- *Periodic borrowing from the West.* As noted in Chapter 2, the question of whether Russia should emulate the West or present a superior alternative is a recurrent feature in Russian history. Borrowing from the West entails an ambiguity, with a desire to take the best that the West can offer while retaining Russian identity and resisting the overwhelming of Russian culture. Russia since the later 1990s has demonstrated this ambiguity in many areas, with a broad opening up to the West resulting in the cautious embrace of many of the facets of 'globalization', combined with a determined resistance to what the more extreme opponents of Westernization have called 'cultural genocide'.

- *A special feeling for land and nature.* Russia was urbanized more recently than most other European nations, and in most families it is only a matter of going back a couple of generations or so to find rural, predominantly peasant, roots. Furthermore, the vast expanse of Russia's territory means that it contains some of the most sparsely populated areas on earth. Nature and the land continue to play a part in many lives, even for urban inhabitants. The celebrated *dacha* (summer house) beyond the boundaries of the cities is the destination for millions of Russians in the summer months. Trips to the countryside to pick berries and mushrooms in season are standard motifs in Russian literature, and continue to be regular occurrences for many Russians. At the *dachas*, and even within the environs of the cities, private plots where vegetables and fruit can be grown are common – indeed, there is strong evidence to suggest that such private agriculture kept the Soviet Union going when the official state-administered agricultural industry failed.

Alongside the elusive questions of the Russian soul and the Russian Idea, it is also possible to point to identifiable experiences in history and repeated features of everyday life that help to explain contemporary Russia's cultural identity.

Death and martial culture

The experience of violent death and social chaos marked the Russian people as a whole in the twentieth century. From the First World War of 1914–18, followed by revolution in 1917 and the civil war of 1918–20, with its attendant shortages and famines, through the largely self-inflicted famine of 1932–3, and the mass arrests and executions of the Stalinist terror – over 30 million Russians died prematurely even before the Second World War began. Between 1941 and 1945 the war claimed a further 28 million victims, far more than in any of the other combatant nations. Soviet military losses alone were over 8 million, when US military losses were under 350,000 and British losses nearer to 300,000. Such experiences cannot but leave an impact on the Russian people. No family remained untouched by the devastation of war. In comparison, the second half of the twentieth century was relatively less traumatic, with the war in Afghanistan (1979–88) being the major conflict of note. None the less, some observers have portrayed the upheavals of the 1990s as of significant magnitude, with British historian, Christopher Read, writing tentatively of the difficulties involved in comparing the political mass murders of the Stalin years with the 'economic mass murder' of the 1990s (Read, 2001: 230).

The impact of the Second World War on the Russian nation is difficult to overstate. If the veneration of veterans is noteworthy in, say, Great Britain or the United States, then it is doubly so in Russia, which has, of course, a particularly Russo-centric view of the Second World War. The Great Patriotic War, as Russia terms this war, started for the Soviet Union when Germany invaded in June 1941, and ended with the German surrender on 9 May 1945. Little mention is made of the pact between Germany and the Soviet Union in 1939, which led directly to the occupation of a divided Poland by invading Nazi and Soviet forces. Nor is much made of the continuation of the Second World War outside Europe until victory over Japan in September 1945. For Russians, 'Victory Day' is 9 May, which remains a public holiday in Russia. From 2008 onwards, the Victory Day celebrations saw the restoration of a major military parade through Red Square in Moscow (see Illustration 9.1 on page

207). During the atheistic rule of the Soviet Communist Party, elements of reverence for the military provided key unifying features where perhaps religion might previously have played a role. For example, the tradition developed that, on their wedding day, couples would follow a civil ceremony with a visit to the local war memorial, where photographs would be taken. This practice continues today.

In contemporary Russia, conscription into the military remains in place. As well as providing military training for conscripts and making a significant contribution to Russia's desire to staff a near million-strong army, military service also provides a unifying experience – 'cultural' in the broadest sense of the term – for men across the country. However, it has become increasingly difficult in the post-Soviet era for the practice of conscription to achieve these aims. A large number of potential conscripts manage to avoid conscription by taking advantage of the variety of exemptions and loopholes available, or by simply not responding to the call-up in such numbers that chasing up all the 'no shows' becomes too logistically burdensome for the armed forces. Each year, around half a million young men reach the call-up age of 18. Of these, almost half (244,000 in 2012) do not respond to their call-up notices, and students in higher education are generally exempt. In 2013, the military anticipated recruiting only 153,000 conscripts. The reduction of the period of conscription from two years to one in 2008 was partly designed to discourage such draft avoidance, and included the closure of a number of such loopholes. None the less, current shortfalls have led to calls from some for more students to be called up, and even for women to be allowed to join the annual call-up if they wish. Such measures are proposed by those keen on maintaining conscription. To many others, though, including some within the Ministry of Defence, a conscription-based army represents an anachronism in the twenty-first century. Attempts to move towards professional, rather than conscripted, armed forces have been discussed in government circles since before the Soviet collapse. Current plans anticipate that there will be 425,000 professional soldiers by 2017, up from 240,000 in 2013. However, even were such a rapid increase to be achieved, continued insistence on an armed forces at least double that size implies a continued reliance on the uncertain conscription process.

Widespread respect for the armed forces still exists in Russia, where post-Soviet opinion polls have long shown the army to be the second most-trusted public organization, after the Russian Orthodox

Church. Physical expression of respect for these pillars of Russian identity can be seen in developments in Moscow in the second half of the 1990s. In 1995, in time for the fiftieth anniversary of the end of the Second World War, a vast new memorial, 'Victory Park', was opened. In 1996, a statue of the most famous Soviet commander of the Second World War, Marshal Zhukov, was erected near the entrance to Red Square. Between 1995 and 1997, the Cathedral of Christ the Saviour, in which Pussy Riot performed their anti-Putin punk prayer in 2012 (see Chapter 7), was built in time to mark the somewhat contrived celebratory anniversary of 850 years since the foundation of the city.

Putin's political narrative and the use of history

Since Vladimir Putin first became President of Russia in 2000, Russia's ruling regime has put significant effort into the construction of a national narrative that would make sense of historical developments, explain current policies, and develop a national idea suited to contemporary Russia. National identities partly arise from below, from 'the people', and are partly created from above, by the rulers. Both of these elements draw on history and notions of national consciousness. To understand contemporary Russia, it is vital to know what it says about itself, or, more precisely, what its leaders say to its people.

During the Yeltsin presidency (1991–9), the regime had failed in its attempts to build Russian national identity. In terms of drawing on history and notions of national consciousness, there were three particular problems. First, Yeltsin's national identity narrative was polarizing, not unifying. It centred on a wholesale rejection of the Communist past – a stance particularly evident in the pivotal presidential election of 1996, when Yeltsin was presented as the only hope for preventing a return to communism. Second, symbols are key in the creation of national identity, and the Yeltsin regime struggled to find appropriate ones. At the 2000 Olympic games in Sydney, when Russia's gold medallists stood on the podium, they had no recognizable national anthem to sing. Russia under Yeltsin had adopted a far-from-rousing provisional anthem called 'Patriotic Song', written in the nineteenth century by composer Mikhail Glinka and lacking in words. Nor did the new national holidays of that era strike many Russians as appropriate symbols for national celebration – Constitution Day (12 December) marked 1993's flawed constitutional referendum; and Independence Day (12 June) marked Russia's break with the Soviet Union. The very newness of such symbols meant that they had shallow roots in the national consciousness. Third, the narrative and symbols around the Russian national identity in the Yeltsin years came to mark a period of national decline. They became associated not with Russian greatness but with poverty, lawlessness, a weak pro-Western foreign policy and a corrupt elite.

President Putin's central narrative of power initially sought to define his period in office positively against the alleged failures of the Yeltsin years. The key *leitmotifs* of Putin's national identity discourse became stability, unity and the notion of Russia as a great power. These themes have been to the fore since the beginning of Putin's presidency in 2000, and have developed in substance and prevalence in official discourse.

Perhaps the first issue in the Putin regime's narrative was the question of what was to be done with the Soviet years. Too often in the Western media, the impression is given that somehow contemporary Russia is, for want of a better word, 're-Sovietizing'. In other words, becoming increasingly like the old Soviet Union. We have argued in several places in this book that many developments – centralizing the government, reducing space for opposition and civil society, creating uncompetitive elections, believing that Russia should have a sphere of influence in international relations – have echoes of Soviet-era practices. Let us be clear, though, that such practices are not exclusively Soviet in character. More importantly, when it comes to the core element of the Soviet regime – namely, a belief in the Communist ideology – the Russian government has no time for that at all.

At the beginning of his presidency Putin's 'eve of millennium' address tried to explain the balance he sought in dealing with the Soviet past. On the one hand, he talked about the 'outrageous price our country and its people had to pay for that Bolshevik experiment', and the 'historic futility' of Communism's 'blind alley ... far away from the mainstream of civilization'. At the same time, though, he refused to deny the 'unquestionable achievements of those times'. In adopting state symbols, Putin sought to bring together disparate elements of Russia's past – the coat of arms from the pre-imperial era, the flag from the imperial period, and the Soviet anthem, but with new words. These were a symbolic representation of the commitment to unity, stability and Russia's great-power status, which we have noted as the *leitmotifs* of the official Russian identity today. The political vehicle created to back Putin in parliament in 2000 was given the name Unity, and later, United Russia. The rhetoric of stability is related to that of unity. In his first public statement as acting president on the eve of the millennium, Putin declared that the Russian people had had their fill of cataclysmic events and radical reforms; he promised to bring stability.

These early symbolic statements and gestures set down the base on which the revived concept of Russian national identity was to be built in the Putin era. Its content was then developed by Putin and his colleagues through engagement with Russian history and philosophy, and an ever-widening public promotion of a Russian national identity that embraced the Tsarist era, lauded those who fought against communism, and yet refused to reject entirely the experiences of the Russian people during the Soviet years. Russia's national identity, as still put forward in presidential statements and ever more prevalent in political discourse, emphasizes the notion of a distinct Russian civilization that differs from 'the West'. This allows an emphasis on a 'Russian democracy', suited to the circumstances of Russia, and is echoed in Putin's reactions to criticism from the West that he has taken Russia down an anti-democratic path.

The most stark symbolic break with the Communist era made by President Putin was the abolition in 2004 of 7 November as a national holiday. During the Soviet era this date was Revolution Day, the main Soviet holiday and symbol of Soviet power, with its massive military parades through Red Square in front of the Party leadership. Under Yeltsin, the day remained on the list of national holidays, although in 1996 Yeltsin had renamed it the Day of Reconciliation and Accord. Under Putin, 7 November was removed completely from the list of official holidays, and National Unity Day on 4 November replaced Revolution Day. National Unity Day commemorates the liberation of Moscow from the Poles in 1612. This event ended the civil war and foreign intervention of the 'Time of Troubles' and ushered in the Romanov dynasty, which remained in power until the revolution of 1917.

When National Unity Day was first celebrated in 2005, television programmes were broadcast explaining its significance. Clear parallels were drawn between the civil conflict and crisis of the early-seventeenth-century 'Time of Troubles', which were ended with victory over the Poles in 1612, and the 'time of troubles' experienced by Russia in the 1990s. The implication was that, just as the Romanov dynasty brought stability in 1612, so the Putin era brought stability after the chaos of the Yeltsin years. Other elements were also woven into the narrative around National Unity Day. It celebrates a Russian victory over Western domination, symbolized by Orthodox Russia beating Catholic Poland. Its instigation also facilitated a dig at the oligarchs, who flourished under Yeltsin. The 'seven *boyars*' who reputedly sought their own personal interest, wealth and power in league with enemies of Russia abroad in the seventeenth-century 'Time of Troubles', stood as types for the 'seven bankers', the seven major oligarchs of the Yeltsin era, broadly accused of the same behaviour. For a regime that had identified oligarchs such as Berezovsky and Khodorkovsky as among its chief opponents, such a narrative around Russian national identity was seen as particularly helpful.

The process of re-creating a narrative of Russian national identity involves symbols, discourse and a good deal of official effort in introducing new national holidays, propagandizing a particular version of history through speeches, ceremonies, books and the media, and organizing international conferences and cultural events. The result is a narrative that is in line with the broad policy statements of the current regime. However, this focus on national identity does not have a straightforward political effect. Very little of the effort expended in crafting official narratives around historical figures, philosophical treatises and civilizational dialogues has any direct impact on the mass of Russian people. The discourses of Putin's national identity project are too neat for the complexities of everyday political life. They contain ambiguities and tensions around issues such as the lack of progress in fighting corruption, whether Russia is competing with or working alongside other major powers, and the disjunction between overlapping notions of the West, the US and Europe.

One such ambiguity often picked up on by Western observers relates to the place of Stalin in Russian history. As we have noted, the narrative of Russian identity developed during the Putin years seeks to distance itself from the political elements of the Soviet era while acknowledging that not everything that happened during those decades needs to be disparaged. At the same time, we have seen the central place in Russian identity of the Second World War and its continued position as the key national holiday in Russia. The clear difficulty is that the Soviet Union's leader in this great victory was also its most brutal Communist dictator, Josef Stalin. There remains a degree of ambiguity in the treatment of Stalin in Russia. On the one hand, the deaths of millions during the Stalinist dictatorship are acknowledged – for example, there is a Gulag (forced labour camp) museum in central Moscow, and Solzhenitsyn's novel *Gulag Archipelago* is a set text in Russian schools. On the other hand, Stalin is by no means so thoroughly denounced as, for example, Hitler is in Germany today. It is hard to imagine the Nazi equivalent in today's Berlin of the renovation of Kurskaya metro station in central Moscow in 2009, which included, carved atop pillars in the entrance hall, a verse from the old Soviet national anthem declaring that 'Stalin raised us to be loyal to the nation; He inspired us to work and be heroic.'

Culture and contemporary reality

The importance of literature and art in the lived experience of educated Russians was heightened during much of the twentieth century by the strict censorship that the Soviet authorities exercised in these areas. State control of literature, music and art in order to force it into the straitjacket of service to what was a fundamentally utilitarian, anti-spiritual and philistine regime affected the intellectual psyche of the Russian people.

To love art forms for their own sake was to defend a small area of personal independence from the authorities. Literature and music were used to express subtle – and not so subtle – dissatisfaction with the dominant ruling party, and to interpret these messages required a high-level of artistic literacy. Debates still occur, for example, over the precise meaning of passages in Shostakovich's symphonies. In the Soviet era, the heavy literary journals would regularly sell out on publication, and people would pass round carefully copied typescripts of banned works. The word *samizdat* (literally 'self-published') became – like *glasnost* a decade or so later – a term sufficiently well-used to be understood by many in the West, referring as it did to illegal literature of all forms, from heavyweight novels, through political statements against the regime, to religious tracts.

Although strong state censorship was in place for most of the Soviet era, the state education system none the less helped to produce a highly literate population that knew not only the Russian classics of Pushkin, Tolstoy and Dostoevsky, but also a range of foreign classics. Russian knowledge of, and respect for, the works of Shakespeare, for example, can often seem to exceed that in England. In the early 1990s, as the Soviet Union dissolved itself and censorship disappeared, many Russians avidly snapped up those works that had previously not been available. Multi-volume sets of the works of dissident

Soviet authors such as Solzhenitsyn, Pasternak and Bulgakov appeared on the bookstalls swiftly set up around the Moscow metro system, alongside complete works of other literary giants, copies of the Bible, and the ubiquitous 'Teach Yourself English' courses that were increasingly *de rigueur* for Russians seeking to make a life for themselves in the uncertain new world of the market economy.

If at first in the post-Soviet era the bookstalls and kiosks of Moscow reflected the relatively highbrow tastes of the intelligentsia and focused on Russian works, they swiftly branched out as the almost anarchic freedoms of the early 1990s took hold. On the bookstalls, classic literature began to give way to detective stories, thrillers, science fiction and fantasy. Russian translations of Western bestsellers such as Agatha Christie and Tom Clancy elbowed the more highbrow literature out of the way, and Russian authors themselves moved into these more popular genres.

As the 1990s progressed, however, the somewhat naïve excitement of the first flushes of cultural liberty began to give way to a more sophisticated and unique popular culture. The clichés of the late Soviet period revolved around the supposed desire among young Russians for anything Western – scarcely a Western traveller to the Soviet Union in the last decades of its existence was sent off without being advised to pack an extra pair of Levis for selling on arrival – and the apparent preoccupation of Russians with outdated Western music, notably the Beatles and 1970s heavy rock bands. (Former president Dmitrii Medvedev embodies this latter cliché, with a genuine and much publicized devotion to the music of English rock band Deep Purple, who played a private concert for his benefit in the Kremlin in early 2008, forty years after the band was formed.)

Whatever truth exists in these clichés, the younger generation of Russians swiftly blew it away in the 1990s. Russian youth movements emerged with a distinctly indigenous edge; literary genres and musical styles alike drew on Western examples and swiftly added Russian ingredients. Russian detective writers found plenty of material in the crime-ridden business culture of the new Russia, and other genres too (notably fantasy and science fiction) soon identified their own authors instead of merely accepting translations of Western bestsellers. A similar process of adoption and adaptation occurred across musical genres, culminating in the unprecedented – and short-lived – dominance of the UK and European pop and dance charts for several weeks in 2003 by Russian artists, the teenage duo Tatu.

Literature

As with any country, the literature of Russia reflects the state of the nation. The great novels of Tolstoy and Dostoevsky in the second half of the nineteenth century addressed the 'accursed questions' of the human soul, alongside the questions of Russia's place in the world and the social divisions within Russian society. We have mentioned already in Chapter 2 the prescience of Chekhov's play, *The Cherry Orchard* (1904), closing with the sound of an axe striking a tree, symbolizing the blows being struck to the old social order as the revolutionary twentieth century dawned.

During the Soviet era, the Communist regime sought to subjugate literature to its own demands and ideas. From the early 1930s onwards, the genre of 'socialist realism' told stirring tales of devotion to work and building the new industrialized Soviet state; for example, in works such as Nikolai Ostrovsky's *How the Steel was Tempered* (1934). The official policy was that literature should be positive and optimistic. The counterpart of socialist realist literature in painting and sculpture was the healthy, well-proportioned, musclebound worker, male or female, sleeves rolled-up, a smile on the face, and a hammer or sickle raised aloft. Such images fitted the self-conceptualization of the Communist elite, which also controlled all publishers, exhibition halls, concert venues and so on.

Of course, the best artists and writers, almost by their nature, are most unlikely to shape their output in line with such crass strictures. Pasternak and Solzhenitsyn were both awarded the Nobel Prize for Literature, though the Soviet regime persuaded Pasternak to decline his award. Both smuggled their best known works, respectively *Dr Zhivago* and *The Gulag Archipelago*, to the West for publication and were vilified by the authorities at home. Pasternak remained in the Soviet Union until his death in 1960. Solzhenitsyn was exiled until finally returning to Russia in 1994, where he was lionized by successive presidents. He died in 2008, shortly before his ninetieth birthday. Other writers, such as Yurii Trifonov (1925–81), somehow managed to remain within the pale of official Soviet literature and yet touch on topics which, so far as their readers were concerned, were much more 'realistic' than socialist realism's tales of building communism. Trifonov wrote, earlier than most but relatively obliquely, about the difficulties of the Stalin years.

From the 1960s onwards, fiction dealing with the more risqué topics – such as the purges, the drudgery of modern urban life, and the double domestic/professional burden carried by Soviet women – became increasingly common. While the state sought to control and guide the content of literature throughout the Soviet era, the degree of artistic licence that was allowed ebbed and flowed at different times. There was a cultural thaw in the Khrushchev years (1953–64), and in the late 1960s and early 1970s more controversial works, such as Solzhenitsyn's devastating labour-camp critique, *One Day in the Life of Ivan Denisovich* (1962), were published in the Soviet Union, before later being banned.

As the Soviet era came to an end and censorship disappeared, it was something of an irony that the state of Russian literature can be said to have declined initially. There were several reasons for this:

- the new freedoms meant that many readers turned to what had previously been unavailable – the banned works of Soviet dissidents and of Western literature;
- the removal of the dead hand of the state from its monopoly control of publishing meant an end to the focus on more literary works – albeit of varying quality – which the Soviet system encouraged; and
- in the immediate post-Soviet years, there was a tendency among Russia's more literary authors, revelling in their freedom, to become more linguistically experimental, playing with language in a way which was not particularly easy to translate and make accessible to readers beyond Russia.

For most of the 1990s, then, pulp fiction became a force in Russian literature, with a number of authors selling books in their millions, producing novels at a great rate, and being paid royalties far below what would be paid to similarly successful authors in the West. The stories of Aleksandra Marinina, Viktor Dotsenko and many others were set in the world of the mafia and criminal gangs. Liberally sprinkled with the jargon of that milieu, such works did not shy away from the sex and violence associated with the lives they portrayed. The very best-selling authors were set apart from their competitors by the creation of strong hero figures who became the centre of their novels, such as Marinina's female detective, Anastasia Kamenskaya, the eponymous heroine of a successful TV series.

Literary purists bemoaned such a state of affairs, as Russia became far more like the rest of the world in its dealings with literature. No longer were writers quite so venerated and so much a part of public and political discourse as they had previously been. In many ways, the Russian people's special relationship with literature has gone – or at the very least, been put on hold. None the less, the literary scene in contemporary Russia has gradually regained strength since the turn of the century helped to some extent – certainly in terms of publicity – by the establishment of prizes such as the Russian Booker Prize, the Big Book Prize (with a generous cash award, partly funded by the Russian state), and the National Bestseller Award. The Russian state has also put considerable effort into promoting Russian culture, including new Russian authors, abroad. The Russian Federal Agency for Press and Mass Communication sponsors both the 'Яead.Russia' initiative, which publishes Russian authors in translation and backs an annual translation prize, and Academia Rossica, an organization set up in 2000 to enhance cultural links between Russia and the English-speaking world. Along similar lines, the Russkiy Mir (Russian World) Foundation, was established by presidential decree in 2007 to promote the Russian language around the world.

Prominent among the themes apparent in contemporary Russian literature is a future-oriented, often dystopian, vision. Several such works have recently been translated into English, including:

- Olga Slavnikova's 2006 Russian Booker winning novel *2017*, which is set in the mountains of Russia a hundred years after the Russian revolution, and explores the tension between the spiritual, the natural and the material.
- Vladimir Sorokin's *Day of the Oprichnik*, set in 2028, where a New Russia is ruled by a regime that restores the *oprichniki*, a force of men infamously brutal during the rule of Ivan the Terrible (1547– 84), loyal to the monarch and tasked with suppressing opposition, in a future that combines high-tech, drug-fuelled extravagance with brutality and magic.
- Dmitrii Glukhovskii's *Metro2033* imagines a post-apocalyptic world in the Moscow metro system, with Moscow above ground made uninhabitable by nuclear fall-out. The fractured history of Russia is apparent in this subterranean setting where different metro lines are occupied by different groups, such as the Communist Red Line, the fascist Fourth Reich, the Trotskyists and the 1905 Confederation. *Metro2033* became a bestseller and spawned not only a sequel, *Metro2034*, but a first-person shooter video game for Xbox gamers.

• The prolific Dmitrii Bykov has not only written biographies of Boris Pasternak and the author and singer Bulat Okudzhava, but also several novels, one of which, *ZhD* ('ЖД' in Russian), has been translated into English as *Living Souls*, and tells of a future civil war in a Russia that has lost its global standing.

Bykov, Slavnikova and Sorokin would be ranked among the 'big names' of contemporary Russian literature, and the translation of some of their works into English has given them a wider readership and demonstrated that Russian writers, to some extent backed by cultural organizations such as Academia Rossica, are re-taking their place in world literature. In the first post-Soviet decade or so, very few contemporary Russian writers were being translated into English, with two notable exceptions: Viktor Pelevin and Boris Akunin. Viktor Pelevin's prose reflects the chaotic Russia of the post-Soviet era, which his earlier work portrays. Pelevin's writing has depicted a nihilistic world infused with materialism, Buddhist philosophy, drug-taking, computer games, advertising slogans and violence. He writes in a style that is cinematic, episodic and impressionistic. In this approach, Pelevin certainly taps into and reflects a particular strand in Russian literature, his writing in places being reminiscent of Dostoevsky's psychological portraits, such as *Notes from the Underground*, or Pilnyak's portrayal of post-revolutionary Russia in 1919, *The Naked Year*.

Although Pelevin became known outside of Russia, the pseudonymous Boris Akunin made the breakthrough that Pelevin did not, becoming a Russian author – although born in Georgia, he has lived in Moscow for over half a century – who publishes and is a bestseller in Europe and the United States. Akunin writes detective thrillers, but of a slightly more genteel type than the blockbuster mafia novels discussed above. Instead, Akunin's stories are set in the nineteenth century, with his hero, Erast Fandorin, owing more to Sherlock Holmes than to contemporary movie heroes.

Other authors who would be counted among the leading literary figures in contemporary Russia, and have been translated in English, include:

• Mikhail Shishkin, whose novel *Maiden Hair* draws on his own experiences working with asylum seekers for the Swiss Immigration Department.
• Ludmila Ulitskaya, whose best-known work, *Daniel Stein, Interpreter*, presents a fictionalized account of the life of Oswald

Rufeisen, a Polish Jew who survived the holocaust, helping other Jews while forced to work for the Gestapo as an interpreter, and then converted to Christianity and became a Carmelite monk.

- Zakhar Prilepin, the author of *Sin*, for which he won the Super National Bestsellers Award, dubbed 'book of the decade', and which tells, in a series of short stories, its hero's life growing up in post-Soviet Russia's violence and poverty. Prilepin advocates opposition to the Putin regime from a Russian nationalist position, being a long-time member of the National Bolshevik Party.

In giving an overview of the literary scene in contemporary Russia, it is worth noting the movement known as 'new drama', which arose in the late 1990s and early 2000s. New drama is simply that – new plays written by previously unknown, usually young, authors, perhaps the best known being Vasilii Sigarev's 2001 play *Plasticine*, which won the Anti-Booker Prize for contemporary Russian literature. While hesitating to impose a common theme across the plays that would come under the 'new drama' heading, it is broadly the case that they follow much of the serious literature of the late 1990s and 2000s in addressing the dark side of contemporary life in Russia. *Plasticine* deals with urban degeneration, the Presnyakov brothers' best known play is *Terrorism*, and the Durnenkov brothers' Royal Shakespeare Company-commissioned *The Drunks* is built around a vodka-downing soldier returning home from the brutality of Chechnya.

New drama moves away from the traditional approaches – the plays are written very much in contemporary language, have a penchant for monologues, and can be somewhat cinematic in their approach – and away too from the traditional director-dominated theatre system. Some of this approach has spilled over into television, with writers such as Vyacheslav Durnenkov and Yurii Klavdiyev contributing to the controversial TV series *School*, which began on Russia's Channel One in 2010, and takes an uncompromising approach to depicting the sometimes cruel realities of life in some Russian schools today.

Film

As with so much in contemporary Russia, the world of film follows a pattern from the late 1980s to the present day of liberalization, Western influence, and then a rebirth of a more distinctly Russian approach. In the last years of the Soviet era the most noteworthy films were those that began to break the taboos imposed by state censorship. *The Cold Summer of '53* (1988) dealt with the labour camps and Khrushchev's decision in 1953 to release large numbers of criminal – as opposed to political – inmates, and *Little Vera* (1988) tackled the social problems of the late Soviet period, becoming renowned both for this and for breaking taboos by its inclusion of a nude scene.

When the Soviet Union collapsed, so too did its state-controlled and state-funded studio system, Goskino. This meant that funding for Russian films became increasingly scarce. At the same time, Russia opened up to Hollywood blockbusters. Many of the new glossy magazines that began to appear carried the sort of gossip and tittle-tattle surrounding the lives of American film stars that is familiar in the West, and the cinemas showed American films on global release, dubbed into Russian. This state of affairs continues today, but at the same time indigenous film-making has recovered to some extent.

In the 1990s, Nikita Mikhalkov's *Burnt by the Sun* – an account of the brutalities and betrayals of Stalin's terror – and Sergei Bodrov's *Prisoner of the Caucasus* (*Prisoner of the Mountains* in its Western release) were both critically acclaimed and funded by private investors, but made next to no box office impact in the West. *Burnt by the Sun* won an Oscar for best foreign film, and *Prisoner of the Caucasus* was nominated in the same category. Mikhalkov and Bodrov were both nominated again for best foreign film at the Oscars in 2008, with *12* and *The Mongol*, respectively. In a similar vein, in the early years of the twenty-first century, Aleksandr Sokurov's *Russian Ark* (2002) received rave reviews for its cinematographic brilliance. Lavishly costumed and filmed in the Hermitage Museum in St Petersburg, this sweep through 200 years of Russian history is the first full-length feature film ever to be composed of a single unedited shot running uninterrupted from beginning to end. Once again, though, artistic acclaim did not lead to box office success.

However, the Russian film industry began to recover in the second half of the twenty-first century's opening decade. This recovery can be credited to growing audiences and a huge increase in state support. A number of multi-screen complexes were built across Russia's major cities and the film distribution system consolidated, so that by 2012 the latest blockbusters could expect to open in around 2,000 cinemas across Russia. State-funding of Russian film-making increased from around US$17 million in 2000 to over US$200 million in 2013.

It is still foreign films that dominate audience figures in Russia today. In 2012, only one of the top 30 highest grossing films in Russia was Russian – Roman Prygunov's adaptation of Sergei Minaev's story of corporate greed, *Soulless* ('Dukhless'), which came in at number 25 in terms of receipts for the year. 2012 was, though, a particularly poor year for Russian films at the box office, as in all of the previous five years at least one Russian-made film had appeared in the Russia/CIS box office top ten. Nearly all of these films had very Russo-specific themes, for example, biopics of Soviet-era singer Vladimir Vysotsky (see 'Music, theatre and dance' below) and of revolution-era Admiral, Aleksandr Kolchak. However, not all Russian films and film-makers remain focused on domestic audiences. Kazakh-born director Timur Bekmambetov's hit films *Night Watch* (2004) and *Day Watch* (2006) were so successful in Russia that their worldwide distribution rights were snapped up by US distributors, and Bekmambetov himself has worked on Hollywood blockbusters as well as going on to direct two further Russian box office hits – *The Irony of Fate 2*, a sequel to the much loved Soviet film of 1971, and the comedy *Six Degrees of Celebration* (*Ёлки* in Russian).

Music, theatre and dance

Today's popular music scene in Russia mirrors to some extent the world of Russian film – much of what the public watch and listen to comes from the West, there are a number of home-grown stars who are scarcely known outside of Russia, and the occasional Russian singer or group enjoys wider international popularity. Pop duo Tatu made a brief breakthrough to top the charts in Europe in 2003. Tatu were also trail-blazers for Russia in the Eurovision Song Contest, finishing third in 2003, and singer Dima Bilan won Eurovision in 2008, a victory deemed highly prestigious in Russia. Names such as rock group Agata Kristi (who disbanded in 2010), singer-songwriter Nyusha, and alternative rock band Slot (with an English language album released in 2011) are reasonably well known in Russia but scarcely register in the West.

It is fair to say that an essential part of understanding the cultural make-up of Russians whose formative years were the 1960s and 1970s is an awareness of the icons of Soviet popular music. Two names in particular stand out, Vladimir Vysotsky and Alla Pugacheva:

- Vysotsky was a gravelly voiced, hard-living, maverick actor turned singer-songwriter, in some ways a Soviet Bob Dylan, in that he played guitar, had a highly distinctive voice, and – most significantly – wrote lyrics that were a literary and poetic comment on the world around him. Vysotsky died young, aged 42, in 1980. In his lifetime his politically 'unreliable' lyrics meant that none of his songs – with the sole exception of excerpts from a film soundtrack on flexi-disc – were officially released, and his following was built on unofficial cassettes of his music, and *samizdat* publications of lyrics. A biopic film, *Vysotsky. Thank You for Being Alive*, was released in 2011, with the screenplay by Vysotsky's son, Nikita. Its huge box-office success in Russia to a large extent reflected the affection in which he continues to be held by those who grew up in the late Soviet years.
- Alla Pugacheva, on the other hand, is a more traditional figure. She enjoyed official approval in the Soviet era, becoming the Soviet Union's first and greatest pop star. During her career she has sold over 200 million albums, and has successfully made the transition to the post-Soviet era, enjoying a legendary status among Russian citizens and émigrés alike – of a certain age.

In the sphere of classical music, Russia's ability to produce some of the world's finest performers continues unabated. In the Soviet era, the likes of the dissident cellist Mstislav Rostropovich or the pianist Sviatoslav Richter achieved global fame for their virtuosity. Russia can continue to boast some of the greatest of contemporary musicians, such as the conductor Valerii Gergiev, who has a famed commitment to Russian music, the pianist Boris Berezovsky, and the violinist judged by many to be the world's best – at least until an injury forced him to restrict his appearances after 2008 – Maksim Vengerov.

Musical theatre in Russia hit the headlines for all of the wrong reasons in 2002, when Chechen terrorists took hostage the audience at a Moscow performance of the musical *Nord-Ost*, and the culmination of the siege resulted in 130 deaths (see Chapter 3). None the less, musicals remain a staple of Moscow popular theatre, with productions of, for example, *Notre-Dame de Paris*, *Romeo and Juliet* and *Graf Orlov* in recent years.

In the world of Russian arts, it is not only *Nord-Ost* that has been in the news for unwanted reasons. One of Moscow's most famous buildings, the Bolshoi Theatre, underwent lengthy renovation between 2005 and its grand re-opening in 2011. As with other major

Illustration 8.1   The Bolshoi Theatre, Moscow, was re-opened in 2011 after a six-year renovation period

building projects in Russia, a corruption scandal marred the process. Then, shortly after the theatre's re-opening, the Bolshoi ballet company similarly attracted negative publicity, as its artistic director fell victim to an acid attack amid allegations of back-stage intrigue and mafia involvement. At least the opening of St Petersburg's Mariinsky II theatre and concert venue in 2013 attracted only mild criticism – from some who see its glass frontage as akin to a shopping mall. That is a matter of personal taste. What is not in doubt is that, standing just across the canal from the iconic nineteenth-century Mariinsky Theatre, the 2,000-seat Mariinsky II has state of the art acoustics and facilities. It was opened with a gala concert, conducted by Valerii Gergiev and including a speech from President Putin. Leaving aside the talk of terrorism and tawdry scandals, Russia's theatre, ballet and music scenes remain vibrant and world class.

Sport

The Soviet Union devoted impressive resources to the development of leading sportsmen and women, seeing international success as a sign of the supremacy of the socialist system. This socialist supremacy was apparent in some sports more than others, notably gymnastics and athletics. The tradition created in these sports continues today, and in addition new areas of excellence are springing up. What is more, the Russian state, is – like other states – once again using sport as a platform for proclaiming its standing in the world. The 2013 World Athletics Championships took place in Moscow, in a Luzhniki Stadium that was half empty for much of the proceedings. In 2014, the Winter Olympics came to Sochi, in southern Russia, near the now-disputed border with the Georgian region of Abkhazia, which Russia has recognized as independent since summer 2008. The Sochi Games have become a totemic event in Russia, spoken of as a key political marker in Russia's continuing development as a world power and vested with such significance that the authorities dare not let anything go wrong in the preparation for these Games. Unfortunately, however, preparation for them has been marred by costs far exceeding initial estimates, allegations of corruption tied to these increased costs, and the sort of inability to keep construction on schedule which marks many major sporting projects around the globe.

Four years after hosting the Winter Olympics in 2014, Russia will host an even bigger global sporting event, the football World Cup (see Box 8.1). The pleasures of sport aside, countries seek to host Olympics and World Cups for grand reasons of international prestige, local development and perceived economic benefits. As Aleksei Sorokin, the boss of the Russian organizing committee for the World Cup, puts it, hosting the World Cup will open Russia to the world on an unparalleled scale. Russian support for sport, particularly on the international stage, was demonstrated following the London Olympics of 2012 (see Box 8.2). On their return to Russia, all 129 of the country's Olympic medallists were presented with Audi cars – in different models for gold, silver and bronze – and many athletes received state awards.

In terms of spectator sports, football remains the most popular in Russia, although Russian teams have rarely enjoyed huge success either internationally or in European club competitions over the years. As Russia's economy improved in the first decade of this century, so too did Russia's standing in European football, partly boosted by major clubs having the wealth to sign foreign players and pay sufficient wages to retain – at least longer than previously – home-grown talent. Super-rich and merely very rich Russians have

---

Box 8.1   The FIFA World Cup, 2018

In addition to hosting the 2014 Winter Olympics, Russia is also to host what is perhaps the biggest sporting event in the world, the FIFA World Cup, in 2018.

Preparations for this event involve huge infrastructure commitments. The tournament will be held in twelve stadiums situated in eleven cities:

Moscow	Nizhny Novgorod	Sochi
St Petersburg	Rostov	Volgograd
Kaliningrad	Samara	Yekaterinburg
Kazan	Saransk	

In addition to twelve stadiums, most of which will be completely new, the infrastructure requirements for the tournament involve improving the quantity, quality and capacity of roads, airports, hotels and communications.

The overall cost of preparation for the 2018 World Cup has been estimated at US$20.9 billion.

---

come to prominence in European football in recent years through the ownership of football clubs. Roman Abramovich's ownership of English Premier League club Chelsea, who won the UEFA Champions League in 2012, is the most high profile. However, Russian owners back other clubs too, such as Monaco in the French League, and previously little known Russian Premier League club Anzhi Makachkala from Dagestan, whose billionaire owner thrust the club into the spotlight in 2012 by financing the employment of high-profile players and world-renowned manager Guus Hiddink.

Media

The deterioration of press freedom in Russia has been a widely discussed issue ever since Vladimir Putin's accession to the presidency in 2000. In 2013, the press freedom index published by the NGO Reporters Without Borders saw Russia's position drop to 148th out of 179 countries. Such a negative evaluation, although partly formed on the basis of subjective analysis, is the result of an array of pressures on the Russian media in recent years. Polls show that about half the Russian population think the media to be completely or

---

Box 8.2   Russia in sport

Athletics. Russia is a global power, and the leading European nation, when it comes to athletics. Athletics medals at the 2012 Olympic games included eight gold medals, among which were high jump golds for Ivan Ukhov and Anna Chicherova, and track golds for Maria Savinova in the 800 metres, Yulia Zaripova in the steeplechase, and Natalya Antyukh in the 400 metre hurdles.

Basketball. Russia's basketball team came third in the 2012 Olympics tournament, and some of Russia's leading players – notably Andrei Kirilenko and Timofey Mozgov – ply their trade in the American NBA. Perhaps the biggest Russian impact on the NBA, however, has come from the 2010 purchase by Russian multi-billionaire businessman-turned-politician Mikhail Prokhorov of the New Jersey Nets team, which promptly moved to New York and was renamed the Brooklyn Nets in 2012.

Chess. Russia has a celebrated chess pedigree. Only the American, Bobby Fischer, in the early 1970s, briefly interrupted a continuous list of Soviet and Russian world chess champions in the second half of the twentieth century. The world chess federation, FIDE, is headed by Kirsan Ilyumzhinov, until 2010 the president of the Russian republic of Kalmykia. In the 1990s, the chess world was split, as world champion Garry Kasparov refused to recognize FIDE's authority and backed the creation of a rival world championship, which was won in 2000 by Vladimir Kramnik of Russia. In 2006, the World Chess Championship was once again reunited, and Kramnik became undisputed champion until being beaten by the Indian Viswanathan Anand in 2007, who won the championship again in 2012 when it was held in Moscow.

Gymnastics has been a strength in Russia and the Soviet Union for decades. At the 2012 Olympics, 18-year-old Aliya Mustafina won four

⟶

---

mostly under the control of the state. In the twenty-first century, the concept of freedom of information has a wider application than ever before. It applies not only to freedom of the press and broadcast media, but also to state control over, and surveillance of, telephone conversations, e-mails and the internet. In Russia between 50 and 60 per cent of the population uses the internet, and that proportion is rising.

In the 1990s, released from the strict controls and censorship of the Soviet years, freedom of the press flourished relatively unchecked in Russia. The media landscape was transformed by the rise of super-rich oligarchs, the withdrawal of state funding for many medals, and the Russian women's team a silver in artistic gymnastics. In rhythmic gymnastics the Russia team continued its domination of the competition, winning a fourth successive Olympic gold, with Yevgeniya Kanaeva becoming the first woman to successfully defend her individual gold.

Football. In 2005, CSKA Moscow won the UEFA Cup, and in 2007 the traditional dominance of Moscow-based clubs in the Russian league was broken by Zenit St Petersburg (owned and funded by the giant gas company, Gazprom), which won the Russian Premier League, and followed that up in 2008 by winning the UEFA Cup and UEFA Super Cup, beating Manchester United in the latter.

Ice hockey. Russia won the men's world ice hockey championship in 2012. From the early 1990s, top Russian players began to be signed up by National Hockey League teams in the United States and Canada. The biggest Russian NHL star of recent years is Washington Capital's Aleksandr Ovechkin, three times winner of the most valuable player award (2008, 2009, 2013). His compatriot Yevgenii Malkin won the award in 2012.

Judo. Russia's president, Vladimir Putin, has a black belt in judo and has contributed to a judo textbook. The Russian men's judo team won gold in three of the seven weight categories in the 2012 Olympics.

Olympics. In the 2012 summer Olympic Games in London, the Russian team came fourth in the medals table – behind the United States, China and Great Britain.

Women's tennis. Maria Sharapova and Maria Kirilenko were both ranked in the world's top ten in 2013, following in the recent footsteps of compatriots such as Elena Dementieva, Dinara Safina and Vera Zvonareva.

publications, and the endeavours of journalists revelling in new-found freedoms. Of course, this statement represents a broad overview, and the decade of the 1990s was not all rosy for the journalistic profession. As in other areas (for example, freedom of worship, discussed elsewhere in this chapter), the time between the collapse of the Soviet system and the normalization of the current Russian system towards the end of the 1990s presented opportunities and freedoms that were later reined in to some extent. That short period in the early nineties, when the state still funded much of the media and yet its ability and willingness to exert editorial control had vastly diminished, is looked upon as the heyday of press freedom by some observers. Gradually, as the 1990s progressed, several factors began to influence journalistic freedom.

In particular, as a few individuals gained control of a number of the main media outlets in the 1990s, editorial freedom began to diminish. Many of the newspapers that emerged out of the Soviet collapse tried to establish themselves as truly independent, but increasingly economic reality blocked their efforts as they lacked the financial resources to continue. Consequently, several businessmen who had grown very rich very rapidly in the aftermath of the Soviet collapse began to acquire media assets. New Russian 'media barons' arrived, such as Vladimir Gusinsky, whose 'Most' group was built up to include a major national newspaper, *Segodnya*, and the national TV network NTV. Boris Berezovsky gained effective control over a similar profile of media outlets, including the newspaper *Nezavisimaya gazeta*, and became known as the key figure of influence behind the major national TV station ORT, which, although 51 per cent owned by the state, was largely managed by men close to Berezovsky. With the acquisition of broadcast and print media resources, Gusinsky, Berezovsky and others gained a measure of control over editorial policy.

The 1996 presidential election represented a key point in the development of media–political relations in Russia. At the beginning of that year, incumbent president, Boris Yeltsin, languished in the opinion polls. None the less, the months preceding the presidential vote in June 1996 saw concerted support for Yeltsin across virtually all of the main print and – of particular importance – broadcast media. The big three national TV channels (ORT, NTV and the wholly state-owned RTR) all produced coverage heavily supportive of Boris Yeltsin, who, of course, eventually won the election. Yeltsin's victory in 1996, and the vital role of the media in achieving it, strengthened the links between media control and political influence, and increased the determination of other businessmen to build up their media holdings.

At the same time, and particularly towards the end of the 1990s and into the Putin presidency, the state began to gather back control of key information media. In 1998, a state holding company was created that controlled the national RTR TV channel, as well as nearly seventy regional TV stations and a large number of transmitters across the country. The following year, President Yeltsin created a Press, Television, Radio Broadcasting and Mass Communications Ministry, to develop a state policy on advertising and oversee the auction of broadcast licences. An editorial in *The Times* (6 July 2000) declared that 'a healthy and vigorous press was Yeltsin's proudest legacy, the best guarantee of democratic pluralism'. Since the end of the Yeltsin presidency, press freedom in Russia has declined.

By the elections of 2003 and 2004, pro-regime bias in media coverage had worsened, though it was rarely crude and simplistic; rather it was manifest through shorter amounts of time and more negative coverage given to opposition candidates on the national TV channels. By the Duma election of 2007 and the presidential election of 2008, such media bias in election coverage was almost taken for granted. The same can be said for the elections of 2011–12. In this most recent election period, the Russian political establishment had to contend with a series of large opposition demonstrations. Part of the reaction to these by state-supporting television came in documentaries, which set out to show that opposition activists and critical NGOs were in the pay of foreign powers. At the same time, though, it would be wrong to give the impression that opposition voices are not heard in Russia's media. Newspapers and radio stations, particularly in Moscow, publish and broadcast views from an oppositionist perspective. The *Ekho Moskvy* (Echo of Moscow) radio station is renowned for its free and open discussions, and in the mainstream newspapers, *Komsomolskaya Pravda* and *Izvestiya*, among others, have a balanced perspective. None of this freedom, however, means that the reported restrictions and unspoken pressures are absent. Critics point out that what really matters in Russia is control over the major national and regional TV channels, as this is where most Russians get their news. Since 2000, all of the national television channels in Russia have been under the control, either directly or indirectly, of the state

Under state control, television news coverage has become more uniform and more supportive of the ruling regime, with the state demonstrably bringing the television companies back into line on occasions when they are deemed to have overstepped it. One such occasion early in the Putin presidency was the Moscow theatre hostage crisis of October 2002, after which President Putin criticized coverage that he claimed undermined the anti-terrorism operation. It was clear that NTV's coverage upset the authorities, and within three months the head of NTV, who had himself been seen as a government place-man on his appointment, was removed from his post.

As with all developed countries, Russia's media includes not just newspapers and television, but also a burgeoning world of web-based social media. Polls show that half of all Russians use the internet every day, and a further 10 per cent do so several times a week. What is more, Russians who use the internet reportedly spend more time on social networks than do internet users in almost any other country. The political stances of internet users are broadly in line with the population as a whole, which is scarcely surprising, given the level of internet penetration. What this means, though, is that although there are plenty of pro-regime websites, blogs and postings, the internet also offers a vast arena for free speech of many stripes and shades.

Like many governments the world over, the Russian government continues to wrestle with the question of regulating internet content. Where the issue is one of politics, then Russia's stance reflects its government's broader position on political freedoms. In other words, for most people most of the time discussion is free and open, but at the same time government officials are concerned about issues such as the spread of extremism, and the influence of anti-government content allegedly of Western origin. Deputy Prime Minister Dmitrii Rogozin suggested in 2013 that the US State Department actively sought to promote material that might undermine the Russian state. Where the issue is one of a more criminal nature, Russia's stance was to introduce, in 2012, a system for blacklisting websites accused of promoting child abuse, suicide and illegal drug use. In the system's first months of operation, around 7,000 websites were banned, with critics alleging that the vast majority of these cases stemmed from mistakes or technicalities. One such error saw the banning for a few hours of Russia's equivalent of Facebook, vkontakte ('in contact').

9

Russia and the World

Russia's place in the contemporary world is shaped by both permanent and transient factors. Russia is the world's largest country, geopolitically defined by its position straddling the Eurasian land mass. Its size and location have long been central components of its foreign policy thinking, in terms of both potential influence over global affairs and potential threats to the security of Russia itself. Russia sees itself as a 'great power', with the right to a sphere of influence related to its geopolitical position, and to a place at the top table in global affairs more broadly. As one of only five permanent members of the United Nations Security Council, Russia's influential position in global affairs has formal recognition. A regional sphere of influence, however, is not something so straightforwardly recognized. For example, while Russia might – and indeed does – perceive itself as having a legitimate case for preventing any future expansion of the NATO military alliance to countries such as Ukraine and Georgia, there is no formal justification for Russia to have a veto over the alliances formed by sovereign independent states, whatever their historical and geopolitical relationship with their larger neighbour.

While permanent and long-standing factors continue to shape Russia's relations with the rest of the world, such considerations need placing within the contemporary context if we are to accurately trace the development of Russia's place in the world during the twenty-first century, when it has re-emerged as a major power following its relative decline during the immediate post-Soviet decade of the 1990s. The scale of this re-emergence, however, has been limited in comparison with the hegemonic power of the Soviet Union, and has been inconsistent in terms of aims and outcomes. During the Cold War years in the second half of the twentieth century, the West represented the great competitor to the Russian-led Soviet bloc. These adversaries were not just two competing groups of states. Far more than that; they offered contrasting economic systems and ideological frameworks and put forward alternative visions of the future of mankind, while the possibility of nuclear conflict between them threatened the very existence of human civilization. None of this is so in the post-Cold War era. Although there are differences between Russia and 'the West', such differences are no longer so fundamental, and the very concept of 'the West' has, with the loss of the common Soviet rival, become less straightforward to define. Nevertheless, when one looks at Russia's foreign policy in the second decade of the twenty-first century, it still appears to be shaped largely by the concept of the West, and particularly the United States, as 'the other' against which Russia must define itself and its position in the world. That such a view is scarcely reciprocated by the United States and other Western powers – for whom the significance of Russia has declined in recent decades – serves to highlight questions about what lies behind Russia's conceptualization of its place in the world.

Some Russian analysts, chiefly from the more nationalist, Eurasianist camp, would argue that Russia's contemporary foreign policy is still driven by the idea that it represents an outward-looking civilizational model for the rest of the world, a preferable alternative to Western consumerist liberalism. Others see Russia's stance as increasingly inward-looking, even moving towards isolationism, driven primarily by domestic political advantages to be gained by the Putin regime from setting itself up as the patriotic defender of Russia's national identity, and from seeking to enhance the prestige of the Russian military. No overview of Russia's place in the contemporary world, however, can be comprehensive without taking into account economic links. Economic growth in Vladimir Putin's first two presidential terms (2000–8) came from energy exports. Yet, as Chapter 6 sets out, Russia's longer-term economic plans depend on diversification and modernization, which in turn require foreign direct investment and global linkages rather than isolationism. Such conflicting factors obfuscate the fundamental values that drive Russia's foreign policy. Foreign policy analyst Jeffrey Mankoff (2011) talks of tactics rather than strategy being to the fore. In this picture, Russia's alliances and policy decisions derive from the perceived benefits to the national interest in each case, rather than from a consolidated, constant and value-based conceptualization of Russia's place in the world.

Illustration 9.1   Russia's military remains revered

Preparations for the Victory Day parade, to commemorate victory over the Nazis in 1945. Red Square, Moscow, May 2008.

This chapter considers Russia's place in the world through the prism of relations with different geographical areas and from different viewpoints – Russia as a global power, as a military power, and as a regional hegemon. It starts, however, by considering what Russia itself says about its place in the world in its official Foreign Policy Concept.

Russia's Foreign Policy Concepts, 1993–2013

Russia's current Foreign Policy Concept was signed off by President Putin in February 2013, after the usual round of discussions among the foreign policy elite. The notion that a state should have a clear declaration of its position on foreign policy is one apparently held dear in Russia. In fact, it is not only in the sphere of foreign policy that there is such a statement of position and priorities. There also exist an official Military Doctrine, last promulgated in 2010, and a

National Security Strategy of the Russian Federation, published in 2009. Such overarching conceptualizations of the international and security concerns of the state do not in themselves correspond precisely to actual policy. They are one step removed from immediate decision-making, and allow Russia to strike an international and domestic pose, establishing a set of broad positions that serve to some extent as a diplomatic 'shop window', and to some extent as a guide for detailed policy-making. The Foreign Policy Concept is, then, a useful document for understanding how Russia wants to be seen in terms of its international position, and how the Putin regime understands the world around it. It can less easily be read as a set of policy positions.

The key themes of Russia's foreign policy position are readily apparent from reading the Foreign Policy Concept, both in its latest version and in the earlier iterations of 1993, 2000 and 2008. Looking back over two decades, the 1993 Foreign Policy Concept can now be seen as a transitional and somewhat idealistic document, within which the seeds of later developments are apparent. Towering over all considerations of Russia's foreign policy position in 1993 was the sudden and dramatic loss of superpower status and empire as the Soviet Union collapsed, and the sense that fundamental choices of direction lay before the nascent Russian Federation. The Soviet Union's superpower status drew on a number of factors:

- Military – during the Cold War, global international relations were dominated by the existence of two great opposing military blocs – the Warsaw Pact and NATO. Their military pre-eminence came from their capability of fighting an all-out nuclear war, the consequence of which would be global annihilation. Nuclear weapons were essential for superpower status, but attention was also given to the development and production of conventional weapons. Developments in military technology, from the 1980s onwards in particular, meant that the quality of weaponry became increasingly important, whereas Soviet conventional strength had traditionally been built on quantity.
- Imperial – the Soviet bloc (those countries whose political systems were installed and maintained by the USSR) reached into the heart of Europe and, after 1979, the Soviet empire had begun to extend southwards by means of the eventually doomed invasion of Afghanistan. Furthermore, as the leader of one pole of a bipolar

world, the Soviet Union had significant influence with allies across the globe, notably in South-East Asia, the Middle East, Africa and Central America.

- Ideological – the USSR was an ideological state. Its self-legitimation came from a belief in Marxism–Leninism, and the presumption that the Communist Party of the Soviet Union led the world on the path to communism and workers' power. Though easy to dismiss today, such an ideological underpinning strengthened and guided the international policies of the Soviet leadership. It provided a sense of mission and influenced the decision of some client states to ally themselves with the USSR.
- Economic – although the Soviet economy was rapidly failing by the early 1980s (see Chapter 6), trade relations played a key role in giving substance to the ideology of international relations. Towards the end of the Soviet period some two-thirds of the country's foreign trade was with other socialist countries. Furthermore, the Soviet Union strengthened ties with key countries by subsidizing arms exports. In the Gorbachev years (1985–91) only a third of arms exports were paid for directly; the rest were sold under advantageous credit conditions, subsidized massively, or given away free of charge.

The bifurcated world of the Cold War era finally collapsed in 1989–91. In 1989, anti-Communist revolutions in Eastern Europe broke up the Warsaw Pact as the East European satellite states rejected Soviet communism. In 1991, the nations that had made up the Soviet Union itself became independent. In that same year the United States led a coalition of forces from across the developed world to victory in a short war with Iraq, leading to talk of a 'new world order' and a unipolar system, with the United States being the sole superpower.

It was into this world, and with the legacy of the superpower status outlined above, that Russian foreign policy emerged. There are a number of key ways in which Russia's international relations since 1991 have been shaped by aspects of the Soviet Union's standing in the world. On the break-up of the Soviet Union, Russia became the official successor state to the USSR, and therefore took over one of the five permanent seats on the United Nations Security Council, accepted primary responsibility for fulfilling treaty obligations, and took over elements of the Soviet foreign policy infrastructure (for example, the Ministry of Foreign Affairs (MFA) and its embassies).

Immediately, then, Russia identified itself as a 'great power'. At the time of the Soviet Union's break-up there was little international surprise at, or argument with, the assumption of succession on the part of Russia. In the West, this process alleviated concern that the replacement of a superpower by fifteen independent states would lead to massive instability, particularly with regard to the proliferation of nuclear weapons. Among the clear majority of the 'successor states' themselves there was a recognition that only Russia had the capability and standing to take over the USSR's role on the international stage. Identification as a member of the UN 'permanent five' thereby confirmed Russia's insistence that it is indeed a great power and should be treated as such.

Against this background, the Foreign Policy Concept of 1993 showed a Russia wondering about the challenges and possibilities ahead. That year saw momentous conflict between reformers and conservatives in Russia's domestic politics (see Chapter 2), culminating in armed struggle on the streets of Moscow. In foreign policy terms, the newly developed Concept showed signs of similar tensions between the reformist Atlanticists, who favoured closer integration with the West, and the more conservative Eurasianists, who looked to hold on to Russian influence over the former Soviet space. Overall, the Concept's tone was optimistic with regard to a genuine turn in East–West relations. Hope for the creation of a 'new world order' persisted, with talk of a strategic partnership with the United States intended to lead to an eventual alliance, and of enhancing relations with countries in the Asia-Pacific region. At the same time, though, unsurprisingly the Concept indicated a reluctance to accept that the former Soviet states were fully independent entities. It mooted the creation of a unified military strategic space, and expressed concern for the rights of the millions of Russians who now found that they were no longer living in a Soviet Union ruled from Moscow, but abroad in newly independent states.

By the time Russia's Foreign Policy Concept was revised during the first months of Vladimir Putin's presidency in 2000, much of the optimism of the 1993 version had been diluted, and much of the uncertainty had disappeared. By 2000, Russia's Foreign Policy Concept could bluntly state, in reference to its earlier version, that

> certain plans relating to establishing new, equitable, and mutually advantageous partnership relations of Russia with the rest of the world ... have not been justified.

In the intervening years of economic decline, Russia had seen NATO expand eastwards to take in Poland, Hungary and the Czech Republic. In the conflict in former Yugoslavia in the 1990s, Russia's sympathies towards Serbia had clashed with the notion of a pro-Western foreign policy. This pro-Serbian stance led to a widening gap between the West and Russia, as NATO geared up for, and fought, a war against Serbia in 1999.

The beginning of NATO's bombing campaign against Serbia provided an illustration of the deterioration of relations between Russia and the West by the end of the 1990s. Yevgeny Primakov, who was at that time Russia's prime minister, was informed of the bombing while halfway across the Atlantic en route to a meeting with US Vice President Al Gore. He immediately ordered his plane to turn around and return to Russia, literally and symbolically turning his back on the West. To be in Moscow in those days was to be aware of strong anti-Westernism, and deep anger, expressed in the media by many otherwise pro-Western politicians as well as by the more nationalist-minded. This anger sprang from a variety of sources: a feeling of kinship with Russia's Slavic and Orthodox brethren in Serbia; a fear that, in the same way as action was being taken to protect the Muslims in Kosovo from Serbian armed forces, NATO might take action to protect the Muslims in Chechnya from Russian forces; and, most of all, a feeling of impotence, that Russia no longer mattered and that NATO could wage war in Europe irrespective of Russia's feelings.

Putin's first Foreign Policy Concept, in 2000, firmly established what has been the lodestar of Russia's foreign policy ever since. Against the background of what Russia perceived to be an increasing tendency on the part of the United States to act in a unilaterally domineering manner (and remember this was before the 'war on terror' waged after 11 September 2001), Russia's heavily revised Concept asserted its intention to 'seek to achieve a multi-polar system of international relations that really reflects the diversity of the modern world with its great variety of interests'.

The 2008 Concept, signed by then President Dmitrii Medvedev, continued to emphasize the need for a multi-polar system of international relations to reflect the diversity of the modern world. The latest, 2013, version of Russia's Foreign Policy Concept, talks of a 'multi-vector policy', similarly predicated on 'the creation of a polycentric system of international relations' and 'genuine partnership' between such poles of foreign policy influence as Russia, the European Union, the United States and China.

This stance towards the ordering of international affairs smacks to some of an out-dated recourse to imperialist thinking, and is sometimes characterized as neo-Soviet by those who see the Putin regime as nostalgic for at least an echo of the global standing enjoyed by the Soviet Union. However, although there exists a substantial nationalist literature in Russia promoting the notion of what Mikhail Yurev terms 'the third empire', the Putin regime does not harbour such ambitions. None the less, the gearing of foreign policy to the creation of a world order in which 'great powers' have 'spheres of influence' is central to Russia's worldview. Within this conceptualization, the United Nations should act as a forum for the regulation and co-ordination of international relations, and the status of the five permanent members of its Security Council (the United States, Russia, China, the United Kingdom and France) should remain untouched. This emphasis on the status of the UN, with its focus on regulation and co-ordination, again stems from Russia's view of a world where no single power should be allowed to unilaterally engage with global issues without reference to the other 'great powers'. Russia's concerns in this regard especially relate to resentment of any perceived US hegemony, particularly in what might be seen as the sphere of influence of other powers.

A multi-vectored foreign policy in practice

Russia's long-serving Minister for Foreign Affairs, Sergei Lavrov, has put forward the notion of 'network diplomacy' – a diplomacy of flexible alliances – which can change depending on what problem is to the fore. This approach to Russia's foreign relations is revealing in several ways. It speaks of the absence of overarching ideological factors driving foreign policy. No longer is it the case, as it was in the Soviet years, that Moscow is bound to other nations by a shared commitment to a particular view of the world and its development. Such freedom from ideological encumbrance backs up the stance often proclaimed by the Putin administration that Russia's foreign policy is a pragmatic one. Don't look too deeply, seems to be the message; if in a given international situation Russia seeks a given outcome, then it will direct policy accordingly.

What drives Russian foreign policy is the pursuit of Russia's national interests. This being so, then Russia's international position is changeable. The picture is of a great power that is sufficiently self-contained to not be permanently tied in to any other power bloc. An important element of such an understanding of the world is the idea that, as the 2013 Foreign Policy Concept emphasizes, 'global competition takes place on a civilizational level'. Russia sees itself, with some justification, as a civilizational hub. It is not in the orbit of some other global grouping, but is itself a centre towards which other states might gravitate. As an example of this self-conceptualization, Russia's decision not to participate in the EU's European Neighbourhood Policy reputedly stems from a refusal to be identified alongside many other states simply as a neighbour of the European Union, rather than as an alternative pole of the international system.

The United States

Setting out the basic elements of Moscow's view of a multi-vectored world helps to explain why contemporary Russia's attitude to the West is far more nuanced than a simple 'pro' or 'anti' label allows. When President Putin came to power in 2000, Russia shifted initially towards a more pro-Western stance. Putin's first foreign trip as president was to the United Kingdom, he established good relations with Western leaders, and post-9/11 he was strongly supportive of the US in its 'war on terror'. On 11 September 2001, when New York and Washington were attacked by Al-Qaeda terrorists, President Putin was the first world leader to offer his sympathy and support to President George W. Bush. The strength of this support, then and subsequently, took many observers by surprise, and brought Putin some criticism at home, especially from within the armed forces. Eighteen senior military men wrote an open letter, published in the Russian press, criticizing too close an alignment with the United States and its allies.

Why, then, did Putin respond so favourably to the US 'war on terror' in the aftermath of 11 September 2001? First, the Islamist terrorism of Osama Bin Laden was a mutual threat to Russia, the United States and Europe, and there had reportedly already been discussions about possible joint action against Al-Qaeda before 11 September 2001. Second, in his letter to President Bush immediately after the attacks on New York and Washington, Putin stated that the Russian people, perhaps above others, could empathize with the United States, having experienced terrorist attacks on their capital city. It was exactly two years earlier that terrorists – allegedly Chechens – had blown up two apartment blocks in Moscow, killing hundreds. Russia had been engaged in a second brutal war in

Chechnya since then, in the face of much Western criticism. Throughout that time the line taken by Putin had been that Russia was defending Europe against Islamic terrorism. After 11 September 2001, Putin's views were listened to more in the West rather than dismissed out of hand, and Western criticism of Russian action in Chechnya decreased.

There were clearly Russian interests at stake, then, when the initial decision to support the US-led 'war on terror' was made. However, as noted above, Russia's international position is guided by an ongoing assessment of national interests, rather than fixed alliances. In the early years of the presidencies of both Vladimir Putin and George Bush, relations between the two leaders were good, symbolized by Bush's famous statement after their meeting in Slovenia in 2001, that 'I looked the man in the eye. I found him to be very straightforward and trustworthy and we had a very good dialogue. I was able to get a sense of his soul.' During the US-led invasion of Afghanistan in 2001, Russia raised little objection to the establishment of American military bases in Kyrgyzstan, Uzbekistan, Tajikistan and Georgia.

By his second term as president, Putin had turned away from the United States. The most well-known statement of Russian foreign policy in recent years was made by President Putin six years after 9/11, at the Munich Conference on Security Policy in 2007. Here he attacked the United States for showing disdain for the basic principles of international law and, alluding to the US-led invasion of Iraq in 2003, for militarily overstepping its national borders without the support of the United Nations. The stance taken in Putin's Munich speech, and increasingly thereafter, was one that sought to present the United States, and not Russia, as out of step with 'normal' rules of international behaviour. On some issues, Russia was not alone in taking this view, and indeed had joined with France and Germany among other European nations in opposing the Iraq war.

Other issues were also aggravating US–Russian relations. Moscow interpreted US plans to site missile interceptors in Poland and a radar system in the Czech Republic as aggressive and anti-Russian. Putin had not forgotten US support of the 'colour' revolutions in Georgia in 2003 and Ukraine in 2004, and he blamed the West for supporting the rise to power – in states bordering Russia and deemed to be in Russia's sphere of influence – of regimes considered antagonistic towards Russia and its interests. The rhetoric of confrontation had been ratcheted up by Vice President Cheney in 2006, when he delivered a blistering attack on Russia in a speech in Lithuania's capital,

Vilnius. Cheney accused the Kremlin – with particular reference to the Orange revolution and the gas dispute with Ukraine in January 2006 – of 'blackmail', 'intimidation,' 'undermining the territorial integrity of its neighbours' and 'interference in democratic processes'.

Like Yeltsin before him, Putin too found it ever harder to stomach continuous criticism from the West, particularly the US, of Russia's internal affairs. The difference is that whereas Yeltsin had a tendency to give in to such criticism, Putin does not. There has developed in Russia in recent years, through the Medvedev presidency of 2008 to 2012 and into Putin's third term, a stubborn refusal to pay heed to Western criticism of alleged human rights abuses. Indeed, Russia's response to such criticism has not simply been a refusal to listen, but has instead become markedly active. The ruling regime in Russia has voiced disquiet at what it terms the politicization of the human rights agenda.

The central foreign policy issue at stake for Moscow here is familiar, namely a commitment to a multi-vectored world, where one state – the United States again – must not attempt to dictate to other powers, and if international measures are needed they should be taken through the United Nations. Russia complains that it is unjustly singled out by the West with regard to human rights, and has reacted with a number of specific measures. The activities of international NGOs in Russia have been curtailed, and Russia has begun publishing (in 2011 and 2012) its own negative human rights reports on Europe and the United States. In 2013, the fluctuations of US–Russian relations were exemplified with the long overdue repealing by Congress of the Jackson–Vanik Amendment – a trading sanction imposed in 1975 against Communist states that restricted emigration – only for it to be replaced by the 'Magnitsky law', refusing entrance to the US or use of its banking system to Russian officials deemed implicated in the death of Sergei Magnitsky and other human rights violations. (For details of the Magnitsky case see Box 7.2 on page 169.)

The strength of the US–Russia relationship has waxed and waned in the two decades since the Soviet Union collapsed. This can be explained by the fact that, for every area of disagreement and antagonism, there is an area of mutual interest, such as preventing terrorism or, as the two major nuclear weapon states in the world, ensuring non-proliferation and therefore acting together in relation to the intentions of countries such as Iran and North Korea in this regard. In 2008, the election of two forty-something former law lecturers, Dmitrii Medvedev and Barack Obama, to the presidencies of Russia and the United States respectively, presented an opportunity for the two countries to, in the words of Vice President Biden, 'press the reset button' with regard to their relationship. The metaphor is revealing, in that it suggested that differences between the US and Russia, though substantive, were not fundamental. In other words, there was no great ideological divide between the two states, but rather a series of specific disputes aggravated by differing approaches. The button could be reset in terms of tone and approach. In 2008, President Medvedev gave his own speech in Germany on foreign relations, which was far more conciliatory than that given there by his predecessor the year before.

Fours years later, in 2012, however, with Obama entering his second term and Putin back in the Kremlin as Russia's president, talk was of the need to 're-set the reset' in US–Russian relations. The optimism of the original reset had been undermined by differences on human rights and continuing Russian unease about what it considered unilateral US interference around the world. President Medvedev had reluctantly, and in apparent disagreement with his then Prime Minister Putin, ensured Russia's abstention from the UN Security Council resolution regarding intervention in Libya during the Arab Spring of 2010. As uprisings in the Middle East spread to Syria, however, Russia sided with the regime of President Assad against the wishes of the US and its Western allies. Russia's stance, pushing for UN-backed decommissioning of chemical weapons, was seen by many observers as the crucial factor holding back US military action against Syria in the summer of 2013. Relations between Russia and the United States took a further hit that summer, when Russia granted asylum to Edward Snowden, wanted by the US authorities after he had exposed the extent of mass surveillance activity of which he had become aware while working for the CIA and the NSA. President Obama cancelled his planned summit meeting with President Putin as a sign of US disapproval for Russia's stance.

Behind these headline events, deleterious to the US–Russia relationship, the two countries none the less continue to work together on a range of issues, such as co-operation over Afghanistan, negotiations on easing visa requirements, and ongoing talks about arms control. Since 2008, the transit of non-military NATO equipment across Russian territory en route to Afghanistan has been permitted, and in 2012 Russia even approved the use by the United States and its NATO allies of an air base in the Russian city of Ulyanovsk, Lenin's birthplace, in order to facilitate these transit arrangements.

To sum up Russia's relationship with the United States in the second decade of the twenty-first century, it represents an accommodation between two former enemies with mutual interests, antagonisms and misunderstandings. The US, having 'won' the decades-long Cold War and its battle of ideas, stands as the stronger participant in this relationship. Russia presents itself as a combination of wounded and resurgent, rebuffed in its desire for an equal partnership and insisting on its place as an independent great power of civilizational standing. The picture is complicated, however, when we turn our attention to another 'vector' in Russia's conceptualization of a multi-vectored world, namely Europe.

Europe

Often – too often for sophisticated analysis – Europe is thrown together with the United States to form a geopolitical entity known as 'the West', which stands apart from, and in opposition to, Russia. There is of course long-standing substance and analytical utility to this notion of Russia and 'the West' as opposing civilizations (see Chapter 2). None the less, the relationship between Russia and Europe differs from that between Russia and the United States. The difference stems predominantly from Europe's geographical, mercantile, and – to some extent – intellectual proximity to its larger Russian neighbour. Since the Gorbachev years (1985–91) onwards, Russia has consistently called for the creation of a common space of stability and security in the Euro-Atlantic area, through developing good relations with the United States and Europe. To some extent, both the United States and Russia have sought, with some justification, to claim a civilizational closeness to Europe. In 2005, President George W. Bush stated, in relation to Russia's standing as a European country, that 'European countries embrace those very same values that America embraces'. Russia in turn repeatedly emphasizes its own integral part in European civilization.

Russia's multi-faceted proximity to Europe provides a different set of imperatives from that at play in the relationship between Russia and the United States. In terms of national interest, at the forefront of policy considerations in relation to Europe are economic issues. Russia's largest overall trade partner by some distance is the European Union, with around US$410 billion worth of trade in 2012. In particular, the Russian energy sector's chief customer is Europe; 80 per cent of oil exports, 70 per cent of gas exports and half of Russia's coal exports are currently to the EU. As well as trade relations, Russia's policy priorities of modernization and economic diversification (see Chapter 6) similarly rely on open relations with the countries that make up the European Union. Around three-quarters of all foreign direct investment in Russia comes from these countries, with total capital investment exceeding US$260 billion by the end of 2012. The modernization project also enjoys more formal institutional support from Europe, with the President of the European Union, Manuel Barroso, and the then President of Russia, Dmitrii Medvedev, agreeing a Partnership for Modernization in 2009, resulting in almost US$2.5 billion funding becoming available for loans from the European Bank of Reconstruction and Development and the European Investment Bank.

The formal level of EU–Russian relations can sometimes seem replete with summits and agreements that have a little substance at lower levels of competence, and mask more significant undertones of mistrust and disagreement. For example, the 2013 EU–Russia Summit in Moscow saw the signing of a joint statement on co-operation in civil protection, and an administrative memorandum on the principles, goals and structure of dialogue in the area of protecting consumers' rights. However, the relative lack of progress on more substantive matters at the 2013 summit indicates a continuing strategic unease between the EU and Russia. Discussion on visa-free travel stalled, seemingly endless discussions to update and replace the nearly two decades old Partnership and Co-operation Agreement (1994) between the EU and Russia saw no breakthrough, and crucial energy co-operation concerns were kicked into the long grass with the production of a 'roadmap to 2050'.

The issue of energy co-operation represents a useful prism through which to see Russia's relationship with Europe in a different way from that apparent in the diplomatic niceties of summitry and broad declarations that Russia is integral to Europe. On two occasions in recent years – 1 January 2006 and 1 January 2009 – Russia cut off gas supplies to Ukraine. Ostensibly, and to a large extent genuinely, the disputes leading to the cutting off of gas supplies were commercial in nature, to do with a failure to agree new prices set by Russian supplier Gazprom, which were significantly higher than the previously subsidized rate. The commercial nature of these disputes was, however, clearly augmented by political factors. Gazprom's majority shareholder is the Russian state, and, particularly in the 2009 dispute, then Russian Prime Minister Putin appeared to go out of his way to demonstrate that he was issuing instructions to the company. The not-so-subtle political message in these disputes was that if Ukraine wanted to move politically westward and out of Russia's sphere of influence, it should not expect any help from Russia in doing so. In addition, cutting off gas supplies to Ukraine also affected customers in many European countries, for whom Ukraine is a transit point for supplies of Russian gas.

Russia's attitude to co-operation with Europe comes within the overarching principles of Russian foreign policy that work for, and on the basis of, a multi-vectored world. 'Europe' represents one pole of influence in this world so long as it is understood, roughly speaking, as the European Union and its member countries. When the EU sought to enter into partnerships with former Soviet states such as Belarus, Ukraine, Georgia, Azerbaijan and Armenia, Russia's president complained that these efforts amounted to a partnership against Russia. The focus on the EU as an entity in its own right, however, represents a relatively recent aspect of Russia's approach to Europe, and does not preclude bilateral relations with individual European states. During the Yeltsin years (1991–9), Russia appeared to view relations with the European Union itself as of secondary importance compared to relations with NATO, the G7/G8, or even the Council of Europe, which Russia joined in 1996.

To talk of contemporary Russia's relations with Europe is to encompass a range of differing bilateral relations, even if one uses the term Europe in a political rather than geographic sense, as short-hand for the countries of the EU (or of the European Economic Area). Traditionally, in the post-Soviet era, Russia has had good relations with France and Germany. During the 1990s, there were regular trilateral summit meetings of these countries, and the run-up to the Iraq war in 2003 saw Russia, France and Germany among the European states aligned against military action, with the United Kingdom, Spain and Italy in favour. This chapter began by noting Russian Foreign Minister Lavrov's preference for 'network diplomacy' where alignments shift according to the issue at stake. Following this notion, positions taken on the Iraq war do not necessarily indicate permanent preferences for Russia in terms of relations with European states. Close relations with Germany under Chancellor Schröder (1998–2005) have taken on a sharper tone under Angela Merkel's chancellorship. Vladimir Putin has enjoyed particularly warm relations with sometime Italian Prime Minister Silvio Berlusconi, and relations with the United Kingdom have been at a very low ebb for the past decade (see Box 9.1).

Box 9.1   UK–Russian relations

Relations with the United Kingdom became particularly tense and difficult during the first decade of the twenty-first century. This was partly a factor of the UK being seen as the United States' most loyal ally, and therefore serving as a proxy state for Russian displeasure. However, it was mainly related to specific UK–Russian disputes.

Russia wanted to extradite a number of its citizens from the UK, including advocates of Chechen independence and 'oligarchs' from the Yeltsin years, but these requests were rejected by the UK courts, who granted political asylum to a number of figures who were viewed as criminals or even terrorists by the Russian authorities. London came to be seen as a refuge from the Kremlin for many opponents of the Putin regime, or – as the Kremlin might have put it – enemies of Russia. While the UK government explained that it could not influence the decisions of the courts, the Russian leaders found this hard to believe, perhaps because such influence over their own courts would have been easy for them.

Those granted political asylum included a former KGB officer, Aleksandr Litvinenko, who had made enemies in the Russian secret service, and had accused some of its officers of being behind the Moscow apartment bombings of September 1999, which had been blamed by the authorities on Chechen terrorists. In 2006, Litvinenko died of polonium poisoning in London and the British media, with the odd exception, implied that the Russian state, or even Putin himself, was behind this death. A police investigation led to the UK requesting the extradition of a suspect from Russia. This was refused by Russia, on the grounds that the Russian Constitution did not allow for such an extradition. The UK government found this hard to believe.

In Moscow, the Russian authorities launched raids on the offices of the British Council, alleging financial irregularities, and the British ambassador experienced regular harassment by a political youth organization loyal to the Kremlin.

There were a number of other disputes involving the refusal of visas to British businessmen, mutual accusations of espionage, and commercial disputes, all of which served to deepen the crisis in UK–Russian relations.

The Russo-Georgian war of 2008 saw swift condemnation of Russia's actions from the UK government. Nothing unusual there, except that it was accompanied by a visit to refugee camps in Georgia by Foreign Secretary David Miliband. Even more unusually, the then leader of the opposition in the UK parliament, David Cameron, similarly made a rapid visit to Georgia. When Cameron became prime minister he oversaw the beginnings of a slight thaw in relations, with a visit to Moscow focused on specific trade-related agreements rather than broader and more contentious matters.

China

Russia is, of course, not just a European country; it is Eurasian. In terms of international relations, the Asian aspect of this term has become increasingly important in recent years, particularly in relation to the rise of China. China's significance to Russia stems from its rapid economic growth, its proximity to Russia, its geopolitical position, its embodiment of an alternative mode of development to liberal democracy, and its potential as a future ally or enemy. At the beginning of the twenty-first century, a Goldman Sachs analyst, noting the economic rise of Brazil, Russia, India and China, coined the acronym BRICs to refer to these states. Within eight years the acronym had become, with the addition of South Africa extending it to BRICS, a formal international grouping with its own summits. Despite the real economic and political differences between the BRICS states, the rise of identifiable new forces in the world very much suited a Russia concerned about a hegemonic United States, supported by its European allies, putting forward its model as the appropriate developmental path for the world. Among these states, China in particular matters to Russia. The two countries share a land border, which has led to inevitable concerns over security, migration, and – an issue eased by a series of bilateral agreements signed in the first decade of the century – the precise location of the border.

As a formally Communist authoritarian state developing a market-based economic system with substantial state oversight, China also represents an alternative politico-economic development model from that apparently chosen by Russia when the Soviet Union collapsed in 1991. Under President Yeltsin (1991–9), Russia made the choice for market democracy and the abandonment of communism. Over two decades later, the Putin regime in Russia repeatedly speaks of the economic hardships of the Yeltsin years and puts much of the blame on the Western advisers guiding Moscow at the time. While retaining a formal commitment to market democracy, today's Russia has unquestionably moved in a less democratic, more state-centric, direction. The existence of a Chinese model of development has some attraction for Russia, appearing to demonstrate that economic growth need not conflict with a strong state showing some degree of authoritarianism, and that there are other global powers that are ready to ignore Western castigations about human rights.

The Chinese model, however, also has concerns for Russia. China's economic growth has seen its manufacturing base expand rapidly. Whereas in the 1990s and the early years of this century, Russian exports to China included an element of technologically advanced and manufactured goods, particularly in the form of weapons sales, as the twenty-first century progresses the trend in the trade relationship is for Russia to be the raw materials supplier and China the manufacturer. Such a trade balance does not present immediate problems for Russia, which in particular is actively seeking to diversify its energy exports so as not to be entirely dependent on European customers. The opening of the first Sino-Russian oil pipeline in 2010 was heralded as linking the world's largest producer of oil with the world's largest consumer of energy. At the same time, though, China already constitutes a rival for influence, a stronger economic power, and a potential security threat.

The significance of China to Russia was demonstrated in 2008, when Beijing was the destination for Medvedev's first foreign trip as president, and again in 2012, when Putin visited the Chinese capital shortly after his third-term inauguration. The honour was reciprocated in 2013, when new Chinese President Xi Jinping's first trip abroad was to Moscow, where thirty economic agreements were signed. As the formal establishment of the BRICS summits demonstrates, the Russo-Chinese relationship is not simply bilateral, but seeks also to widen the number of states aligned in organizations separate from the 'old world' Western-led institutions. The development of the Shanghai Co-operation Organization (SCO), established in 2001, is a case in point. The SCO is made up of China, Russia, Kazakhstan, Kyrgyzstan, Tajikistan and Uzbekistan, with Afghanistan, India, Iran, Mongolia and Pakistan having observer status. In 2007 and 2010, the SCO conducted joint military manoeuvres, and some in Russia see it as potential counter to NATO as a military alliance in the longer term – although others see the Collective Security Treaty Organization filling that role (see Box 9.2).

Russia's near neighbours

Russia's increasing insistence over the last decade on having a 'sphere of influence' in terms of international politics raises the question of how far this influence should extend. In the Soviet era, it could be seen as having a core, an inner ring and an outer ring. The core was the Soviet Union itself, which broke up into fifteen independent states in 1991. The inner ring was the 'Soviet bloc' consisting of those Central

Box 9.2   The Commonwealth of Independent States and related organizations

- The closest formal relationship is between Russia and Belarus, who are committed to a treaty on the formation of a Union State, though with little sign of anything of real substance coming of this in the near future.
- In October 2000 – building on a 1996 CIS customs union between Belarus, Kazakhstan and Russia – these three countries plus Kyrgyzstan and Tajikistan formed the Eurasian Economic Community. Its early years saw sporadic progress, with a planned common economic space with Ukraine coming to nought. The establishment of the EU's Eastern Partnership programme in 2008 saw a renewed effort from Russia to work against what it sees as EU encroachment on its own sphere of interest.
- In 2009, Russia, Belarus and Kazakhstan formed a Customs Union. This was strongly driven by Russia, with the Putin regime seeing it as a stepping-stone towards wider integration.
- Ahead of his re-election to Russia's presidency in 2012, Vladimir Putin called for the establishment of a Eurasian Union. In office, he continues to push for the same, with the intention of creating a free economic zone and an eventual currency union. In 2012, a Eurasian Commission was established with representatives from Belarus, Kazakhstan and Russia. A widening of this group – to include Kyrgyzstan and Tajikistan – might begin to make a Russian-led Eurasian version of the EU more feasible.
- A slightly wider grouping than that engaged in economic co-operation and union makes up the Collective Security Treaty Organization (CSTO), founded in September 2003. Its members are Russia, Armenia, Belarus, Kazakhstan, Kyrgyzstan and Tajikistan. Russia would like the organization to expand further to include the Georgian Republics of Abkhazia and South Ossetia, which Russia recognizes as independent states following the conflict in August 2008, and perhaps Serbia.
- The outer ring of the Commonwealth of Independent States was made up for a decade of a loose, semi-official grouping of countries, known by the acronym GUAM (Georgia, Ukraine, Azerbaijan and Moldova), and founded in 1998. This group had originally included Uzbekistan, which withdrew in 2005 and moved closer to Russia in terms of its external relations by joining the CSTO. Uzbekistan then withdrew from the CSTO in 2012. Georgia, on the other hand, moved in the other direction and left the CIS following the Russo-Georgian conflict of August 2008.

This conceptualization of the CIS as an inner core and outer ring is useful, but does not convey the full complexity of relations between the former Soviet states.

and Eastern European countries with Communist governments, under Moscow's control until 1989. The outer ring was a looser and more fluid grouping of countries around the world that relied on Moscow for military, economic and political support. Contemporary Russia's policy of seeking a clear 'sphere of influence' has been manifest in several ways, primarily focusing on the core of former Soviet states, but also exhibiting a degree of grievance that the countries of the former Soviet bloc have now clearly aligned themselves with Western Europe.

In the immediate post-Soviet years, the formation of the Commonwealth of Independent States (CIS) represented a solution to the problem of how to organize (most of) the states that had made up the Soviet Union. Drawing on the historical and geographic context set out above, it is easy to understand why Russia's initial priority in terms of regional leadership is those countries that were formerly part of the Soviet Union. This is not a view based wholly on grand perceptions of geopolitics and great power status. It also had a basis in the objective realities of economic and military infrastructures remaining from the Soviet era, and in the moral claim to influence given by the existence of a Russia diaspora up to 25 million strong in the former Soviet states in 1991. Such realities, however, diminished over time, and most of the Russians who wanted to have returned home (see Chapter 3). None the less, the desire to retain influence over most of the former Soviet states remains at the top of contemporary Russia's foreign policy agenda .

Of the successor states to the Soviet Union, eleven of these, along with the Russian Federation, have made up the CIS for most of the post-Soviet era. The three Baltic republics of Estonia, Latvia and Lithuania declined to join the CIS on the break-up of the Soviet Union, and consistently pursued membership of NATO and the EU, gaining both in 2004. In 2005, Turkmenistan changed its CIS status to that of associate member. In 2008, Georgia announced, after the August conflict with Russia, that it was leaving the CIS.

In the short term, immediately after the collapse of the USSR, Russia and the other post-Soviet states were faced with concrete issues of disentanglement and the reorganization of relations that inevitably result from the fracture of what was one country into fifteen. Military deployment had to be disentangled, property had to be shared appropriately – leading, for example, to disputes over the Black Sea Fleet in Ukraine and the Baikonur space-launch facility in Kazakhstan – independent currencies were established, and even such apparently minor matters as representation at the 1992 Olympic

Box 9.3	Russia's foreign ministers
Andrei Kozyrev	November 1991–January 1996
Yevgeny Primakov	January 1996–September 1998
Igor Ivanov	September 1998–March 2004
Sergei Lavrov	March 2004–

Games and the establishment of national football teams involved careful negotiation, resolved by the creation of interim CIS teams. There has never been any serious suggestion that the other former Soviet states would re-unify as a single state, with the possible exception of Belarus and Russia, which since 1996 have been negotiating – with very little progress other than a formal agreement – elements of a supranational confederate union.

The CIS was formed in December 1991 and included most of the states emerging from the Soviet Union. From its very inception some members – Russia in particular – saw it as a means of holding on to some aspects of the Soviet Union, while others saw it as a means for achieving a 'civilized divorce', a dividing-up of what once belonged to the Soviet Union, before the newly independent states went their own ways. The CIS is not a state itself, and the differing aims of its members have seriously undermined any effectiveness as a united body able to act on the international stage. It rests on a mix of formal multi-lateral treaties and a network of more substantial bilateral agreements between Russia and individual states. Each member state has interests that deviate to different degrees and at different times from those of Russia. There are complicated dynamics in a series of relationships, and any attempt by Moscow to make the CIS a tighter organization would risk its disintegration from centrifugal forces. For simplicity's sake, the CIS countries can be represented as an inner core of countries that want closer ties, and an outer ring joined primarily by the desire for greater freedom from Russian influence, and indeed from the CIS itself (Box 9.2).

If the short-term difficulties of imperial break-up are complex and fraught with tension, they are at least readily identifiable. The longer-term legacy has been a forced retraction of the Russian sphere of influence. What were republics within the Soviet Union are now independent countries, and therefore subjects of international law and objects of international relations. If the Russian Federation were to engage in expansionist policies, these are now front-line countries to

Table 9.1 Russia in international organizations

Organization	Established	Number of Members	Purpose / Comments
Arctic Council	1996	8	forum for Arctic co-operation
ASEAN (Association of South East Asian Nations) Regional Forum	1994	27	regional co-operation
Asia-Pacific Economic Co-operation (APEC)	1989	21	promotion of regional economy
Black Sea Economic Co-operation Zone (BSEC)	1992	12	regional stability and economic co-operation
BRICS	2009	5	acronym from Brazil, Russian, India, China, with the 'S' for South Africa added in 2011
Collective Security Treaty Organization (CSTO)	2002	7	military and political co-operation among former Soviet member states
Commonwealth of Independent States	1991	11	co-ordination of relations between former Soviet states
Conference of Interaction and Confidence-Building Measures in Asia (CICA)	1999	23	co-operation for peace and stability in Asia
Council of Europe	1949	47	to increase unity and quality of life in Europe
Council of the Baltic Sea States (CBSS)	1992	12	support for democracy development in Baltic Sea states
East Asia Summit (EAS)	2005	18	co-operation for political, security, economic development in East Asia
Eurasian Economic Community	2001	6	creation of a common economic space
Euro-Atlantic Partnership Council	1997	50	co-operation on political and security issues

Organization	Year	Members	Purpose
European Bank for Reconstruction and Development (EBRD)	1990	65	facilitation of post-Communist transition
Financial Action Task Force (FATF)	1989	36	combating money laundering and terrorist financing
Group of 20 (G-20)	1999	20	facilitation of global economic stability
Group of 8 (G-8)	1975 (as G6)	9 (inc. EU)	Russia joined in 1997, creating the G-8
Inter-Parliamentary Union (IPU)	1889	161	fostering inter-parliamentary relations across the globe
International Atomic Energy Agency (IAEA)	1957	162	promotion of the peaceful use of atomic energy
International Chamber of Commerce (ICC)	1919	131	promotion of free trade and business interests
International Criminal Police Organization (Interpol)	1956	190	police co-operation
International Development Association (IDA)	1960	189	support for developing economies
Organization for Security and Co-operation in Europe (OSCE)	1975 (renamed 1995)	57	international co-operation for security, democracy, rule of law, etc.
Paris Club	1956	19	national debt negotiation
Partnership for Peace	1994	22	co-operation between NATO and former Communist states
Permanent Court of Arbitration (PCA)	1899	115	settlement of international disputes
Shanghai Co-operation Organization (SCO)	2001	6	regional co-operation, including military
United Nations Security Council	1945	15	Russia one of the 5 permanent members (along with China, France, the UK, the US)
World Trade Organization (WTO)	1994	157	Russia joined in 2012 after protracted negotiations

be expanded into, rather than launching pads for further aggrandisement. Russia did not use military force to directly expand its influence until the Georgian conflict in 2008, and then the crisis in Ukraine, particularly in the Crimea region, in 2014. The post-Soviet equivalent of the Soviet Union's war with Afghanistan (1979–88), in terms of the attempt to secure Russia's southern flank, has been two wars with the Chechen Republic, which is not even one of the post-Soviet states but legally a component of the Russian Federation. When Russia has wanted to base troops in surrounding republics, it has had to do so by means of careful negotiation, combined with activities such as peace-keeping and border guarding, with the exception again of the incursion into Georgia in 2008 in response to Georgian troops' actions in South Ossetia and Abkhazia. Furthermore, it is not only Russia that has stationed troops in the former Soviet republics. During its invasion of Afghanistan in 2001, the United States established a military presence in Kyrgyzstan, Uzbekistan, Tajikistan and Georgia.

Clearly, therefore, Russian foreign policy has become more closely focused on a reduced sphere of influence compared to that of its Soviet predecessor. This provided something of a post-imperial psychological shock for Russia's policy-makers. The very concept that, for example, Ukraine is a foreign country, was a difficult conceptual leap for elite and masses alike to make, as was made dangerously clear when Russia allegedly attempted to interfere in Ukraine's presidential election in 2004.

By the end of 2004, the determination of Russia to hold on to, or indeed to re-create, its influence in Europe's second largest country, Ukraine, became evident in its initially staunch support for the more pro-Russian candidate, Viktor Yanukovych, in Ukraine's disputed presidential election. Viktor Yushchenko eventually defeated Yanukovych in a re-run following mass protests against electoral fraud. President Putin's backing for Yanukovych represented a serious error of judgement, serving to emphasize Russian impotency in its supposed sphere of influence. The events in Ukraine in 2004 became known as the 'Orange revolution', after the colour adopted by the Yushchenko campaign. The 'colour revolutions' – chiefly Ukraine's Orange revolution and Georgia's 2003 'Rose revolution' – are seen by Russia's ruling regime as Western inspired provocations, designed to undermine Russia's influence in its 'near abroad'.

In December 2013, Ukraine's President Yanukovych strengthened ties with Russia rather than with the European Union. This move sparked mass protest in the capital Kiev, the intensity of which saw Yanukovych overthrown in February 2014. A crisis in Russia's relations with the West resulted, as its troops in Crimea secured pro-Russian control of the region, determining not to simply acquiesce to changes in Ukraine which it saw as counter to Russian interests. In contrast, Russo–Georgian relations became more stable following the election of President Giorgi Margvelashvili in 2013.

This chapter has presented an overview of contemporary Russia's place in the wider world which reveals the multi-faceted approach taken towards external relations by the Russian Federation. As all states do, Russia draws on its history, traditions, economic interests, geopolitical situation, public opinion and cultural values in its inter-action with other countries. Russia, though, is not like the vast majority of states. Its recent history is as a global superpower. Its traditions are imperial. Its economic interests affect vital energy supplies to much of Europe. Its geopolitical situation is as the world's largest country, the biggest country in Europe, the biggest country in Asia, bordering fourteen states, and with legitimate interests across much of the northern hemisphere. Its public opinion and cultural values reflect these factors, and throw into the mix a sense of disappointment at national decline in the 1990s, of grievance – warranted or not – at perceived Western enmity, and of national pride built on notions of Russia as a great power, fated to lead and guide lesser nations.

It is scarcely surprising, then, that contemporary Russia's international policies can appear on occasions to be contradictory, given that so much has to be held in tension. Trade-offs have to be made between different priorities. In conclusion, though, to understand Russia's relationship with the wider world, it is important to be able to pick out Russia's own priorities from among these countervailing factors. Among the twists and turns in relationships with different states that we have noted (and, for that matter, with the many states not covered here in detail but included in Table 9.1), and underpinning broader shifts in attitude towards concepts such as 'the West', contemporary Russia needs to be understood as a country which sees itself as a regional leader of global significance. We can argue over whether this self-perception is accurate, legitimate or delusional, but it is essential to acknowledge its hegemony within Russia. When trade-offs are made in Russia's international relations, regional leadership and 'great power' status are only tradable in extremis. And even then, as the history of post-Soviet Russia shows, every effort will be made to trade them back at the earliest opportunity.

10

Conclusion

Headlines about contemporary Russia in the international press revolve around familiar themes – authoritarianism, the struggles of the opposition, controversial legal cases, and international relations. Whatever their accuracy, they bring forth polarized responses and create a generic impression of the Russian Federation. The survey of contemporary Russia presented in this book presents a fuller and wider picture. While not ignoring the headline issues, I have sought to emphasize too the elements of what we might call 'normal life' in Russia. Behind the political questions that are the focus of media attention, almost 150 million citizens of Russia go about their daily lives: working, being educated, bringing up families, drinking, travelling, surfing the internet and so on.

Just taking these activities, we have seen in the preceding chapters that in terms of working life, Russia's unemployment rate in 2012 was a little over 5 per cent, compared to 7 to 8 per cent in the United Kingdom and the United States, and around 10 per cent in the European Union as a whole. Some 65 per cent of employed Russians are now working in service industries. The figure of 70 per cent of 17- to 22-year-olds in Russia enrolled in higher education is notably high in terms of international comparison. From the same comparative perspective, a lower percentage of Russians are bringing up children compared to many other countries, due to the demographic decline of the post-Soviet years. That situation is changing, though, with 2012 being the first year since the Soviet Union collapsed in 1991 when the Russian population grew on the basis of the birth and death rates alone – that is, discounting migration. Drinking remains a serious problem in Russia, particularly among men, with the World Health Organization estimating that one in eight deaths can be attributed to alcohol-related diseases. More and more Russians are travelling abroad for their holidays. Around half of all Russians use the internet every day, with surveys showing the percentage of internet use devoted to social media to be particularly high compared to other countries with mass internet access.

Taken as a generality, this all approximates to 'normal life' in a developed twenty-first-century country. Russia has its defining features – in the above snapshot, high levels of alcohol consumption and participation in higher education – but is recognizably familiar as a modern state in the globalized world of today. Perhaps it seems unnecessary to point this out. However, given a long-standing obfuscatory tendency to mythologize Russia among many analysts, and considering the elemental upheavals experienced by Russia's citizens in the past century (see Chapter 1), the comparative normality of the lives of most Russians merits emphasis. Such an emphasis by no means intends to deny or disregard authoritarian tendencies, legal abuses, corruption and so on. It does, however, seek to add another dimension to the characterization of Russia today.

In the introductory chapter we noted the call from some experts for Russia to be judged on the basis of 'plain facts'. Such a plea is reminiscent of a debate within academia's Russian studies community in the 1990s, when area studies scholars clashed with specialists in specific disciplines over how best to understand the newly independent Russia. The latter sought to consider Russia using the same approaches, types of data, and comparators as they would any other country. The area studies specialists, steeped in knowledge of Russia from across the disciplinary range, averred that understanding required insight into the culture, history and commonplaces of life. As in many academic debates, it is worth combining the salient points from both sides. The 'plain facts' tell us a good deal and facilitate the comparisons that are essential to truly locate and evaluate contemporary Russia. The 'insider knowledge' helps us to understand symbols, moods and trajectories.

If some plain facts show many aspects of Russians' lives to be recognizably common and contemporary at the level of global comparison, then specific knowledge of the Russian experience illuminates some of the significance in this finding. The introduction to Chapter 5's consideration of politics and government noted that President Putin and Leonid Brezhnev (Soviet leader, 1964–82) shared both longevity and popularity. Polls have fairly consistently, although declining a little in his third term as president, given Putin an approval rating in the 60–70 per cent range. Polls asking Russians to name their most popular leader of the past century have regularly placed Leonid Brezhnev at the head of the list.

Knowledge of Russia's history helps to explain these results. Considering the past hundred years or so, it is only really only under Brezhnev and Putin that Russians have enjoyed extended periods without fundamental national calamity. Tsar Nicholas II's reign saw the First World War and the revolutions of 1905 and 1917; under Lenin (1917–24) there was civil war; the Stalin years (1928–53) visited on Russia famine, terror and 28 million dead in the Second World War; Khrushchev's (1953–64) policy of placing missiles on Cuba brought the world to the brink of nuclear war; Andropov (1982–4) and Chernenko (1984–5) died swiftly in office – embodying the sick and failing nature of the Soviet state as they did so – but none the less superpower relations still had time to plummet dangerously during these short interregnums; Gorbachev's reform programme (1985–91) ushered in the collapse of the Soviet Union and of the Communist project in Europe; in the 1990s under Yeltsin the Russian people felt the effects of that collapse in economic disaster, two wars in Chechnya, international decline, regional fragmentation, and the state's inability to do much of what a state should do in terms of providing security, law and order, healthcare, education and so on. While the Brezhnev years (1964–82) and Putin's first two terms (2000–8) were not lacking in incident, as periods through which to live they offered relative calm combined with oil-powered economic growth and an increase in consumer comforts. Not a bad offer when set against what went before.

History does not always represent a sound guide to the future. None the less, drawing on the Brezhnev years for analogy does usefully provide one perspective on where contemporary Russia might be heading today. For all the nostalgia-infused popularity of Brezhnev among Russians of a certain age, by the end of the Brezhnev years the Soviet economy was in decline and many Soviet citizens – particularly among the young and the intelligentsia – were deeply frustrated at the lack of opportunities in Soviet life, at the longevity of their ageing leaders, and at the corruption prevalent in everyday exchanges. What is more, among the political leadership, figures were emerging who shared these thoughts and wanted an honest and open debate about the country's direction. On coming to power, Mikhail Gorbachev famously declared 'we cannot carry on this way' and labelled the Brezhnev years 'the era of stagnation'.

Potential parallels, though by no means precise analogies, can be drawn with the Putin regime in its third term. Any leader who has been in power for eighteen years, as Putin will have effectively been if he serves out his current term as president until 2018, risks welcome stability morphing into irksome stagnation. Putin's return to the presidency in 2012 was not accompanied by any great narrative explaining his purpose. When he came to power in December 1999, Putin had immediately set out a clear narrative that resonated with many, calling as it did for a strong state, national unity and increased international standing. He then consistently followed the narrative that he established. He strengthened the Russian state, centralized the institutions, oversaw economic growth, restored Russia's status internationally, and then, in keeping with a stated commitment to the Russian Constitution, stepped aside after his legally allowable two consecutive terms as president in favour of a young and apparently more liberal successor, Dmitrii Medvedev (2008–12). Putin's decision to stand again for the presidency in 2012 delivered a plot twist to the narrative of the Putin years that has never been explained with the same detail and resonance as when he first appeared at the apex of the state.

Long-term leaders who come to power, as Putin did, declaring that their task is to correct someone else's mistakes, become at some point the people held responsible for the current state of their country. This will be the case especially if, as is entirely possible, Russia's economy plateaus during Putin's third term. Opinion polls in 2013 showed signs of Putin fatigue, with the majority of respondents saying that someone else should take over the presidency in 2018 rather than Putin standing for yet another term. Polls also showed that more people agreed with Aleksei Navalny's characterization of Putin's United Russia as the 'party of crooks and thieves' than did not. A regime deemed corrupt and presiding over a period of economic difficulty will, as happened in the later Brezhnev years, meet with increasing dissatisfaction. Perhaps more important than public opinion in a managed democracy is elite opinion. At the elite level, in-fighting between factions has become more apparent in the early years of Putin's third term.

To emphasize, the analogy with the Brezhnev years is by no means precise. Contemporary Russia and the world in which it exists are very different from the Soviet Union and the milieu of the Cold War. None the less, the analogy's central point – that longevity can become stagnation – holds validity. There will be voters in the 2018 presidential election who were born after Putin came to power, and it is natural that the desire for change will grow.

The perils of prediction are legion, and perfectly feasible scenarios exist in which President Putin leaves the presidency before his third term ends, or steps down at the end of his term, or stands again for a further six-year term in 2018. Whenever it happens, however, it is indisputable that at some point, probably in the next decade, further political change will occur at the highest level of Russian power. Perhaps more important than the question of when this will be, is the question of how it will happen. As we have seen in Chapter 5, contemporary Russia has a democratic constitution. It conducts elections, and formally has a clear separation of powers between the executive, the legislature and the legal system. We have also investigated the informal ways in which such institutions have been undermined to create a self-perpetuating elite within a democratically deficient polity.

It is possible – though public opinion at the time of writing, 2013, suggests it is unlikely – that dissatisfaction with the Putin regime could grow and create a revolutionary situation, with mass demonstrations and calls for real democracy forcing a change of government. It seems more possible, though again there are few signs of it now, that the call for greater democracy could come from within the regime itself: from liberal elements who sensed a thaw during the Medvedev presidency (2008–12) and feel let down; from those engaged in business or concerned about the economy, who see democratic progress as essential to engaging in global commerce and attracting foreign investment; or simply from astute politicians, Putin perhaps amongst them, deciding that the maintenance of power requires some opening up of the system, either in response to public pressure or to breathe some new life into the regime. Pressure for change within the regime might result in a quasi-revolutionary crisis situation, or instead take a slower, more controlled, evolutionary approach. Whatever happens, however, democratic change in Russia does not require the sort of systemic transformation seen at the end of the Soviet Union. Russia already has a democratic system in place. Indeed this democratic system functions – albeit imperfectly – and is used to legitimate the ruling regime. A serious and effective reform process in Russia requires that the role of the formal institutions and regulations increases and the influence of informal practices and distortions decreases.

From the perspective of the Putin regime, and indeed – so opinion polls tell us – most Russians, support for political stability rather than change has been a defining feature of Russia's twenty-first century so far. Given the experiences of the 1990s, it is little wonder that stability has been at the heart of the narrative that contemporary Russia's regime has promoted. From the perspective of critics – and this is the standard view found in most Western media – what we have seen since the turn of the millennium is the gradual, firm, and occasionally brutal, removal of plurality from politics, the media, and even big business in Russia. Whereas elections in Russia in the 1990s were genuinely competitive and unpredictable, the decision that President Medvedev would step down in favour of Putin in 2012 was a deal done behind closed doors. Once announced, six months ahead of the election, it was clear that it would be so. The regime's often stated line argues that Russia has been expected to cope with too much too quickly, that democratization took much longer in the West, and that change is slowly happening in Russia. Critics point instead to other former Soviet and Eastern bloc countries that managed to become fully fledged democracies with remarkable alacrity. They argue that the problem with Russia is not that it is moving too slowly towards democracy, but that it has actually stopped moving in that direction at all and has turned back.

It is difficult to envisage contemporary Russia experiencing a democratic change of regime in the near future. Members of Russia's ruling elite have a commitment to stability – surely shaped to some degree by a predilection for the personal perquisites of power – which translates into a fear of political pluralism. They toy with the notion, some may even believe that in the longer term it is the way to go, but then they persist in the view that the time is not yet right for Russia to risk a genuinely competitive election. They persist, too, with the state paternalism that is rooted in Russia's history, with the idea that the state knows best and – as we noted in Chapter 3 – that opposition is a rather unnecessary diversion away from fulfilling the vital tasks standing before the country. We also noted in Chapter 3, however, that the flip-side of a political and popular culture that tends to venerate the capabilities of the state, is that disillusionment sets in rapidly when the state fails. Of course, this happens the world over, but in mature democracies there is an opposition waiting in the wings to replace the failing regime, and an established mechanism by which this process takes place. Russia lacks the sort of opposition that looks ready for power and its formal process for the transfer of power to an opposition by elections remains untried.

The declared policies of Russia's ruling regime in the second decade of the twenty-first century envisage building on the Russian economy's lucrative raw materials base to create a diversified and technology-driven national economy. As part of this process, Russia itself would become more widely developed, with investment in its physical infrastructure opening up more and more of its vast territory to the advantages of economic growth, and the continued implementation of plans to improve the provision of health care, education and housing across the country. Implicit in the regime's 'Russia 2020' plan is the notion, backed up by the constitutional elongation of the presidential term to six years from 2012 onwards, that the state should not be distracted in its vital tasks by too much in the way of politicking, elections and democratic choice. Overall, what 'Russia 2020' is supposed to be about is another of those concentrated periods of modernization so familiar in Russian history (see Chapter 2). History, however, never runs as smoothly as the implementation of a plan to 2020 might imply. As discussed above, with or without an economic downturn, the Russian people might become disillusioned with the state and its leaders. In the longer term, political and economic stagnation bring back on to the agenda potential political outcomes of a revolutionary, or more likely evolutionary, nature seeking to remove or reshape the ruling regime.

Equally, however, there is the possibility that Russia's position as a producer of raw materials means that, even though terms of trade may decline, it none the less has a secure medium- to long-term resource to provide the basis for economic development. Whatever the precise outcome of economic development in Russia, though, it will have to deal with demographic decline over the next fifty years or so. Related to this, the question of immigration – particularly with regard to the Far East and its proximity to populous China – will require political skill to deal with it effectively. Russia's national identity as a 'great power' both influences and depends on wise navigation through these problems.

These are the challenges that lie ahead for Russia, and, of course, the future is always uncertain. What is absolutely certain, though, is that these challenges will be addressed increasingly by a post-Soviet generation. The younger generation of Russians has grown up in a comparatively open country, indeed far more open in so many ways than that in which their parents lived. The task for the coming generation is to let stability evolve into the change necessary to develop a modern twenty-first-century state, economically diverse, technologically advanced, securely pluralist, and yet still recognizably Russian.

Recommended Reading

There is a wide range of literature on Russia. Aside from academic writers, Russia is one of those countries that is sufficiently distinctive for it to make a keen impression on Western journalists and travellers, leading to a steady stream of memoirs, travel books and so on. This brief guide sets out a few key texts that will enable you to widen your knowledge of the themes covered in this book.

General books

Russia often finds itself the subject of books by journalists and writers, as well as by academics. Such books vary in their nature. Sweeping journalistic introductions offer accounts for the general public, such as Dimbleby's (2008) book to accompany a television series on journeying across Russia, or Sixsmith's (2012) book to accompany a radio series on Russian history. Roxburgh (2012) covers the rise and rule of Vladimir Putin, 'the strongman' of Russian politics. Ben Judah's (2013) account of contemporary Russia argues that Putin is not the strongman he appears to be. Both books provide excellent accounts, matching similar work from earlier eras, such as David Satter's (2003) account of the 'rise of the Russian criminal state' in the 1990s and into the 2000s, and David Hoffman's (2011) revised and updated book on the oligarchs, originally published in 2002.

The historical context

A series of three books covering Russian history from 1649 to the present has been published in recent years: Wirtschafter (2008), Weeks (2010) and Lovell (2010). As well as providing up-to-date scholarship, this series seeks to bring a degree of originality through defining eras that do not follow the standard subdivisions of Russia history. Also well worth looking at for a good overview of Russian history is Hosking (2001), and an accessible overview of the period between 1812 and 2001 is available in Westwood (2002). The most up-to-date history of the period from late Tsarism to contemporary Russia is Service (2009). There is a vast amount to choose from in terms of histories of the Soviet era, from books covering the entire period, such as Volkogonov (1998), to those devoted to particular leaders. For Lenin, Stalin and Trotsky, recent comprehensive biographies are those written by Service (2000, 2004 and 2010 respectively). A definitive account of Khrushchev and his time in power is that by Taubman (2003). For the Brezhnev era, books by Bacon and Sandle (2002) and Tompson (2003) give useful introductions. The Gorbachev years are well-served by authors such as Brown (2007) and Sandle (2009), and by Gorbachev's own memoirs (1996). Yeltsin, aside from the three volumes of his memoirs (1990, 1994, 2000), is the subject of useful biographies by Aron (2000) and Colton (2008). There are many accounts by participants and observers of the years around the collapse of the Soviet Union, and perhaps particularly engaging for Western readers are those by the British and US ambassadors of that time, respectively Braithwaite (2002) and Matlock (1995). For an assessment of the Soviet era through a study of its ideology, I recommend Sandle (1998). For an accessible overview by the same author of the ideology that guided the Soviet Union, read *Communism* (Sandle 2012). Far heftier works on this topic on a global scale are Service (2007) and Brown (2009). Also very much worth a look for a politics-focused overview of the Soviet years and beyond, including the Soviet successor states, is Suny (2011).

Land and people

A recent and comprehensive geographical overview of 'Russia and its neighbours' is available in Blinnikov (2011), and there is a similarly comprehensive analysis of post-Soviet Russia's geography in Shaw (1999). Environmental matters are dealt with by Henry (2010) and Oldfield (2005), with an excellent historical account available in Josephson (2013). The story of the development of Moscow is provided by Colton (1996), and updated in a fascinating insight into life in contemporary Moscow by Shevchenko (2009). Reisinger (2013) presents an assessment of the regional policy pursued by Vladimir Putin, as do Ross and Campbell (2009). A useful account of the conflict in Chechnya and the wider north Caucasus is available in Schaefer (2010). An up-to-date assessment of religious matters can be found in Fagan (2013). For stories of travels into the Russian heartland in the post-Soviet years, Richards (2009) reaches aspects of the Russian land and people not touched by most academic authors.

Social structure and social policy

Compared with overviews of Russian politics, the number of book-length accounts of Russian society is relatively small. Health issues are covered well in Manning and Tikhonova (2009), and the same authors' 2004 book on poverty and social exclusion similarly provides a fine overview of its topic. A more popular – as opposed to academic – work, which looks at demography and alcoholism, is Bullough (2013). An account of developments in the judicial sphere is available in Smith (2009) and Smith and Sharlet (2008). The Khodorkovsky case and its implications are covered in definitive detail by Sakwa (2014). For a harrowing, non-academic narrative of an Englishman caught up in Russia's judicial system during the Putin years, Tig Hague's *The English Prisoner* (2009) does not stint on graphic description. For an assessment of education reforms in the Russia, Johnson (2010) is fairly comprehensive, and Maximova-Mentzoni (2012) covers university reform.

Politics and government

A vast amount has been written about the politics and government of contemporary Russia, with the most recent and comprehensive academic textbooks being Shiraev (2013), Remington (2011), Sakwa (2010) and White (2010). An informed critique of the Putin era, focusing on Putin himself, is contained in Hill and Gaddy (2013). Michael Stuermer's (2008) readable account of the Putin years takes a less stringently critical line than some. Bacon and Renz (2006) consider the growing authoritarianism of Putin's Russia from a security perspective. The informal side of Russian politics, and of Russian socioeconomic life more widely, provides the theme for a recent edited volume by Kononenko and Moshes (2011).

The economy

The economic developments of the Putin era are covered excellently by Robinson (2012) and Sutela (2012). For a more business-focused approach, see Glazunov (2013). A trilogy of books by Ledeneva (1998, 2006, 2013) looks in detail at the connections, networks and customs of socio-economic and business life in Russia, and their impact on wider politics. A fine guide to the workings of the Soviet economy is to be found in Hanson (2003). There are a number of assessments of the reform attempts in the 1990s, largely focused on a 'where did it all go wrong?' theme. For coverage of this period, see Freeland (2002). An insight into the criminality and corruption of the early post-Soviet years is available in Brzezinski (2002).

Rights, freedoms and civil society

The best analysis of civil society in contemporary Russia is Chebankova (2013), which is more up-to-date than a fine edited volume from Evans *et al.* (2005), though the latter covers a wider range of civil society groups. The situation in the Soviet Union in relation to rights, freedoms and civil society is dealt with well in an account of the life of Sergei Kovalev, Boris Yeltsin's human rights commissioner in the 1990s; see Gilligan (2004). Bowring's recent book (2013) covers rights in Russia from the imperial period to the present day. Arutunyan (2009) provides a useful assessment of the development of the media under Putin, and Burrett (2010) focuses on television and its political role in Russia.

Culture and media

An overview of Russian pop culture in the Yeltsin and early Putin years can be found in Borenstein (2008). Beumers *et al.* (2011) explore developments in Russian media since the Soviet collapse. Hutchings and Rulyova (2009) focus on the culture of Russian television. Beumers (2005, 2009), and Beumers and Lipovestkii (2009), offer insight into popular culture, cinema and drama. Concepts of the Russian Idea and the Russian approach to life are the subject of McDaniel (1996) and of Pesmen (2000). Alena Ledeneva (1998, 2006, 2013) explains much about contemporary Russian political and economic life through her studies of social interaction. An excellent literary narrative of Russian perceptions of life on the threshold between the Soviet and post-Soviet eras is to be read in Hobson (2001). Russian identity in the post-Soviet era is surveyed in Billington (2004) and the place of death and memory in Russia is splendidly evoked in Merridale (2000). Of the contemporary Russian literature covered in the chapter on ideas and culture, the following are available in English translation: Bykov (2010), Glukhovskii (2010), Prilepin (2012), Shishkin (2012), Slavnikova (2010), Sorokin (2011) and Ulitskaya (2011). In terms of 'new drama', English texts are available for Durnenkov and Durnenkov (2009), Presnyakov and Presnyakov (2003) and Sigarev (2002).

Russia and the world

For excellent detailed overviews of Russia's foreign policy, see Gvozdev and Marsh (2013), Tsygankov (2013) and Mankoff (2011). Sherr (2013) provides a good thematically oriented assessment. An insider's account of US–Russian relations for most of the Yeltsin era can be found in Talbott (2002), and on the decline in these relations, Tsygankov (2009) provides impressive clarity. Perspectives on Russian foreign policy towards Europe are available in Engelbrekt and Nygren (2010). Bobo Lo (2008) concentrates expertly on the relationship between Russia and China. Lo (2003) also delivers the best account of Russia's foreign relations during Putin's first term.

Russia Online in English

A small selection of useful websites covering various aspects of Russian affairs is listed below.

Academic analysis

Carnegie Moscow Centre: www.carnegie.ru/en

Program on New Approaches to Russian Security: http://www.ponarseurasia.com/

Royal Institute of International Affairs – Russia programme: www.chatham-house.org.uk/research/russia_eurasia

Russia in Global Affairs: http://eng.globalaffairs.ru/

Russia Votes: www.russiavotes.org

Blogs and podcasts

Robert Amsterdam: www.robertamsterdam.com

Russia Other Points of View: www.russiaotherpointsofview.com

The Power Vertical: http://www.rferl.org/archive/The_Power_Vertical/

Culture

Read Russia: http://readrussia2012.com/

Russkiy Mir Foundation: http://www.russkiymir.ru/russkiymir/en/

Economics

Bank of Finland Institute for Economies in Transition – Russia forecast and statistics:
http://www.suomenpankki.fi/bofit_en/seuranta/venajatilastot/Pages/default.aspx

RBC Business Information Space: http://rbcholding.com/

Government and politics

The official presidential website: http://eng.kremlin.ru/

The Federation Council website has some English content (http://council.gov.ru/en/), as does the government website at: (http://government.ru/en/)

The State Duma website (www.duma.ru) is in Russian only.

Miscellaneous

Forum 18 (religious freedom): www.forum18.org/index.php

Levada Centre (Opinion Polling): www.levada.ru/eng

Moscow Metro: www.metro.ru

Russian Orthodox Church: https://mospat.ru/en/

Russian religious news: www.stetson.edu/~psteeves/relnews

News

Radio Free Europe: www.rferl.org

RIA Novosti: http://en.ria.ru/

Russia Today: http://rt.com/

The Moscow Times: www.moscowtimes.ru

The Voice of Russia: http://voiceofrussia.com/

Bibliography

Aron, Leon (2000) *Boris Yeltsin: A Revolutionary Life* (London: HarperCollins).

Arutunyan, Anna (2009) *The Media in Russia* (Maidenhead: Open University Press).

Bacon, Edwin and Mark Sandle (eds) (2002) *Brezhnev Reconsidered* (Basingstoke: Palgrave Macmillan).

Bacon, Edwin and Bettina Renz, with Julian Cooper (2006) *Securitising Russia: the Domestic Politics of Vladimir Putin* (Manchester: Manchester University Press).

Beumers, Birgit (2005) *Pop Culture Russia!: Media, Arts, and Lifestyle* (Santa Barbara, CA: ABC-CLIO).

Beumers, Birgit (2009) *A History of Russian Cinema* (Oxford: Berg).

Beumers, Birgit, Stephen Hutchings and Natalia Rulyova (2011) *The Post-Soviet Russian Media: Conflicting Signals* (London: Routledge).

Beumers, Birgit and Mark Lipovestkii (2009) *Performing Violence: Literary and Theatrical Experiments of New Russian Drama* (Bristol: Intellect).

Billington, James H. (2004) *Russia: in Search of Itself* (Baltimore, MD: Johns Hopkins University Press).

Blinnikov, Mikhail S. (2011) *A Geography of Russia and Its Neighbors* (New York: Guilford Press).

Borenstein, Eliot (2008) *Overkill: Sex and Violence in Contemporary Russian Popular Culture* (Ithaca, NY: Cornell University Press).

Bowring, Bill (2013) *Law, Rights and Ideology in Russia: Landmarks in the Destiny of a Great Power* (London: Routledge).

Braithwaite, Rodric (2002) *Across the Moscow River: The World Turned Upside Down* (Newhaven, CT: Yale University Press).

Brown, Archie (2007) *Seven Years that Changed the World: Perestroika in Perspective* (Oxford: Oxford University Press).

Brown, Archie (2009) *The Rise and Fall of Communism* (London: Bodley Head).

Brzezinski, Matthew (2002) *Casino Moscow: a Tale of Greed and Adventure on Capitalism's Wildest Frontier* (New York: Free Press).

Bullough, Oliver (2013) *The Last Man in Russia and the Struggle to Save a Dying Nation* (London: Allen Lane).

Burrett, Tina (2010) *Presidential Power and Television in Putin's Russia* (London: Routledge).

Bykov, Dmitrii (2010) *Living Souls* (Richmond: Alma Books).

Chebankova, Elena A. (2013) *Civil Society in Putin's Russia* (London: Routledge).

Central Intelligence Agency (2013) *World Factbook.* URL https://www.cia.gov/library/publications/the-world-factbook/

Colton, Timothy J. (2008) *Yeltsin: A Life* (New York: Basic Books).

Colton, Timothy J. (1996) *Moscow: Governing the Socialist Metropolis* (Cambridge, MA: Harvard University Press).

Dillin. John (2001) 'World Confronts an Aging Population', *Christian Science Monitor*, 1 March 2001, p. 21.

Dimbleby, Jonathan (2008) *Russia: A Journey to the Heart of a Land and its People* (London: BBC).

Durnenkov, Mikhail and Vyacheslav Durnenkov (2009) *The Drunks* (London: Nick Hern).

Economist, The (1999) 'Special article: Russia in default: Money can't buy me love' 6 February pp. 23–5.

Engelbrekt, Kjell and Bertil Nygren (eds) (2010) *Russia and Europe: Building Bridges, Digging Trenches* (London: Routledge).

Evans, Alfred B., Laura A. Henry and Lisa McIntosh Sundstrom (2005) *Russian Civil Society: A Critical Assessment* (Armonk, NY: M. E. Sharpe).

Fagan, Geraldine (2013) *Believing in Russia: Religious Policy after Communism* (London: Routledge).

Freeland, Chrystia (2000) *Sale of the Century: Russia's Wild Ride from Communism to Capitalism* (New York: Random House).

Gilligan, Emma (2004) *Defending Human Rights in Russia: Sergei Kovalyov, Dissident and Human Rights Commissioner, 1969–1996* (London: RoutledgeCurzon).

Glazunov, Mikhail (2013) *Business in Post-Communist Russia: Privatisation and the Limits of Transformation* (London: Routledge).

Glukhovskii, Dmitrii (2010) *Metro2033* (London: Gollancz).

Gorbachev, Mikhail (1996) *Mikhail Gorbachev: Memoirs* (New York: Doubleday).

Guardian, The (2008) 'Real Lives: Hell on Earth' 18 April, Features, p. 4.

Gvozdev, Nikolas K. and Christopher Marsh (2013) *Russian Foreign Policy: Interests, Vectors, and Sectors* (Washington, DC: CQ Press).

Hague, Tig (2009) *The English Prisoner* (Harmondsworth: Penguin) (also known as *Zone 22*, and in the United States as *Tomorrow You Go Home*).

Hamilton, Alexander, and James Madison, *et al.* (2008) *The Federalist Papers* (Oxford: Oxford University Press).

Hanson, Philip (2003) *The Rise and Fall of the Soviet Economy* (Harlow: Longman).

Hanson, Philip and Elizabeth Teague (2013) *Liberal Insiders and Economic Reform in Russia* (London: Royal Institute of International Affairs). Available at: http://www.chathamhouse.org/publications/papers/view/188985

Harrison, Mark (2002) 'Economic Growth and Slowdown', in Edwin Bacon and Mark Sandle (eds), *Brezhnev Reconsidered* (Basingstoke: Palgrave Macmillan).

Henry, Laura A. (2010) *Red to Green: Environmental Activism in Post-Soviet Russia* (Ithaca, NY: Cornell University Press).

Hill, Fiona and Clifford G. Gaddy (2013) *Mr. Putin: Operative in the Kremlin* (Washington, DC: Brookings Institution).

Hobson, Charlotte (2001) *Black Earth City: A Year in the Heart of Russia* (London: Granta).

Hoffman, David (2011) *The Oligarchs: Wealth and Power in the New Russia* (New York: PublicAffairs).

Hosking, Geoffrey (1997) *Russia: People and Empire, 1552–1917* (London: Fontana Press).

Hosking, Geoffrey (2001) *Russia and the Russians: A History* (London: Allen Lane).

Howard, Marc Morjé (2003) *The Weakness of Civil Society in Post-Communist Europe* (Cambridge: Cambridge University Press)

Huntington, S. P. (1991). *The Third Wave: Democratization in the Late Twentieth Century* (Norman: University of Oklahoma Press)

Hutchings, Stephen and Natalia Rulyova (2009) *Television and Culture in Putin's Russia: Remote Control* (London: Routledge).

IFAD – International Fund for Agricultural Development (2007) *Sending Money Home: Worldwide Remittance Flows to Developing and Transition Countries* (Rome: IFAD).

Johnson, David (2010) *Politics, Modernisation and Educational Reform in Russia: from Past to Present* (Oxford: Symposium Books).

Josephson, Paul R. (2013) *An Environmental History of Russia* (Cambridge: Cambridge University Press).

Judah, Ben (2013) *Fragile Empire: How Russia Fell In and Out of Love with Vladimir Putin* (London: Yale University Press).

Kolesnikov, Andrei (2007) 'Razve Putin mozhet byt' neprav?' *Kommersant* 9 April 2007 p. 1

Kononenko, Vadim and Arkadi Moshes (2011) *Russia as a Network State: What Works in Russia When State Institutions Do Not?* (Basingstoke: Palgrave Macmillan).

Kornai, János (1992) *The Socialist System: the Political Economy of Communism* (Princeton, NJ: Princeton University Press).

Lane, David and Cameron Ross (1999) *The Transition from Communism to Capitalism: Ruling Elites from Gorbachev to Yeltsin* (London: Macmillan).

Ledeneva, Alena V. (1998) *Russia's Economy of Favours: Blat, Networking and Informal Exchanges* (Cambridge: Cambridge University Press).

Ledeneva, Alena V. (2006) *How Russia Really Works: The Informal Practices That Shaped Post-Soviet Politics and Business* (Ithaca, NY: Cornell University Press).

Ledeneva, Alena V. (2013) *Can Russia Modernise?: Sistema, Power Networks and Informal Governance* (Cambridge: Cambridge University Press).

Levada Centre (2012) *Obshchestvennoye mneniye 2012 ezhegodnik* (Moscow: Levada Tsentr).

Lo, Bobo (2003) *Vladimir Putin and the Evolution of Russian Foreign Policy* (Oxford: Blackwell/Royal Institute of International Affairs).

Lo, Bobo (2008) *Axis of Convenience: Moscow, Beijing, and the New Geopolitics* (Washington, DC: Brookings Institution).

Lovell, Stephen (2010) *The Shadow of War: Russia and the USSR, 1941 to the Present* (Oxford: Blackwell).

Mankoff, Jeffrey (2011) *Russian Foreign Policy: the Return of Great Power Politics* (Lanham, MD: Rowman & Littlefield).

Manning, Nick and Nataliya Tikhonova (eds) (2009) *Health and Healthcare in the New Russia* (Aldershot: Ashgate).

Manning, Nick and Nataliya Tikhonova (eds) (2004) *Poverty and Social Exclusion in the New Russia* (Aldershot: Ashgate).

Matlock, Jack (1995) *Autopsy on an Empire: The American Ambassador's Account of the Collapse of the Soviet Union* (New York: Random House).

Maximova-Mentzoni, Tatiana (2012) *The Changing Russian University: from State to Market* (London: Routledge).

McDaniel, Timothy (1996) *The Agony of the Russian Idea* (Princeton, NJ: Princeton University Press).

Merridale, Catherine (2000) *Night of Stone: Death and Memory in Russia* (London: Granta Books).

Oldfield, Jonathan (2005) *Russian Nature: Exploring the Environmental Consequences of Societal Change* (Aldershot: Ashgate).

Pesmen, Dale (2000) *Russia and Soul: an Exploration* (Ithaca, NY: Cornell University Press).

Presnyakov, Oleg and Vladimir Presnyakov (2003) *Terrorism* (London: Nick Hern).

Prilepin, Zakhar (2012) *Sin* (London: Glagoslav).

Putin, Vladimir (2000) *First Person: An Astonishingly Frank Self Portrait by Russia's President* (London: Hutchison).

Read, Christopher (2001) *The Making and Breaking of the Soviet System* (Basingstoke: Palgrave Macmillan).

Reisinger, William M. (2013) *Russia's Regions and Comparative Subnational Politics* (London: Routledge).

Remington, Thomas F. (2011) *Politics in Russia* (London: Pearson).

Richards, Susan (2009) *Lost and Found in Russia: Encounters in a Deep Heartland* (London: I. B. Tauris).

Robinson, Neil (2012) *The Political Economy of Russia* (Lanham, MD: Rowman & Littlefield).

Ross, Cameron and Adrian Campbell (2009) *Federalism and Local Politics in Russia* (London: Routledge).

Roxburgh, Angus (2012) *The Strongman: Vladimir Putin and the Struggle for Russia* (London: I. B. Tauris).

Sakwa, Richard (2010) *The Crisis of Russian Democracy: The Dual State, Factionalism and the Medvedev Succession* (Cambridge: Cambridge University Press).

Sakwa, Richard (2014) *Putin and the Oligarch: The Khodorkovsky–Yukos Affair* (London: I. B. Tauris).

Sandle, Mark (1998) *A Short History of Soviet Socialism* (London: UCL Press).

Sandle, Mark (2009) *Gorbachev: Man of the Twentieth Century?* (London: Hodder Arnold).

Sandle, Mark (2012) *Communism* (Harlow: Longman).

Satter, David (2003) *Darkness at Dawn: the Rise of the Russian Criminal State* (London: Yale University Press).

Schaefer, Robert W. (2010) *The Insurgency in Chechnya and the North Caucasus: from Gazavat to Jihad* (Santa Barbara, CA: Praeger Security International).

Service, Robert (2000) *Lenin: a Biography* (Basingstoke: Palgrave Macmillan).

Service, Robert (2004) *Stalin: a Biography* (Basingstoke: Palgrave Macmillan).

Service, Robert (2007) *Comrades: A World History of Communism* (Basingstoke: Palgrave Macmillan).

Service, Robert (2009) *The Penguin History of Modern Russia: From Tsarism to the Twenty-First Century* (Harmondsworth: Penguin).

Service, Robert (2010) *Trotsky: a Biography* (Basingstoke: Palgrave Macmillan).

Shaw, Denis (1999) *Russia in the Modern World* (Oxford: Blackwell Publishers).

Sherr, James (2013) *Hard Diplomacy and Soft Coercion: Russia's Influence Abroad* (London: Chatham House).

Shevchenko, Olga (2009) *Crisis and the Everyday in Post-Socialist Moscow* (Bloomington, IN: Indiana University Press).

Shevkunov, Archimandrite Tikhon (2012) *Everyday Saints and other stories* (Dallas, TX: Pokrov Publications)

Shiraev, Eric (2013) *Russian Government and Politics* (Basingstoke: Palgrave Macmillan).

Shishkin, Mikhail (2012) *Maidenhair* (Rochester, NY: Open Letter).

Shleifer, Andrei and Daniel Treisman (2004) 'A Normal Country: Rethinking Russia', *Foreign Affairs*, March/April.

Sigarev, Vasilii (2002) *Plasticine* (London: Nick Hern).

Sixsmith, Martin (2012) *Russia: A 1,000-Year Chronicle of the Wild East* (London: BBC).

Slavnikova, Olga (2010) *2017* (London: Duckworth).

Smith, Gordon B. (2009) 'Legal Reform and the Dilemma of Rule of Law', in Stephen White, Richard Sakwa and Henry Hale, *Developments in Russian Politics 7* (Basingstoke: Palgrave Macmillan).

Smith, Gordon B. and Robert Sharlet (2008) *Russia and its Constitution: Promise and Political Reality* (Leiden: Martinus Nijhoff).

Sorokin, Vladimir (2011) *Day of the Oprichnik* (New York: Farrar).

Stuckler, David, and Lawrence King *et al*. (2009) 'Mass privatisation and the post-communist mortality crisis: a cross-national analysis' *Lancet* 373: 399–407

Stuermer, Michael (2008) *Putin and the Rise of Russia* (London: Weidenfeld & Nicolson).

Suny, Ronald Grigor (2011) *The Soviet Experiment: Russia, the USSR, and the Successor States* (Oxford: Oxford University Press).

Sutela, Pekka (2012) *The Political Economy of Putin's Russia* (London: Routledge).

Talbott, Strobe (2002) *The Russia Hand: A Memoir of Presidential Diplomacy* (New York: Random House).

Taubman, William (2003) *Khrushchev: The Man and his Era* (New York: W. W. Norton).

Tompson, William (2003) *The Soviet Union under Brezhnev* (Harlow: Longman).

Tsygankov, Andrei (2009) *Russophobia: the Anti-Russian Lobby and American Foreign Policy* (Basingstoke: Palgrave Macmillan).

Tsygankov, Andrei (2013) *Russia's Foreign Policy: Change and Continuity in National Identity* (Lanham, MD: Rowman & Littlefield).

Ulitskaya, Ludmilla (2011) *Daniel Stein, Translator* (London: Duckworth).

United Nations Development Program – UNDP Russia (2012) *National Human Development Report for the Russian Federation, 2011: Modernization and Human Development* (Moscow)

Volkogonov, Dmitri and Harold Shukman (ed.) (1998) *The Rise and Fall of the Soviet Empire: Political Leaders from Lenin to Gorbachev* (London: HarperCollins).

Weeks, Theodore R. (2010) *Across the Revolutionary Divide: Russia and the USSR 1861–1945* (Oxford: Blackwell).

Westwood, J. N. (2002) *Endurance and Endeavour: Russian History 1812–2001* (Oxford: Oxford University Press).

White, Stephen (2010) *Understanding Russian Politics* (Cambridge: Cambridge University Press).

Wirtschafter, Elise Kimerling (2008) *Russia's Age of Serfdom 1649–1841* (Oxford: Blackwell).

World Health Organization (2010) *The World Health Report 2000 – Health Systems: Improving Performance* (Geneva: WHO).

Yeltsin, Boris (1990) *Against the Grain: An Autobiography* (London: Pan Books).

Yeltsin, Boris (1994) *The View From the Kremlin* (London: HarperCollins).

Yeltsin, Boris (2000) *Midnight Diaries* (London: Weidenfeld & Nicolson).

Index

65637004R00152

Made in the USA
Middletown, DE
ber 2019